IT'S ALL IN YOUR NUMBERS

IT'S ALL IN YOUR NUMBERS

The Secrets of Numerology

Kathleen Roquemore

Harper & Row, Publishers
New York, Cambridge, Philadelphia, San Francisco
London, Mexico City, São Paulo, Singapore, Sydney

I dedicate this book to people everywhere, in the hope that it may aid them on their path. Love and light abundant.

A hardcover edition of this book is published by Harper & Row, Publishers, Inc.

IT'S ALL IN YOUR NUMBERS: THE SECRETS OF NUMEROLOGY. Copyright © 1975 by Kathleen Roquemore. All rights reserved. Printed in the United States of America. No part of this book may be used or reproduced in any manner whatsoever without written permission except in the case of brief quotations embodied in critical articles and reviews. For information address Harper & Row, Publishers, Inc., 10 East 53rd Street, New York, N.Y. 10022. Published simultaneously in Canada by Fitzhenry & Whiteside Limited, Toronto.

First PERENNIAL LIBRARY edition published 1985.

Designed by C. Linda Dingler

Library of Congress Cataloging in Publication Data

Roquemore, Kathleen.
  It's all in your numbers.

  "Perennial library."
  Includes index.
  1. Symbolism of numbers. I. Title.
BF1623.P9R58   1985   133.3'35   85-42589
ISBN 0-06-091305-3 (pbk.)

87 88 89 MPC 10 9 8 7 6 5 4

ACKNOWLEDGMENTS

I give thanks to all my loved ones, and in particular to Dr. Neva Dell Hunter and all of her group from Quimby Center who introduced me to numerology; to Fran, who gave me the faith to start; to Kathy and Jerry, for without their generosity a word would never have been typed; to Nikki and Doyle, who allowed themselves to be displayed in print; and to Cris, Anna, Don, Carol, Hazel, Byron, Bettie, and Joy—all my dear friends who gave me the encouragement to go on. I must also include my friends in spirit who gave me the idea in the first place and who came to my rescue many times.

Most of all, I give thanks to my children—to Jaimy who helped me realize my own strengths, and to Patt, Tom, Penne, and Stacy, who through their help gave me the time to research and write this book.

My love and God's blessings to you all.

CONTENTS

I

BASIC INFORMATION—THE MAJOR NUMBERS

One

INTRODUCTION
TO NUMEROLOGY

Most of us have a desire to know more about ourselves and the people around us. We want to understand our lives better, to know why certain things happen to us and why we respond to them the way we do. There are many well-known sciences that can tell us something about ourselves and others. Among them are astrology, palmistry, and handwriting analysis. Perhaps the least-known science is numerology, yet like the others it is a definite science based upon facts and governed by certain rules.

Numerology is the science of numbers or vibrations and was one of the sciences practiced by men of great wisdom in ages long past. They realized that everything is made up of vibrations. They knew that this universal law applied to people as well as to things and that it could be used to determine a great deal about individuals. It is in fact part of what makes us individuals. Each number has its own vibratory influence and therefore its own characteristics. Through a few simple rules and formulas we can begin to see how these influences come into play in our lives and have a definite influence over us.

The palmist will tell us that the way the lines in our hands are formed is by no means a matter of chance, that they have been formed in a definite and individual pattern so that we may be able to tell certain things about ourself and our life. When reading palms the palmist adheres to rules that say what certain lines pertain to. An astrologist will tell us that we were born at a certain time and therefore are governed by certain planets, and the fact that we are under the influence of these planets is not a matter of chance. You may argue that you were born prematurely because of an accident that befell your mother, but the true occultist knows that nothing really happens by chance. The same is true of the handwriting analyst, for he or she knows that you do not write the way you do because you liked the way your grandmother wrote and tried to pattern your writing after hers. He or she is well aware that handwriting is governed by the brain, and by applying certain rules it is possible to tell a tremendous amount about the person that you now are.

Numerology has in common with these sciences the belief that a person comes into a life at a certain time and with a certain name, not as a matter of chance but as a matter of choice, and that from these things much can be told about the person and his life. Even if you cannot agree with the idea that your birth name and birth date are not a matter of chance, there is no reason to argue with the theory that they have a definite effect upon your life, and upon this fact numerology is based. You may be surprised to find out just how much your numbers can tell about you and your life, as many have been when they read the work-ups that I have prepared for them. It may tell you some things that you already know, others that you only suspected, and some things that you have only thus far hoped were true. This information is based upon calculations made from the numbers derived from the birth date and from the letters of the name given at birth. Not only can much be told from one's name at birth, but also from nicknames and name changes made through life.

Numerology gives us a chance to see ourselves better, to realize just what talents and abilities we possess, what our limitations are, what we are here to do and how best to accomplish that destiny, what jobs we are best qualified for, what lessons we came into this lifetime to learn, and what debts we are here to pay off. We can learn about situations and people, what forces rule us, what our greatest area of power is, the cycles of our life and the vibrations governing them, our challenges, what each year holds in store for us, and what it is best for us to do and not do.

Not only can numerology tell us these things about ourselves, it can also tell us the same things about the people around us. When we understand them and ourselves better, we are much more able to get along with each other. Through numerology parents can understand why their children are the way they are and can therefore handle them more efficiently and aid them in growing up. It is a tool that can be used to help achieve greater harmony between the one you love and yourself. Young people can use it as an aid in deciding upon a vocation and eliminate a lot of the trial and error in trying to find a satisfying field in which they can perform well. For the teacher it is a way of understanding students and helping them to be better students. It can be an invaluable aid to the businessman regardless of his line of business. No matter who you are or what you are doing, it can be used to better your life and your relationships with others. Even difficult people become easier to get along with when we know the forces that govern them, because then we can see how to deal with them.

Part of the beauty of numerology is that you do not have to study long and hard before you can begin to put what you have learned to use. You can quickly learn a few basic facts and formulas that will immediately help you to begin to understand yourself and others better. From there, you can go on to learn more and more up to any point you wish. Of all the sciences, it is probably one of the easiest to learn. If you can add, or even just count on your fingers for that matter, you are able to use numerology. Perhaps its simplicity is the reason that it is less often used than some other sciences. We are in an age when people seem to believe that anything worthwhile has to be complex.

The value of something is determined by how well it works, and so the only way for you to tell the value of numerology is by trying it. See for yourself if it doesn't tell you things about yourself and your life that you are already aware of—and a lot that you are not. It was in this exact way that I began to use numerology, for things have to prove themselves to me, and I believe that in the same way you will also begin to use it and continue to do so.

I am of the belief that no one science of this nature gives a complete picture, consequently I do not feel in competition with any of the other sciences. With numerology, one is able to get part of the picture. Add astrology and your picture becomes more complete. Palmistry gives you another view; handwriting analysis adds still more. By putting them all together you finally have the total. I do not believe that you can have a complete picture without numerology, because although each of these sciences may cover some of the same areas, they also specialize. They each have a way of reinforcing the other and at the same time tell something that cannot be found elsewhere.

In numerology we work with the numbers 1 through 9 and the master numbers 11, 22, and 33. The master numbers are never reduced, but all other two or more digit numbers are reduced to one digit. For instance, if we have the number 25, we add the 2 and 5 together: $2 + 5 = 7$. So the number we work with is 7. With years, such as 1941, we add all of the digits together: $1 + 9 + 4 + 1 = 15$. Then we must add the 1 and 5 together: $1 + 5 = 6$. Thus the number we work with is 6. The exception to this rule would be in the case of such dates as 1948, where the sum would be 22. As this is a master number, it is not reduced.

When we are considering dates we have months to deal with, and each month has a number of its own. We know that the number for March is 3 because it is the third month. The number for December is 12, but because 12 is a two-digit number we must add the 1 and 2 together. This makes December a 3 month in numerology. October is the tenth month, and with 10 and other numbers ending in zero (20, 30, 40, 50), we have only to strike out the zero to have the number we are to work with.

Each letter of the alphabet has its own number or vibratory influence, although there are letters with the same numbers. Below is the table for the letters.

1	2	3	4	5	6	7	8	9	11	22
A	B	C	D	E	F	G	H	I		
J		L	M	N	O	P	Q	R	K	
S	T	U		W	X	Y	Z			V

Now that we have a guide for the vibratory influence of each letter, we can begin to take a look at how we arrive at the influence of words. We first figure the influence of each letter and then add them together until we have one digit to work with.

```
G  E  O  R  G  E                K  A  R  E  N
7 + 5 + 6 + 9 + 7 + 5 = 39      11 + 1 + 9 + 5 + 5 = 31
3 + 9 = 12   1 + 2 = 3                3 + 1 = 4
```

```
            O  H  I  O
            6 + 8 + 9 + 6 = 29
                2 + 9 = 11
```

```
        N  E  W                Y  O  R  K
        5 + 5 + 5 = 15         7 + 6 + 9 + 11 = 33
            1 + 5 = 6    +           33 = 39
                3 + 9 = 12   1 + 2 = 3
```

With the sums reduced to one digit we see that *George* is a total of 3, the total for *Karen* is 4, the number we have to work with for *Ohio* is 11 (which we do not reduce because it is a master number), and the total for *New York* is a 3. Notice that in calculating *New York* we also do not reduce the number 33, but that when it is added to the 6 it is no longer a master number, and then is reduced. We must not lose sight of the fact that within the 3 of *New York* is the 33.

In the numbers from 1 to 9 are to be found all of the experiences that life can present. Here are to be found all the things we must learn about, and in one life or another we carry all of the vibrations in each of the positions in our chart. In this way we learn about all of life's experiences from different angles. Although there are basic characteristics for each of the numbers, they do vary some, depending upon where in the chart they appear. One is the number of beginning, and some aspect of the 1 is to be found in each of the other numbers, for the 1 is contained in them all. Nine is the number of completion, and in it can be found some of all the rest of the numbers, for the 9 is all numbers.

Each number has both positive and negative aspects, because nothing is all positive or all negative. The master numbers are far more powerful than the other nine numbers in both positive and negative aspects. When you find these numbers in your chart you must take care and watch closely, lest they begin to produce the negative aspects of these vibrations. The negative aspects of the master numbers are far more destructive than the negative aspects of the others.

The true mission of the master numbers is that of service to their fellowman, each in their own way. If the power of these numbers is used for any other purpose, the results can be very bad for the holder of the number. Despite how it may seem to those of us who judge others from material standpoints, these numbers are only given to souls that are quite old and who have lived through experiences that make them fit to handle such vibrations. They have actually come as leaders and masters, though they themselves are often unaware of this. They too can get lost in the confusion of the material world and so lose sight of the path, but generally this is temporary. Because they are numbers of considerable power, they also contain a lot of tension and are not at all easy to live up to. They require a lot of control. Since all numbers have both positive and negative aspects, each vibration has to be carefully studied and the negative aspects guarded against.

Not all books on numerology include the number 33, perhaps because it is so rarely found and because it has such an extremely powerful vibration. It can be said to be the master of the master numbers; it is truly a combination of the 11 and 22 and carries the power of both. Only the oldest and most advanced souls are ever given this vibration, for if it is not used correctly it is definitely destructive. It is as complex as it is powerful and very difficult to understand and explain. It is not only the 11 and 22, but it is the 3 doubled, and the 6, and the 9, and all of these are elevated far above themselves into the realm of the purely spiritual. I am including the 33 because in the times in which we now live, in this new age with the coming of the Christ close at hand, many master souls are now incarnating upon the earth to help us through the times that are to come, and some of them will be carrying this vibration. For those of you who pursue numerology, this will help you to identify some of these souls and will in turn aid them in seeing their path.

As you begin to study the characteristics of the numbers you will note that many of them have things in common. Generally we find that an even number has more in common with the other even numbers, and to some extent this is very true of odd numbers with odd numbers. It can be said that for the most part the even numbers are the doers and are more concerned with the things of the material world, and the odd numbers are the dreamers and are concerned more with unseen worlds. The doers are interested in success in the material world and test things for their use and efficiency. The dreamers love things of beauty and spirituality; they are idealistic and emotional and test things subjectively.

There is no doubt that people are changing, no matter how it may seem on the surface. For example, in all of the charts that I have done, I have found almost no doers. This is a sign that the world is beginning to change from the very materialistic outlook it has held for so long. When considering the even and odd numbers, realize that the 11 is one of the odd numbers but that the 22 and 33 are dual. While the 11 is a master number, it has not yet progressed to the point where it truly sees the best of both worlds nor has it learned how to really function in the material without losing sight at least partially of the spiritual. The 22 and 33 have achieved a balance by which they can function in both worlds at the same time and achieve a harmony where nothing is lost. This is especially true of the 33. The goal of the 9 is to begin to see that this is possible, even if it may not reach the point of understanding how.

No number is ever limited to what it is, neither is a person limited by the numbers in his or her chart unless that is his or her choice. If we can learn to attune ourselves to the highest aspects of any vibration, we can elevate that vibration to the one above it, so that there really is no limit to the heights we can achieve. We have only to set a goal and begin to work toward it, discarding any thoughts of limitations we may have, for in truth the only limitations we have are in our own minds. You have the ability to be anything that you would like to be, and numerology can help to show you the way to reach your goal. Your today is a product of your yesterday, and so your tomorrow will be a product of your today. Let's get on with building a better tomorrow, and the time to start is right now.

Two

BASIC CHARACTERISTICS
OF THE NUMBERS

For each number, key words are given that can quickly begin to give you an understanding of the vibration and an idea of the other characteristics of that number. But to truly understand yourself or anyone else with numerology, you must go into these numbers in greater depth.

There is negative in all of us, but those who are vibrating to several of the negative aspects of a vibration all have one thing in common: they are in a rut. Those with considerable negatives are parasites. They are so lazy or self-satisfied that they do not care to contribute anything worthwhile to life, and rarely do. All too often they tend to think that the rest of the world owes them a living. If a negative is allowed to remain unchallenged, it eventually becomes destructive. The true purpose of all negatives is to force us into destruction. It is in this way that so-called evil in the end destroys itself. When we get tired enough of the consequences that it brings upon us we will begin to fight it and bring it to its own end.

If we take a look at ourselves and feel that because we are mainly in tune with the positive aspects of our vibrations, and if we ignore the negative and do nothing to rid ourselves of it, we can add the negative laziness to our list. None of us is totally positive, but we can at least strive continually in that direction, ridding ourselves of any negative that we can. After all, we are the ones who will reap the rewards of our efforts.

1—THE INDIVIDUAL

The 1 stands alone, generally out in front. One is the beginner, the creator, the instigator, a person who is truly independent and individual, original and progressive. You are a pacesetter, leader, and director. This is a vibration of activity, stimulation, willpower, initiative, positiveness, force, and invention. You have courage, faith in yourself and in your own ideas, a desire to be different, a style and mind all your own. You are quick-acting and clever. You are pioneering and rebel at commands.

If vibrating to the negative, the 1 is procrastinating, stubborn, lazy, dependent, selfish, and weak. He is prone to egotism, stagnation, tyranny, antagonism, and bullying, regardless of who or what it hurts. The greatest danger of the 1 is self-centeredness.

The 1 needs most to develop a friendlier attitude and increased interest in others.

2—COOPERATION AND DIPLOMACY

The 2 is definitely not a loner, in fact to you companionship is almost essential. You are full of love and service and are tactful, charming, receptive, gentle, quite emotional and sensitive, and studious. You show a liking for detail and order. You can be quite an analyst, and you have a desire for balance and a dual nature that is the blending of opposites. Generally adaptable, you are also unassuming, patient, and friendly. You like rhythm and music. The 2 is often interested in things of the occult world.

The negative 2 is indifferent, careless, discontent, oversensitive, imitative, and critical. You lack courage, are shy and sulky, have a bad temper, and can be sullen, sly, and cruel. Apple-polishing, mischief-making, and an inclination toward pessimism and lying are other unpleasant aspects of your nature.

The 2 needs to learn the value of discipline, to be more positive, and to decide with conviction upon a purpose and go toward it with force.

3—EXPRESSION AND WORDS

The 3 has a need for self-expression that often exhibits itself in art, literary work, or in the field of entertainment. You are always a talker, usually with your hands as well as with your mouth. The 3 is filled with a joy of living and rarely worries; you are by nature an optimist. You represent youth, happiness, imagination, inspiration, talent, and charm. You have good taste and are friendly, loving, popular, kind, emotional, clever, and a genial host. You like dancing, color, rhythm, and things of beauty. Basically the 3 has three parts: the physical, the mental, and the spiritual, and these generally manifest themselves as imagination, intellect, and intuition.

The negative 3 is whining, extravagant, vain, trivial, critical, jealous, wasteful, intolerant, and superficial. You are inclined to be a gossip and a hypocrite, to be full of worry and silly pride, and to have a yellow streak. There is the constant danger that in your great desire to express yourself, you may make yourself an unwelcome bore by continually talking, saying what you want when you want, for as long as you want, without consideration for others.

The 3 needs to show self-control and patience and to acquire the ability to concentrate.

4—WORK AND DISCIPLINE

The 4 is practical, patient, exacting, regular and dependable, enduring, economical, organized, conservative, loyal, conscientious, punctual, energetic, and generally the perfect employee. You are hard-working, logical, analytical, busy mentally and physically, and accurate. You show a liking for detail and proportion and are devoted, patriotic, and dignified. Not emotional, you are trustworthy and like things that require concentration. You are a person who believes that nothing is gained without a lot of hard work.

The negative 4 can easily become narrow-minded, repressed, plodding, crude, cruel, vulgar, jealous, rigid, stern, and dull. You can become too concerned with minutiae. You can be too brisk, violent, unfeeling, inhuman, destructive, and full of hatred and animalistic emotions.

You must take care that you do not get into a rut and forget the lighter side of life. You must learn tolerance and to discard the outdated and to keep an open mind.

5—FREEDOM AND VARIETY

Freedom of thought, word, and action is what most 5s display. The 5 is versatile, progressive, adaptable, understanding, adventurous, mentally curious, and a keen judge of human nature. You like travel and to experience life. You enjoy social events and companionship, particularly that of the opposite sex. You are clever and amiable; you are the rejuvenator and have the ability to handle others without ever seeming to do so.

In the negative aspect of this vibration, the 5 is irresponsible, careless, self-indulgent, thoughtless, inconsistent, and procrastinating. You also have poor taste. If really let go, the negative 5 will indulge in perversion, drink, and dope and abuse things of a physical nature like sex and food.

The 5 needs to work at developing loyalty and patience, and you need to have a purpose in life.

6—RESPONSIBILITY, HOME, AND SERVICE

The 6 could be said to be the cosmic parent who is full of love, concern, sympathy, understanding, and domesticity, and who wants to "mother" all who come along. You like harmony, stability, firmness, and justice. You are a home-body and a born adviser, who wants to raise standards. You are idealistic, conscientious, poised, devoted, a good conversationalist, and often a healer. The 6 wants to give service to others, but has to be careful not to give it when it is not needed or wanted.

When not positive, the 6 can be full of anxiety and worry. You tend to be interfering, smug, despondent, meddlesome, and too conventional. You give unwillingly because you feel you are forced to. You can be cynical, egotistical, suspicious, a domestic tyrant, jealous, and full of misplaced sympathy that does no one any good.

The 6 can be far too personal and should guard against this. You must learn to recognize when it is best to let others struggle by themselves so they can learn to handle things themselves.

7—THE ANALYST—INNER WISDOM

Seven is the number of the true mental analyst who is introspective and who likes technical matters and scientific research. You are interested in the facts. Seven is also the number of inner wisdom and guidance and so is spiritual, intuitive, and generally full of faith and trust. You like silence so you can meditate upon the things that are important to you, and you like activity where quality is what counts. You have poise, an inner peace, perseverance, confidence, refinement, wisdom, and a desire for perfection. From the 7, expect the last word. You are usually an authority on the things you talk about. You are also gracious, sensitive, and have the ability to keep confidences.

If negative, the 7 is melancholy, aloof, sarcastic, skeptical, confused, nervous, faithless, and deceitful. You are inclined to drink and steal. You need to be careful so that you don't become something of a hermit.

Although you like to be alone, you must learn to be alone but not lonely. You should work at developing your understanding of others and should guard against fear and becoming depressed.

8—MATERIAL SUCCESS AND EFFICIENCY

The 8 is power on the material plane, and thus represents success in this area. This success is achieved through judgment, executive ability, tact, and zeal. The 8 shows material freedom, authority, management, practicality, discrimination, self-reliance, control, executive diplomacy, and dependability. You are polite, and intelligent, and your good judgment makes you a fair critic. The 8 is best suited to the world of business and finance.

The 8, if negative, can be hard, material, intolerant, scheming, and power-loving. You may be prone to strain, worry, carelessness, poor judgment, and misspent energy and have a desire for recognition. When you are at your lowest, you can be cruel, unscrupulous, and a bully.

The 8 must learn to be tolerant and fair and to guard against becoming overly materialistic.

9—HUMAN UNDERSTANDING AND COMPLETION

The 9 is to learn about and demonstrate love on a universal scale. This is really not as impossible as it sounds, especially for the 9. You are by nature charitable and compassionate and give selfless service because you are something of a humanitarian. You are spiritual, romantic, emotional, magnetic, intuitive, efficient, responsible, cooperative, creative, and independent. You understand the true meaning of freedom and the value of discipline, and have a lot of artistic talent and a broad outlook on life. You should think of others before yourself, and if you put the welfare of others first, you should possess health, money, and love.

In most cases the 9 is an indication that the other numbers have been experienced. As the 9 is a composite of the other numbers, it is considered the completion number.

The lower aspects of the 9 are emotionalism, impracticality, aimless dreaming, egocentricity, sentimentality, fickleness, bitterness, immorality, vulgarity, indiscretion, coldness, and an uncaring, selfish nature.

The 9 needs balance, emotional control, and a purposefulness that it does not naturally possess.

11—REVELATION AND INSPIRATION

The 11 truly possesses intuition and spirituality. You are full of fire and zeal and are generally inventive and idealistic. You are a dreamer and a mystic who may well be clairvoyant. Eleven is electrical and high-strung, and you can have dynamic power if you put it to use. Intuitive penetration, insight, and a capacity for leadership and quick decisions all are part of the make-up of the 11. You like things of beauty like music, poetry, and art and appreciate contact with stimulating minds. You can be an inspiration to others.

The 11 is powerful and if not handled carefully easily falls into the negative and is then impractical and aimless with no real goal or purpose. You can be miserly, shiftless, and lacking in understanding—you can impose your will on others. You can be fanatic, full of pride, dishonest and devilish.

The mission of the 11 is selfless service to mankind, and therefore you need to develop your human understanding.

22—THE MASTER BUILDER

This vibration conceives the tremendous plan and achieves tremendous results. You see the inspired vision and then put it into practical use. Here is power on all planes, understanding of human nature, direction and uplift, organization, highly developed intuition, skill, and diplomacy. You like people, travel, accomplishment, and coordinating. The 22 can be the master analyst in any field if you vibrate to the highest aspect of this number.

The negative 22 is full of big talk and schemes to make money fast for self-promotion. You are indifferent, give grudging service, often have an inferiority complex, are vicious, and may be involved in black magic or crime. The great power of the 22 is there to be used; the way in which it is used is up to you.

The mission of the 22 is also selfless service, and in the midst of the materiality of our world you need to hold strongly to your ideals so that they will not be lost.

33—SPIRITUAL CONSCIOUSNESS AND POWER

The master of the numbers, the 33 is the vibration of spiritual service. It is love in the divine sense of the word; it knows no bounds. Complete tolerance, patience and understanding, realization of the laws of universal harmony, service to mankind on the largest and most selfless scale of all, and devotion to nothing of the material world are all attributes of the 33. This number is capable of the greatest inspiration and revelation and usually possesses great psychic powers. There is very little that the 33 is not capable of, and the use of this tremendous power depends upon the soul who carries this vibration.

The negative aspects of the 33 are the negative aspects of the 6, intensified to a very destructive level. Because this vibration is only given to the oldest and most qualified souls, it is doubtful that you need to consider the negative. If you should by some remote chance succumb to it, you will surely be made to realize your error very quickly.

You need to work at gaining a full realization of the fact that you are indeed a master soul and that you have great powers and abilities. You must also consider at the same time the enormous responsibility that goes hand in hand with these gifts.

Three

THE INNER SELF

Within each of us there is a "best self," which creates desires and urges. This best self has a lot to do with what we would like to be. The "inner self" is concerned with what makes up this best self. This is the part of us that others do not see, but we feel it within ourselves. It has much to do with our feelings, thoughts, and actions, and so is closely related with our personality. It affects our judgment, our outlook on life, our principles, and is generally our motivating force. The number of the inner self has great power and influence in our life. Basically, we can say that the inner self is what we want to do and be, and therefore is largely what we are.

The inner self is found by considering the vowels of our complete name at birth. No matter how many names we may have in a lifetime, the inner self remains the same. To accurately figure someone's soul urge, we must know his or her exact name at birth.

The main vowels are *a, e, i, o,* and *u. W* is a vowel when it is used with another vowel and together they are sounded as one, as with *aw, ew,* and *ow.* Thus *w* is a vowel in words like *Lewis* or *Dow. Y* is a vowel if it follows another vowel and is sounded as one, as with *ay, ey, oy.* Thus *y* is a vowel in words like *Gayle* or *Roy. Y* is also a vowel when there is no other

vowel in the syllable, as each syllable must have a vowel. So
Y is a vowel in words like *Smyth* and *Tyrone*.

One other thing to consider when we are working with
someone's name is *junior*. *Junior* is calculated only if it was part
of the name at birth. If it was a later addition, then it is not used.
If someone was named David Harvey Williams, Junior, at
birth, we must use all four names when doing his chart. This
holds true for names given at christenings and the like; they
were not given at birth, and therefore we don't use them when
working up a chart.

Now let's look at an example of how we find the inner self:

```
6 7   5 5   1       1   5
D O Y L E   E D W A R D   W A L K E R
```

First we add together the vowels of Doyle: $6 + 7 + 5 = 18 =$ 9
Next we add together the vowels of Edward: $5 + 1 =$ 6
Then we add the vowels of Walker: $1 + 5 =$ 6
Now we total these sums: $9 + 6 + 6 =$ 21
Lastly we reduce this figure to one digit: $2 + 1 = 3$

In this manner we find that the inner self of Doyle Edward
Walker is a 3. This is the formula that is always used to find
the inner self, remembering that only the vowels from the full
name at birth are used to calculate the inner self. Now use this
formula to calculate your own inner self, and then look at the
chart of the numbers of the inner self to see just what your inner
self is.

THE NUMBERS OF THE INNER SELF

1—You want to be creative, original, in control of all situations in which you are involved—the leader, manager, director.
You are proud of your capabilities and like to be praised. Independent, you would rather work alone, but if you must work
with others, you want to be the boss. Thus you are a better
employer than employee. You are inclined to be an introvert,
but you can also be very outgoing. You like others to be aware

of your talents. You can accomplish great things, even though at times it may only be for self-glory. You do not like detail work and may ignore it to concentrate on main issues. You are very proud and want your family to live up to your standards so that you will look good to others. You hate disgrace and can be easily humiliated and embarrassed. You are not generally emotional, and love may not be a necessity to you. You are usually fair in business dealings, a loyal friend, and an able leader. You like to go continually forward and are inclined to be active and forceful to the point of boldness. You are good at starting things, and if you use your strong willpower, you will be good at finishing them too.

2—Sensitive and emotional, you like peace and harmony in all things, and so you are very diplomatic and careful of the feelings of others. You are thoughtful, loving, and devoted and often are considered "soft" because you are easy-going, kind, and friendly. You hate to work alone, and you like doing things for others. You prefer to leave center stage to others, are not very ambitious, and seldom discipline either yourself or others. You may fall in love easily and be in tears over seemingly nothing because you have such a sensitive nature. You do not like things that are rigid or set and are content with small things. While enjoying comfort and the like, you do not expect wealth and a life of luxury and generally do not strive for them. You can be studious and with your learning end up with much wisdom. Your desire for collecting things may manifest itself in many ways, and you seem to attract things to you. You can keep a confidence and are good at sharing problems because of your caring nature.

3—You are generally happy and optimistic, and because you do not let life's problems get you down, you set a good example for others. You are inclined toward looking at life as a game, laughing at the bad times, and you rarely if ever worry. You are very emotional and loving, and if you cry, it's not for long. You are very social, loving crowds and people in general, and like to do a lot of entertaining. You don't care much for being alone and want to be popular and have a lot of friends. You may be artistic, and you definitely love things of beauty and want them around you. You can be like a butterfly—flitting from here to there—but you spread happiness wherever you go because of your sense of humor and your interested, entertaining nature. You give your mistakes and failures little thought and go out to try again. You like to do things to make others happy, and although you are rarely unfaithful, you truly enjoy flirting. Usually satisfied with what you find or get, you tend to just give thanks for whatever comes your way. You are a talker, rarely at a loss for something to say, though at times you may talk a lot and really say nothing. Normally a favorite of children and animals, they are usually a favorite of yours too. In many ways you may seem to others to still be a child yourself because you possess many of their characteristics and qualities.

4—You are the solid, conservative, respectable citizen upon whom others may depend. You love your home, family, and community and like to be of service. You do not take easily to new things and prefer everything to be well ordered. You are very punctual and hate to be kept waiting. Conventional, you bow to your conscience, traditions, and usually your superiors. You work best when your work is outlined for you and if you do not have to get in on the planning end of things. You are very good with details and matters that require concentration. You tend to do things in a slow, sure, and systematic manner with great efficiency. You are thorough and dislike haste and waste. You take great pride in your family and are strong in the area of discipline—you discipline yourself as well as others. You will generally give up almost anything for the good of others, often to the point where your self-denial is foolish and harmful to yourself. You are faithful, constant, and loyal, and if people really want to make you angry, they have only to confront you with pretension, deceit, or insincerity. To others you may seem cold and unfeeling, but they shouldn't be fooled by that hard exterior. Underneath you have a great need for love, although you may find it hard to respond when it is given.

5—Your greatest desire is for personal freedom in every area of life, and you should never tie yourself down very tightly. You are bored easily and should keep your life active and varied. You love to be on the go—traveling and seeing new people, places, and things. You always adapt quickly to changes. Life fascinates you; it's an adventure and you love adventures. You are intellectual, curious, emotional, and as changeable as the wind and as fast-moving. You like sunshine and the outdoors, pleasure, crowds, sports, art, music, and science. You do not like details, routine, restrictions, waiting, and remaining when you are ready to go. You can be spiritual, but you see things in your own way. It is hard for you to take responsibility seriously and you may not give it a second thought. You let go of things easily and will not be bound by the conventional or the ideas of others. Wherever you go you add a spark, and so you're usually the star of any group—no matter how brief your stay. The opposite sex draws you like a magnet. You love quickly and even deeply, then suddenly you're on to new worlds, not realizing you've left broken hearts behind. You are the modern-day gypsy, just wanting to roam and be free.

6—As a professional counselor you'd be in seventh heaven because you love to give advice, to manage other people's lives, and to turn all wrong into right. It's not that you're bossy, you just truly love, care, and feel concern for others and want to help. For you your life is your home, family, and friends. You are a good counselor and a very loyal friend because you are kind, sympathetic, understanding, generous, devoted, and broad-minded, even though you're generally conventional. You love to do things for others, though you do appreciate thanks and even praise. You're happiest when working with others, or when someone is in need and you can open your arms, door, or purse strings. You can be artistic and love beauty, music, and comfort. You're inclined to put everything on a personal level and are easily involved emotionally. You want to heal everyone's wounds and see justice done in all things. No matter how large your home, it will probably be full—if only with strays—be they animals or people, for you're too tenderhearted to turn anyone away. Because you need a place to call your own and "roots," you try to give others the same.

7—You are the thinker who has to look at something from all sides and then take it apart to see the middle as well. If you see the top, you must see the bottom. Because of this you gain much wisdom, and although you may not speak often, when you do you usually know what you're talking about. You have an intellectual and scientific approach to things. You value silence, peace, and meditation, and therefore you are spiritual and philosophical, possibly interested in metaphysics and the occult. You can be intuitive and possess great inner wisdom— a quiet kind of *knowing*. You love old things, poetry, flowers, the country, and being alone, though you fear being lonely. Often withdrawn, you are secretive, reserved, conservative, and refined. You like things that have "class," be it cars, clothes, furniture, or people. The business world with its material attitude and confusion is not for you, nor is manual labor, for you prefer using your head to your hands. You are a perfectionist and like to see all things done correctly. Often sought because of your wisdom, you are normally shy and give forth little unless asked. You are extremely emotional, but you hide it as you do all of your feelings, making it hard for others to really get to know or understand you.

8—The born businessman or businesswoman, you truly shine when you're wheeling and dealing in the financial world or managing some business affair—the bigger the better. What you dislike is taking a back seat while someone else drives. You make a good driver because you're efficient, organized, a keen judge of people and what will be successful, exacting of both yourself and others, courageous, and determined. You have the ability to be bossy without ever really seeming to be so. This is because your ideas are sound, your orders fair, and you're a hard worker yourself. Ambitious, you love money and success, and have the strength, enthusiasm, imagination, and vision to go after them and to get them. You are generally one of the pillars of the community because you are dependable, trustworthy, and honest. You want to achieve great heights and have no fear of the climb or battles along the way, for you are sure of winning, regardless of the obstacles you may encounter. You see things on a grand scale and have the power and ability to attain them. You are most at home in the commercial world where your thorough, practical nature can best be put to use—hopefully from a position of authority if we are to see a happy you.

9—Everybody's "big brother"—because of your understanding, thoughtful, sympathetic, and loving nature. When you're not being a big brother then you're being a "great lover" because you truly love people. You desire personal love, which may forever seem to escape you because you belong to the world as a whole. Until you learn to give of yourself to the world, you will never have anything that you can call your own. Because you are attractive and give of yourself so freely, you are easily loved, and unless you understand that love you're going to keep going around in circles. You really feel for others and are always trying to help. Take care that you don't spread yourself too thin and do no one any good. Intuitive and even psychic, you often know other people's thoughts and can be easily hurt because you have trouble looking past personality. You want to share with others, especially your knowledge, talents, beliefs, and wisdom. You have a way with words and people and an understanding of life that you can best get across by personal example. You are spiritual and have faith and a driving need to know the answers and to perceive truth. You rarely meet a stranger because you look upon everyone as a member of one big family. You are not materialistic, and you feel drawn by the unseen worlds. What you want most is to find some way to do something really great for your fellowman—something that will benefit mankind.

11—You are a dreamer. And since dreamers are not always practical, so it is with you. The visions you have are great, but you need to learn to make them a reality if they are to do anyone any good. Idealistic and spiritual, you'd like to save the world and tell everyone your ideas about God and religion. Your ideas for bettering the world would be more workable if you'd take a closer look at the needs of your fellowmen and then consider them. Right to you is as you see it, but remember that everyone is not ready for your level of thinking. The difference is mainly that you live in another world. You can live there, but you are still a part of this one too and must learn to live here. Don't be too upset if others don't understand the revelations that come to you, or see the beauty in things as you do. You have great inner strength and an inventive mind that you need to put to use. Because you like to choose your friends from among your own kind, you may not have very many. There aren't many people who are as immaterial as you. You are intuitive and need to follow your hunches and feelings. You need to associate more with people in general to increase your understanding of them and to be able to help them, which is what you would really like to do. You also need to learn to share more with those who are less fortunate. Have faith. The world you see and wish for will one day be a reality, but you have to help make it.

22—Along with your vision and imagination you have the practicality to put them to use. Whatever you're a part of, you want it to be beneficial to others and to be as perfect as possible. Living in two worlds, you see the best of both and realize that they really aren't separate. You love people and give help whenever needed. You are a kind and patient leader, a master of any situation that comes along. You restore harmony and order in your very individual way. Spiritual and progressive, you use your great power for improvement in all areas and for enlightenment when possible. Others respect you because they realize your fairness and know you can be trusted. You have beautiful ideals and must never let others sway you from them. Trust your own judgment and seek your own counsel, for your guidance is sure. Always appreciated because you realize that others must be free to travel their own paths, do not fail to follow yours, for you have great things to accomplish and you have the power to do so. Do not underestimate yourself. One person can do wonders if his or her faith is strong enough. You are the master builder, so get busy and begin to build something worthy of the great power of your vibration.

33—Your faith and way of looking at and living life may be hard for others to understand because they cannot see the divine order in all things as you can. As complete as your understanding is, you need to find a way to simplify it so that you can teach others. You see harmony and good where others see disharmony and evil. You are able to perceive and love the inner person, regardless of what the outer person may appear to be. You live in a world most of us know nothing about. There are powers at your disposal that we cannot even comprehend. You are a leader and a teacher who demonstrates lessons rather than preach them. Others either love you deeply or hate you fiercely out of jealousy, yet people can see the great good in you. There will always be those who hate what makes them feel inferior. Never thinking of yourself or caring for one instant about what comes your way, you live for others and consequently are always provided for and protected. You have come to show others how to put the spiritual to use in the material world and to share the things you know. Although your way may be quiet and unassuming, you will always have a following of those who are aware of the light you are here to shed. So, let your light shine, for there are many waiting to be shown the way.

Four

THE OUTER SELF—THE PRESENT SELF

The outer self is the you that others generally see—the you they know the best—and thus could be called your impression. Because this is the part of you that is usually brought to the outside, it tells us your greatest talents, abilities, and possibilities. It has much to do with the kind of work you are best at and happiest doing, the way you look (your appearance), and the "equipment" you have been given to help you through life.

The outer self is determined from the birth name, but it is also the only vibration in our chart that can change. Actually it never really changes, for we always carry the influence of our original outer self, but it can be "added to," so to speak. When we change names or use only a part of our birth name, we take on an added vibration—another outer self. Most often this brings about changes in us, not immediately, but over a period of time. Sometimes these changes cause disharmony in our chart and therefore in our lives. You will understand this when you have studied numerology to a greater extent. When you are calculating the outer self, you need to work with both your original name and your present.

To arrive at the outer self we must find the sum of all of the letters of the name, both vowels and consonants. The original, which is calculated from your full birth name, is called the outer self. The outer self that is calculated from your present name is called the present self. When you have figured both, as in the example given, then consult the numbers of the outer self to see what the characteristics of each vibration are. Remember that your actual outer self, or that of someone else, may be the original, or the present, or a combination of the characteristics of both.

$$
\begin{array}{ccc}
\text{N I K K I} & \text{K A R E N} & \text{C A B E} \\
\underline{5 - 9 - 11 - 11 - 9} & \underline{11 - 1 - 9 - 5 - 5} & \underline{3 - 1 - 2 - 5} \\
45/9 \quad + & 31/4 \quad + & 11 \; = 24/6
\end{array}
$$

The outer self calculated from the full birth name of Nikki Karen Cabe is a 6.

$$
\begin{array}{cc}
\text{N I K K I} & \text{P I T T} \\
\underline{5 - 9 - 11 - 11 - 9} & \underline{7 - 9 - 2 - 2} \\
45/9 \quad + & 20 \; = 11
\end{array}
$$

The present self calculated from the name Nikki is presently using is an 11.

   The outer self can help us decide what we are best fitted to do in life. When considering an occupation, keep in mind your preferences and the things you have a natural tendency for, plus the things that you have already learned to do. Sometimes it is helpful to list these things and then list the jobs or professions that appeal to you. Then investigate the opportunities that are available to you. If what you would really like to do, and feel you're fitted for, isn't open to you at present, do not give up the idea of reaching that goal. Proceed to work toward it in any way you can and watch for the chance to have the job. Be aware that to get the job you really want you may have to take one that leads to it, which may not be all to your liking. You will like it a lot better if you keep in mind what the job will lead to and do your very best at it. There is a law that says we must give to get, and we must not do it grudgingly or with resentment. The suggestions for occupations which follow are just that, *suggestions,* and should not be taken as the only things that you should consider doing. They are merely meant to be guidelines to indicate areas where you may be well suited.

THE NUMBERS OF THE OUTER SELF

1—A tower of strength, you walk boldly, head held high, for you know just where you are going—and it's probably to stand in front. Once there, you will take charge because you have definite ideas about how things ought to be run, and you feel you are capable of running them. You like things to go your way, which is forward quickly. You'll never be happy if things are at a standstill, and you have far too much energy to be still for long. If others aren't willing to follow where you lead, or if they cannot keep up with your pace, then you'll probably leave them behind. You'd prefer to be alone anyway. Usually a sharp dresser, you like bright colors and bold patterns, all in the latest styles, and your personality is strong enough that such things suit you. You have your own ideas about things, and the opinions of others are not likely to sway you from your convictions. You need to be your own boss or somebody else's. If that isn't possible at first, at least pick a job where you can eventually advance to such a position. Keep in mind that you are creative, original, clever, inventive, and able to make quick decisions, and above all, you are an individual. Find a place where these qualities can best be put to use.

The 1 Child—It strives to be independent, asserting itself whenever it can. It needs to develop in its own way and does not take orders well. Often bossy, especially with other children, it may be the neighborhood bully and instigator. It is creative, active, strong-willed, and energetic and needs to be directed. It is often concerned with its own desires and feelings and consequently can be thoughtless. If it runs with a crowd, it will only be because this child leads it, because it probably won't have a lot of close friends. In school it will do well if it isn't allowed to get bored and if it doesn't have to sit still for too long a time. It has an inquiring mind and a quick one. It may well be hard to raise, but if it is properly guided, it can grow up to be a true leader of men, and a good one.

Possible Occupations for a 1—Writer, inventor, designer, editor, musician, actor or actress, specialist in internal medicine or psychiatry, lawyer, contractor, director or manager, promoter, salesperson, buyer, guide, politician, illustrator, geographer, inspector, architect, analyst, pilot, explorer, business owner, credit worker, farmer, idea person, manufacturer, telephone operator and repairer.

2—The quiet type, you appear to others to be sweet, shy, and reserved. And you probably are. When you walk into a room you don't make others sit up and take notice, but you really don't want them to anyway. You would rather that someone else be the center of attention, and if the spotlight should be on you, you are likely to be very uncomfortable. Whatever the crowd decides is usually OK with you, and so you're known for being agreeable and easy to get along with. Very sensitive, your feelings can be easily hurt, and you are careful not to say things to hurt others. Most of your clothes are conservative—you aren't one to be gaudy since you don't like to call attention to yourself. You tend to walk like you aren't too sure of yourself, and you may not be. You are happiest when working with others in an atmosphere of harmony, and you really don't like being alone. When looking for employment consider your abilities and interests. You like detail work and order. You have an analytical mind, possess tact and diplomacy, patience, a studious nature, and show a fondness for music and a possible interest in the occult.

The 2 Child—Usually easy-going and agreeable, this child can be a mother's joy. It is loving and likes to do things to please others and to gain praise and approval. Often overly sensitive, you will need to be careful of its feelings, or tears may be frequent. Submissive, this child is easily led—sometimes too much so—and it needs to be taught not to let others influence it too much. In school this child is usually a good student if not a fast or bright one and has a liking for detail. It concentrates well and its patience keeps it from becoming bored easily. Studious and quiet, it may read a lot. It enjoys playing with toys that can be assembled. It needs friends and little time alone, and if an only child will be a lot happier if it has a pet or two. It needs to be of service, so don't be upset if sometimes it is too helpful.

Possible Occupations for a 2—Musician, bookkeeper, librarian, diplomat, politician, teacher, poet, collector, secretary, civil servant, novelist, companion, psychologist, office worker, singer or dancer in a group, statistician, biographer, columnist, club organizer, physicist, composer, sculptor, bacteriologist, tour director, merchant, producer, landscaper, analyst, publisher, psychic or medium, or anything in the occult world, astronomer, and any job providing service: repairman, mechanic, waitress.

3—You are a fashion-setter, and people rarely forget you or fail to notice you. And you would be upset if they did. In appearance, you are attractive and well dressed and have a liking for jewelry and accessories. In manner, you are friendly, animated, full of personality, witty, and usually talkative. How could you not be noticed, and maybe envied? We can rely upon you to tell us what you believe in, how you feel about things, and anything else that comes to mind. You have a way of making the dullest story interesting and life's problems look a lot smaller. A job for you depends upon which aspect of this number you vibrate to: the mental, the physical-emotional, or the social. You can even be quite spiritual. However, don't forget your charm, imagination, love of people, ability to talk, cleverness, liking for beauty and music, need for expression, and your sense of humor.

The 3 Child—Rarely quiet and often loud, it is full of personality and cuteness. It's a real charmer and is often spoiled.

Relishing every minute of attention it can get, it'll do a lot to get it. It's not inclined to be studious and learns better by seeing and doing than from books. Among its favorite activities may be painting, coloring, craft projects, and working with clay. Its artistic ability and imagination may surprise you. In fact it is so imaginative that it may be great at inventing tall tales—often it believes them. It likes people, pets, lots of friends, and social gatherings. Not always easy to manage and very apt to say whatever it thinks, one should encourage this child's artistic ability and not be taken in by its charm.

Possible Occupations for a 3—Writer—especially fiction, jeweler, entertainer, lecturer, clergyman or evangelist, designer, humorist, actor or actress, artist, dressmaker, salesman, beautician, welfare worker, decorator, doctor, lawyer, promoter, photographer, chemist, linguist, worker in advertising or newspapers, worker in arts and crafts, druggist, cartoonist, electrician, handler of animals, dog trainer, rancher, poultry farmer, and teacher.

4—Never flashy, you're the tailor-made suit in conservative colors and styles. To some you may appear plain, but it's really quiet dignity that they in their bright and gaudy clothes do not understand. You are neat and walk with a slow, sure step. All of your actions are very definite, as if planned thoroughly in advance. You're not one to talk a lot, or loudly—you're no show-off. You may even be self-conscious at times. When you go job-hunting, look for a position where your love of detail work, routine, order, and perfection are usable. Work that requires much patience could be right up your alley. If you're intellectually inclined, you might enjoy teaching others how to do something the right way, though you'd be an exacting teacher who disciplined strongly and probably would grade hard. But then, you're not easy on yourself either.

The 4 Child—It likes routine and will be at its best as long as the routine is established and fairly well kept. This child may assert its preferences where clothes or food are concerned.

Quiet and studious, it may not be too tolerant if disturbed. It needs a lot of love, but don't expect it to come to you for love, and it may not act grateful when it is given. Don't be fooled by its bluff. Give it something complicated to do, work that requires concentration, and watch it go to town. It should do well in school and with things that require manual dexterity. Watch for jealousy so that it will not get out of hand. And don't expect this child to be too social.

Possible Occupations for a 4—Builder or contractor, architect, accountant, dispatcher, author—generally technical, banker, factory employee, service station attendant, inspector, military officer, instructor, economist, bricklayer, doctor or nurse, electrician, plumber, technician, printer, dentist, tailor, post office clerk, cashier, office worker, watch repairer, waitress, manufacturer of well-made items, skilled laborer, proofreader, linotype operator, engraver, buyer, draftsman, engineer, farmer, gardener or landscaper, and mechanic.

5—You'll generally be noticed wherever you go, if not for your striking appearance, then for your friendly nature and your way with people. You dislike looking like everyone else and may wear some combinations and colors that others would be afraid to try—but on you they usually look great. Your moods change with a snap of the fingers and so does everything else about you. People do not have to know you for long to realize they can never second-guess you—you can be depended upon to be different and changeable. Sell an Eskimo a freezer? You could do it with ease, especially if the Eskimo was of the opposite sex. For you a job must offer variety, a chance to associate with people, and some way to put your mental ability and curiosity to work. You'd really like to be in a position of authority so your good judgment and your liking for and ability to handle people could be made to work for you.

The 5 Child—A bundle of energy who is bored almost before it's involved, it'll probably keep you hopping and guessing. Always on the go and so curious, and just when you've had it, this child flashes a big smile and cuddles up to you, and you melt inside. You can get mad at it, but you'll rarely stay that way for long. Even rarer is finding something that will hold its interest for long. It's a free spirit and there's little hope of caging or repressing it—it'll only rebel all the more. This child has to learn about life on its own, probably starting young, and you can only hope it'll learn from experience. School won't be easy because it moves far too slowly. Try to keep a variety of things on hand for this child to do. One child now, another the next minute—maybe ten in a day or less—it'll make life a merry-go-round, going so fast you may get dizzy.

Possible Occupations for a 5—Salesman of anything, lawyer, inventor, correspondent, detective, promoter, Secret Service agent, reporter, claims adjuster, broker, booking agent, tour guide, aviator, navigator, geographer, surveyor, photographer, writer, politician, entertainer, lecturer, psychologist, personnel director, merchant mariner, explorer, critic, mining or electrical specialist, theatrical manager or director, civic leader—even a bum!

6—You're not one to start an argument—in fact, you prefer settling them. You'd like to make everything better for everyone, and you try to do so in your quiet way. You usually display good taste in all you say, do, and wear. When shopping, you are inclined toward things that will wear well and provide comfort. Style is fine only if it is sensible and durable. In appearance you have a look of maturity that says, "I'm reliable, sensible, responsible, and definitely adult." Because of this and your understanding nature, others tend to look to you for advice and for answers to their questions and problems. You have the ability to talk well, counsel others, command respect, manage, and bring order out of confusion. Keep these things in mind when you're looking for employment.

The 6 Child—The easiest way to manage this child is to make it feel important by giving it responsibilities. Don't be surprised if it tries to tell you how things should be done, for it starts advising at a young age. Generally it is mature beyond its years. It's a home-body and makes room for all the orphaned pets it can find. You'll break its heart if you say no when it hauls them home. Having a pet of its own to care for would be very good. Usually agreeable, it's not much for fighting or creating disturbances. It's not generally studious but usually does well in school because it feels that it should. It is inclined to want others to adhere to its rules and see things as it does. Often a worrier and maybe overly proud, this child is really loving and devoted and very attached to its family.

Possible Occupations for a 6—Doctor or nurse, teacher, welfare worker, counselor of any kind, personnel director, hotel manager, governess, nursery school worker, director of a youth group, student adviser, cosmetician, social director, professional housekeeper, librarian, minister, actor or actress, musician, chef, publisher, costume designer, song writer, poet, merchant, public service employee, receptionist, hotel clerk, union official, economist, instructor, decorator, chemist, therapist.

7—Dignity and refinement describe you fairly well, although you can seem aloof and even cold at times. You're not ruffled easily and take everything in your stride. You enter a room quietly, analyzing and taking everything in. You are usually graceful and poised and dress stylishly. You see all sides of everything, and so your opinion is usually valued and sought. You dislike people who talk about things they know nothing about, so when you speak you know your ground and may even be considered an authority. You value knowledge and wisdom and are a lover of books. Your studious, mental nature should be taken into account when looking for work, as well as your liking to be alone. Things of perfection, technique, spirituality, quality, confidence, and a scientific nature appeal to you. Never forget to use your intuition, heed your inner guidance, and radiate your inner peace.

The 7 Child—If it seems to live in a world all its own, shutting all else out, don't worry or try to change it. This child is very mental and needs quiet to think about things. Give it a toy and it'll take it apart to see what makes it work. Usually wise for its years, it may make you feel like the child at times. A true bookworm, it'll do well in school but may not shine socially. It loves being loved, but it's hard for this child to show it. And you may never really understand or know it because it keeps so much to itself. It is sensitive and emotional, but it'll usually go off alone to cry. It is secretive and full of faith and trust and has an inborn spirituality that needs to be encouraged. It has a scientific nature and will prefer toys that stimulate mental activity and provide an outlet for its curiosity.

Possible Occupations for a 7—Librarian, judge, writer, preacher, university dean or administrator, psychoanalyst, scientist, appraiser, antique dealer, banker, accountant or auditor, watchmaker, historian, teacher, geologist, lawyer, designer, architect, investment counselor, florist, superintendent or foreman, editor, occultist, dentist, astronomer, doctor, technical expert, engineer.

8—You have an air of efficiency, authority, and power that usually causes others to turn to you for leadership. Normally prosperous-looking, you dress with care and are particular about details. You like clothes that look expensive and will be if you can manage it. You appear strong and your personality is often dominant at times. You are sociable. You want respect, admiration, and acknowledgment of your abilities. You're an excellent judge of what can be successful. You know what will make money, the best way of organizing things, and what will be efficient and progressive, and you know the diplomatic thing to say or do. You're a born business person and are happiest when in a position of control or have any job involving money.

The 8 Child—Its prize possession may well be its piggy bank, which usually won't be empty. In fact, it is likely to collect anything that is worthwhile, and it will take great pride in its possessions. Often this child is a trader who usually ends up with the best of the deal. Among its favorite activities: the lemonade stand, collecting pop bottles—anything that makes money. Encourage the child to use good judgment in spending its money. Explain how a savings account works, for example; it'll probably jump at the idea. Good at school, it is generally neat and efficient and often is active in groups. It has good judgment but must learn to use it and not let its ego get in the way. This child prefers to do things for itself and even may try to run things at a young age because it loves to control.

Possible Occupations for an 8—Banker, manufacturer, buyer, paymaster, cashier, business analyst, accountant, military officer, broker, compiler, head of a school, band leader or orchestra leader, newspaper executive, engineer, statistician, critic, corporation lawyer or tax lawyer, coach, office manager, purchasing agent, contractor, insurance agent, shipper, consultant, promoter, judge, financier, employee of loan or credit office, public official, financial adviser, merchant.

9—You're a romantic and wear clothes that make you look the part. Always well-dressed and neat, you like beauty and harmony in all things. Generally youthful-looking, others are rarely sure of your real age. Your actions are graceful and sometimes even dramatic, so that your personality leaves a strong impression. You are impulsive and emotional; you may laugh one moment and cry the next. You'd enjoy a job that made the most of your artistic ability, understanding, and sympathetic nature. Working where you could help others would interest you. Put your human understanding, your magnetic personality, your charm and kindness to use wherever you go.

The 9 Child—Often confused because it doesn't understand its own feelings, you too may find this child hard to understand. It has a desire to please and a loving nature; it responds sympathetically to the hurts others suffer. Its extremely emotional nature often confuses it. It can be moody at times and can also be easily depressed. It may not care much for school or for too much detail or routine. It's full of energy and possibly nervous. Artistic, it loves things that are pretty and also loves the outdoors. Learning to play a musical instrument, dancing, and athletics interest this child. It is inclined to daydreaming and is not practical. Let it grow a garden, have a pet to love, and cry when it feels the need.

Possible Occupations for a 9—Artist, circulation manager, broker, entertainer, composer, writer, teacher, doctor, lecturer, publisher, mail clerk, ranger, beautician, decorator, freight dispatcher, receptionist, navigator, social worker, preacher, healer, illustrator, astronomer, occultist, chemist, resort owner, publicist, promoter, aviator, salesman of decorative items, designer, conductor, judge, reformer, adviser, lighting engineer, reporter, lawyer, correspondent, humorist.

11—You are the charge of electricity that brings light and life to any gathering. In your eyes is a look that says, "I'm really in another world." When at your best there's a spiritual quality about you that others respond to. You're refined and never showy in dress, but your tastes can run to the exotic and mysterious. You're really not adapted to the business world because you're too impractical, high strung, and dreamy. If you seek employment there, pick your position carefully. You are inventive, intuitive, perceptive, and have the qualities necessary for leadership and quick decisions. Don't forget your love of beauty and intellectual stimulation, and your purpose of service.

The 11 Child—You'll never know where it gets all its energy —most of it will be used in playing. Often the possessor of imaginary playmates, as are the 7 and 9 children (don't be too sure they're imaginary), just let the child have its friends. It may know a lot that you don't, so try listening and asking questions instead of ignoring its "silly" talk. Give it a box and it will probably invent ways to play with it for hours. Don't talk down to this child because it will quickly begin to talk up to your level. Not generally very good in school, it just can't stay in this world long enough to really concentrate on such things. It may often seem out of reach, not seeing or hearing you. It is very bright and can learn quickly when interested. It can be a nervous child and out to have its own way if not properly directed.

Possible Occupations for an 11—Charity, welfare or social worker, inventor, leader of an inspirational enterprise or movement, teacher, telephone operator, lecturer, preacher, lawyer, character analyst, philosopher, beauty specialist, poet, biographer, composer, psychoanalyst, explorer, publicist, auctioneer, promoter, revenue collector, novelist, psychologist, political campaigner, writer on religious subjects, actor, reformer, musician.

22—There you are, the supercharged human being—radiating power possibly because you possess it. Full of nervous energy, you keep in control by doing something to benefit others. You generally look the picture of perfection. Your clothes are in flawlessly good taste. You are poised, and self-assured, and others just sense this. If people want a great idea on a really big scale, they should look you up, especially if it's going to help mankind. You not only have ideas, you know how to put them into action. You are able to organize and control, to understand others and their needs. You can accomplish almost anything, work well with and for others, cheer up those around you, and analyze all things well. Any job you choose should give you the opportunity to make use of your talents. Your intuition and skill make you valuable, and others look to you for guidance.

The 22 Child—Rarely satisfied because it knows that things can be better, this child is too young to understand how to make them that way. Even as a child a 22 may use power for self-gain, and it needs to be shown how to put power to use constructively. This child is probably the one who will start the neighborhood club or come up with plans for a tree house. One way or another, it's a busy person. Help it stay on the right path by keeping it occupied with good activities. It no doubt does fairly well in school—it wants to know all it can. Its big problem may be feelings of inferiority and therefore needs reassurance. This is a lot of power for a child to handle, and it needs all the help you can give.

Possible Occupations for a 22—Statesman, writer, analyst, C.P.A., economist, diplomat, military officer, practical reformer, politician, efficiency expert, supervisor, exporter, organizer of public works and utilities, engineer, Secret Service agent, psychiatrist, builder, doctor, stage manager, shipper, bank inspector, architectural engineer, job counselor, appraiser, translator.

33—Your inner knowledge is something most people can perceive, and when you speak, others generally listen. Your speech is usually quiet but authoritative and carefully worded. There is a humility about you that commands more respect than your power. You walk with pride because you know who and what you really are, and you treat others with respect because you see the real self in all. Your concern for others makes you well loved by many. So little concerned with the material world, you don't fuss with your personal appearance. You are so dynamic that few people will really notice the kind of clothes you wear. You have almost every quality to some degree and can adapt yourself to the needs of the moment and do a good job. Your real job is service to mankind by teaching and example, and this is the only work you should be concerned with. How you sustain yourself in this physical world is not important, for a way will be provided.

The 33 Child—The power of its vibration may well make it a problem child because it doesn't know how to cope with this gift. Be patient, understanding, and loving. Provide as much guidance as you can. Generally quiet and thoughtful, it may have a terrible temper underneath it all. Although usually loving and eager to please, this child has such depth that it may seem to be a "strange" child. It is doubtful that it will be much like other children. It possesses a keen mind and should do well in school except when it's daydreaming. It may be far more interested in studies of other things, like the stars. Full of wisdom and spirituality, it will probably spend a fair amount of time alone with its thoughts building its understanding.

What you think is important to it may not be. Maybe you need to take a closer look at your set of values and not those of the child.

Possible Occupations for a 33—Social or welfare worker, politician, teacher, lecturer, metaphysician, instructor, writer, healer, occultist, artist, musician, statesman or diplomat, salesperson of products beneficial to the public, counselor, analyst, conservationist, ranger, tour guide, personnel director, doctor, a helper of people.

Five

THE DESTINY

The number of your destiny shows where you should be going with your life. If you don't head in the direction it points, life will bring frustration, dissatisfaction, and problems of various kinds. When we ignore our destiny, or any other major number of our chart, we cause great disharmony because we are working against one of our main influences.

Our destiny shows why we are on earth, or what we came to do with our life. Consequently, if we do not follow our destiny, we are wasting our life. We will not accomplish our goal—and anything else we might happen to accomplish is of no value when the destiny is neglected.

Besides showing us what we came to do, the destiny shows the main area we picked to learn about and where we will find our opportunities to fulfill our purpose, and thus help ourselves and others. Other numbers in our chart tell us about our talents and abilities—especially that of the outer self. The destiny shows us where to put these gifts to use for the greatest benefit. For instance, if your outer self shows you are creative, you need to know whether you should put the ability to use in art, literature, or in the world of business.

Please remember that your destiny is not a matter of chance, any more than any of your other vibrations. You chose your destiny yourself, even though you do not remember doing so and may think otherwise. You may not care for the path you chose, you may wish your destiny were some other number, but your soul knew what you needed to do and picked your destiny with that in mind. If you wish to make this lifetime count, then be sure you are following your path. If you do not, you will only have the same path at some later time—in some other life. As a means of progressing, each soul must learn all of the lessons and master each of the paths.

The destiny is derived from the birth date. It is the total of the month, day, and year of your birth. For example:

$$\begin{array}{ccc} \text{July} & 29 & 1941 \\ 7 & + \ 11 \ + & 6 \ = 24/6 \end{array}$$

From this birth date the destiny we work with is 6. When you have calculated your destiny, check the numbers of the destiny to find out about your purpose, path, lessons, and opportunities.

NUMBERS OF THE DESTINY

1—Self-Development—You are to learn about individuality in this lifetime. This means you must learn self-reliance, you must become independent, and you must become aware of your own powers. It is a time to create, originate, take the initiative, strengthen your willpower, stand alone and always ahead of the rest. To fulfill your purpose you must learn about yourself; develop all aspects—body, mind, and spirit—to their greatest ability. Learn to be a leader. Your abilities are a part of the you you are to develop, so by discovering, using, and perfecting them you are advancing toward your goal. Use these abilities to help make yourself as indispensable as possible to others, in all areas of life. Do not feel bound by the patterns others have set. Be inventive. Discover and establish new ways. Opportunity also lies in freeing yourself of any thoughts of limitation. Remember you have the power to go forward at great speeds.

In activity—both physical and mental—learn to work alone and not depend upon others. Only in realizing your own value can you see anything of value in others, so your path is to find out just how very much you are capable of.

2—Self-Surrender—You are here to learn to put others before yourself. The idea is to cooperate, maintain peace, give of yourself in service, and consider the feelings of others. You must learn to truly respect your fellowman and to concern yourself with getting along with everyone. Learn patience, understanding, kindness, and what it really means to give and receive. You will have to be diplomatic, careful of details, a loyal friend, a peacemaker, a listener. This is not a time for self-glory and praise. You must use your talents and abilities for the benefit of others in any way that you can. They were given to you to help you in your path of service. Learn to be sensitive to the needs and wants of those around you, and then strive to provide whatever is lacking. Your opportunities lie in working with and for others, in community activities, in paying close attention to detail, and in almost any situation that involves others. Make yourself of secondary importance. On this path you must learn of the law that says we can only progress through learning to serve our fellowmen, submitting our will to theirs. Only in this way can we learn to submit to the Divine Will—to surrender the self. This path teaches us much about humility—a necessary lesson and virtue.

3—Self-Expression—The path of learning to give outwardly of what we are inwardly. This means that you must learn to use your talents and abilities in forms of self-expression that can make life better and happier for all. You must learn to express your thoughts, feelings, and beliefs—to share them so that others can really know you. You must learn the value of friendship, beauty, and laughter—all of the aspects of the lighter side of life. You must not give way to worry, fear, or depression. You must learn to take what life doles out and go happily on your way. By the example of your own way of living, give others strength and a brighter outlook. You should do something in the arts, be it painting, writing, singing, dancing, or public speaking. Opportunities lie in looking for beauty everywhere and in seeing the best side of everything. Try to come into contact with other people, especially those of an emotional or artistic nature. Find your own avenue of self-expression; use your imagination and cleverness. Perfect your sense of humor and your use of words, and they will work for you. Seek to really understand life. This is a time of self-expression—not for promotion of the self, but for the benefit and enlightenment of others.

4—Self-Discipline—One of the best means of learning discipline is through work, and your path is largely that of work and service. It is a time when you must learn to make yourself do what needs to be done, to be efficient and organized, to produce through service and self-control. You must learn to build for yourself and others, to attend to duties, to be reliable, prompt, accurate, and attentive. You are preparing for the future, so you must lay a firm foundation that will last. Go slowly, doing all with perfection, paying attention to the slightest detail, putting forth as much effort as is necessary to do the job well, whatever the job may be. Do not be easy on yourself; do not think in terms of hardship or self-pity. Use your capabilities by working them to their greatest extent, for they are your "tools." Your opportunity lies in learning the value of work, in system and routine, in being dependable and patient, in doing what needs to be done and doing it well, in building for others as well as yourself, and in setting an example of discipline. This path can be one of great accomplishment—but it can only be realized when we are the captain of our own ship. Self-mastery comes through discipline.

5—Self-Emancipation—On this path you must learn to be free and must learn what being free really means. But you must not abuse your freedom. You must learn to adapt to change, variety, new things and ideas, new places and people, unexpected situations and experiences. During this lifetime you must not restrict yourself too much in any way. Don't overburden yourself with responsibilities and ties that will limit your ability to learn about freedom. There is adventure and much to be learned in progression and exploration, in varying experiences. You must learn to use your abilities in whatever situation you find yourself. Keep an open mind and a watchful eye; don't miss any chance to learn. Opportunity for you comes through travel, from the new and different, and from people who are intelligent and progressive, often scientific. Take your freedom seriously, value it highly, and don't overuse it. Birds migrate, but they build nests and stop in flight to feed. Learning the proper use of freedom truly makes you free. Then it is not your master, but you are master of it, and can go on to greater things. We have to understand and experience our own freedom so that we can allow others to have theirs.

6—Self-Harmony—This life is to teach that we are only in harmony when we are meeting our responsibilities. You must learn to accept responsibility, not with resentment but with an attitude that allows you to do so willingly and well. Burdens they may be, but you must bear them gladly. You must learn to be understanding, sympathetic, and helpful; to be in balance with everyone and everything. You must learn to solve your own problems and help others solve theirs as well. On this path you must learn the value of a home, family, friends, and society, and of aiding others. Use your abilities to bring harmony into the lives of those on your path and to the situations in which you find yourself. Be willing to give mental, spiritual, or material aid when needed. Learn to run a home efficiently and to make family life enjoyable for all. Your opportunity is to be found by accepting responsibility, giving service, adjusting differences, providing whatever others need, in loving and caring, in home and family situations, in things that involve your community, in striving to improve whatever you feel needs improvement, and in giving careful advice. Open your heart to others and do not limit yourself only to those you love. Reach out to help, but learn to know when it is best to let others manage on their own. Only when we help others find harmony can we find it for ourselves.

7—Inner Self—The path of this life is within; it is discovering the self inside. It can be called the path of inner wisdom because once we have truly gone within, we find great wisdom. You must learn about the power of the mind, the value of analysis and knowledge, the reality of the unseen worlds, and the benefit of study. You must really learn to think, to look at things carefully, and to see all there is—to see the material world in its proper perspective. This is the time of introspection, meditation, worship, and true spirituality that seeks the hidden truths. Take nothing at face value, spend time alone and rid yourself of the fear of being alone, strive to know who you really are, and learn all you can about everything you can. Use your talents to increase your wisdom and further your search for truth. They can tell you much about the direction you should search in—for truth is to be found everywhere. You will find opportunity in accumulating knowledge, in the quiet places, in intellectual stimulation—whether from books, people, or experiences—in mental analysis, in the truths you find, in the world within. Let your opportunities be brought to you. This path is to help you find your inner guidance, which will bring you faith, strength, and great peace. This is a path of spirituality, and it matters not what your religion is. All must eventually come to realize that Truth is one and the same, and that it is found within.

8—Self-Power—This is a time for realizing the power you possess and putting it to use in the material world. The ultimate realization of this vibration is that the material and spiritual worlds are really one and that spiritual power can be used for material success. This is the number of success, but the lesson is to learn to use it correctly. The path is that of the business and commercial world and of the money and laws that control it. You must learn to manage, organize, direct, deal with material things, accomplish, achieve, and succeed. Now is the time to realize that you have no limitations. Learn to accumulate and use money wisely and to develop efficiency and judgment. Use every ability you have to aid you in becoming a success, but beware if your only thought is self-gain. You will find your opportunity in the business world, in your executive ability, in coming into contact with those of wealth or power, in large concerns or organizations, and in large-scale operations. Remember the law of giving and receiving. Do not allow materialism to completely absorb you and control you. If you learn to be in the material world but not of it, you can be its master. Take care not to step on others to get where you want to go.

9—Selflessness—This lifetime belongs to others and is meant to be a life of service when you truly sacrifice the self. To understand this vibration fully you must begin by studying the eight before it. You must practice all of those vibrations by giving selfless service, for this is the point to which they all lead. Throughout all time the master souls have come to serve their brethren, and so to go on you must begin to learn the value and meaning of true service. You must place others before yourself, consider the effect of your words and actions upon others, look for ways to be of help, be willing to give up what you have so others may have, and seek knowledge so you can share it. This is the time to learn to be loving, understanding, sympathetic, thoughtful, sensitive, and generous. Give freely and without limitation. You must learn to look upon all people as your brothers and sisters—as children of the one Creator—and put aside all prejudices. Learn not to judge and condemn, to restrict, limit, or control. Develop your human understanding and use patience, tolerance, and tact with all. Use your abilities to give of yourself, for your opportunity lies in being of service. Make the world a better place in which to live by starting in your own little corner and by being what you would like others to be.

11—Self-Illumination—This is the time for activity that will aid in your understanding of life. It is also a time for revelation. Seek both in the quiet, look for them in the confusion, find them wherever they wait for you. Learn to trust and to use your intuition, have faith in your inner guidance, and see the best in others and the good in all things. The path is meant to be primarily spiritual, though you can make of it what you wish. You will be rewarded accordingly. You are to learn how to handle the first of the master vibrations, to share your revelations, and to discover the psychic world and its proper use. Seek truth, a greater understanding of life, and inspiration. Be compassionate. Walk your path boldly, but do not seek glory. Leave accumulation to others. Opportunity is to be found in your inventiveness, in spiritual things and people, in the sharing of knowledge received and found, in living truth as you understand it, in heeding your inner guidance, in contact with the unseen, and in your mental ability. Use your talents in these areas and you could possibly achieve great fame—but do not strive for it.

22—Self-Mastery—When the self has been mastered all things are possible, and in this life you are to learn that this is true. To you has been given the power to accomplish great things. You will be guided by great ideas meant to benefit many, which you are to put into use. The power you have must be used in a spiritual way—to aid others. This is best done in the construction of what is needed or useful. Learn to base your thoughts upon human needs so that the resulting ideas will be beneficial to others. Do not limit your concept of what you are capable of doing; think on a truly large scale. You have the power to affect the whole world with what you do if you will only put it to use. Your abilities can tell you much about the best areas in which to proceed and can aid you with any idea you conceive. Opportunity lies in areas that touch the lives of many, such as large organizations and government. You have large-scale ideas, the ability to accomplish what you envision, and a desire to aid others. This is a very powerful vibration and if the power is not put to constructive use, it can lead you to much unhappiness.

33—Self-Consciousness—To be conscious of what or who the self really is—this is your path. It is the path of knowing that you and the Creator are one. You must come to a total realization that this is true and gain an understanding of the accompanying power. You must learn how to use your power, the laws that govern life, and the demonstration of truth. When you have found that you possess this knowledge, no one will have to tell you anything. You have come to demonstrate what a human being really is and what powers await him or her when he or she comes into a full awakening of self. Opportunity lies in use of the powers you have to aid understanding, teach others, spread truth, demonstrate how to be physical yet spiritual, and do what needs to be done as you see the need. This path is too spiritual to be understood fully by anyone but a soul of this vibration and may not even really be understood by such a soul until it has come into a complete awakening. When that time does come, you will understand all.

Six

THE DESTINY DIRECTION

The function of this vibration is to provide additional information about the destiny, or the purpose we have come to fulfill. The destiny, in a very general sense, tells us where we are supposed to be going with our life, while the destiny direction points us more specifically toward the goal we need to aim at. It sheds more light on our path, which makes the trip easier because we can better see where we are headed.

This is an area in which numerology combines with astrology to give us greater guidance. Originally numerology and astrology were used together as one science, so harmony exists between them. In time, they came to be used separately because competitive feelings arose, and so the formulas that blend the two have largely been lost or forgotten. To determine the destiny direction we start with the number of the destiny and add to it the number of the astrological sun sign. Take the number of your destiny as figured in Chapter Five and add to that the number of your astrological sign. If the destiny is a 9 and you are a Cancer, you would add the 9 to Cancer's 4. Together they total 13, which would be a 4 when reduced to a single-digit figure.

Destiny Cancer

$$9 + 4 = 13 = (1 + 3)\ 4$$

1—Aries (Mar. 21–Apr. 20)
2—Taurus (Apr. 21–May 21)
3—Gemini (May 22–June 21)
4—Cancer (June 22–July 23)
5—Leo (July 24–Aug. 23)
6—Virgo (Aug. 24–Sept. 23)

7—Libra (Sept. 24–Oct. 23)
8—Scorpio (Oct. 24–Nov. 22)
9—Sagittarius (Nov. 23–Dec. 21)
10—Capricorn (Dec. 22–Jan. 20)
11—Aquarius (Jan. 21–Feb. 19)
12—Pisces (Feb. 20–Mar. 20)

If, for example, the destiny is a 6 and the sun sign is Leo, we add the 6 + 5 (destiny 6 + Leo 5) and get a total of 11 for the direction. When the direction is one of the master numbers (11, 22, 33), it is not reduced to a single digit. As an illustration of how this works, let's consider the example above. The 6♒ destiny indicates a path of service, acceptance of responsibility, attendance to duty, love, counseling, an interest in home, family, friends, and community affairs.

The 11→destiny direction points to spirituality, intuition, inspiration, psychic ability, invention, and power and energy in abundance. So, by combining the two, we see that the path is one of service to others through acceptance of responsibility, sharing of revelations, counseling through psychic ability and intuition, with energy directed toward spiritual matters and power used to aid people in domestic, community, and spiritual affairs.

Those born on the cusp have allotted themselves a choice in direction through choosing that time to be born. The cusp is a period of approximately five days at the changing of any two astrological signs; there are two days on either side of the change plus the actual date of the change. People born during these periods are most strongly influenced by the particular sign that they are born under, but they are also strongly influenced by the closeness of the other sign. Again, for example, let's suppose we are dealing with someone born on July 23. This person is a Cancer on the cusp of Leo and has not one or two choices, but actually three. First, there is the choice using the numerical value of the zodiacal sign of Cancer. If the destiny was an 8♒for instance, then we would add the 4 of Cancer to the 8 ≈ to determine that direction, which would be the strongest of the three choices because it is the sign the person was actually born under.

Cancer
$$8≈ + 4 = 12/3$$

Then we repeat the procedure, using the 5 of Leo instead of Cancer's 4.

Leo
$$8≈ + 5 = 13/4$$

The third choice is determined by adding to the destiny the numerical value of both zodiacal signs.

Cancer   Leo
$$8≈ + 4 + 5 = 17/8$$

The three choices then are, 3, 4, and 8. The 8, being the same vibration as the destiny in this case, gives us no additional information and thus can be eliminated as a choice. The 3 says business or commercial concerns of an artistic, expressive nature, such as a clothing manufacturer, owner of an art gallery or a jewelry store, or manager of a resort. The 4 tells us its choice is a business of a constructive or productive nature, with considerable work involved, as in any area dealing with the construction of buildings or homes, manufacturing of almost any kind of goods, especially those where great attention to detail is needed—all of these to be run in a very orderly, systematic, efficient manner.

Although the explanation of how to combine the characteristics of both vibrations has been brief, I trust you'll be able to understand how to co-relate the various influences.

THE NUMBERS OF THE DESTINY DIRECTION

1—You are independent, progressive, creative, inventive, determined, and forceful. You are a leader who forges ahead on

new paths, in new areas, with new ideas and methods. Often
you need to work alone, to be an individual and do things your
own way. Whatever the destiny, the message is to look for
progressive new ways to fulfill it, always going forward with
courage and imagination. Activity, both mental and physical,
and ideas should be keynoted. Never let other people or accepted methods stand in your way. Keep your eyes, ears, and
mind open for any new ideas that could be worthwhile; examine
them carefully and use them if they appear of value. Take the
initiative. Leadership is indicated and reforms in the area the
destiny outlines could well be your path to fulfillment of your
purpose. Your ideas can bring changes that could prove beneficial to many. Shed convention, tradition, the tried and true,
fear, doubt, and all concepts of limitation. Blaze a new trail for
the use of those who will follow.

2—You are being told to direct your efforts to fulfill your
destiny with cooperation in mind. Keep peace and harmony by
surrendering your will and desires to those of others if necessary. The glory of center stage is not for you—seek your place
behind the scenes, for without those to back up the star per-
formers, the show would never go on. Someone must attend to
the details, must be sure that all things receive attention and
nothing is ignored or forgotten. Helping others in the area your
destiny outlines is your specific path and can best be done by
putting concern for them first. You must develop your ability
to sense other people's needs, desires, and feelings rather than
wait for them to tell you. Anticipating and providing what is
needed when possible can smooth the way for many and keep
the show going. The wheels of progress have been slowed by
many a rut that no one noticed. Working with others diplomati-
cally, giving of yourself in service, making concessions in an
effort to keep peace, aiding others to work out personality
clashes, being patient and tolerant, doing the jobs others ignore
because they are dull or appear unimportant—these are your
claims to fame. Giving and sharing can open doors for you and

make life happier for all you come in contact with. When considering your particular path, don't rule out the metaphysical, psychic, or mystical, as it could hold great promise for you.

3—Your path should include contact with emotional, artistic, and creative people who have found or who are searching for a means of expressing their inner beauty, ideas, and beliefs. With them you should be able to let your own shine forth with greater brilliance. People of all kinds, and the ability to relate to them and talk to them, play a big part in your purpose. There is a need to go forth with an outlook on life that is optimistic and cheerful. See the value and humor in all situations. Your own sense of humor should be used to lift the spirits of others and aid them in seeing things in their proper perspective. Helping to soothe a troubled soul, giving others strength to face life's adversities, spreading happiness and beauty, using your ability to love and laugh to heal others' wounds—these things you should learn to do in the world. Opportunity to further your purpose is to be found in social contacts, enjoyment of the lighter side of life, communion with nature, artistic endeavors, and words spoken or written. Reach out to others; touch their lives, their hearts, their minds, their souls, and yours will receive the touch that blesses and fulfills the promise of greater things. Public relations, artistic interests, and self-expression is where opportunity lies for you.

4—Whatever your path, the need for work is indicated—both in the mental and physical areas. Incorporate order and system in your efforts to fulfill your purpose and make use of the gray matter and elbow grease. While others may sit back and toss out ideas or run and play, it is for you to see that something constructive is done—and that could very well mean doing it yourself. Produce well-organized, practical plans for accomplishing what you want and then put them into action. This is the solid foundation upon which all lasting achievements are built. Proceed slowly and with caution if necessary. Develop self-discipline that makes you stick to your plans and the job at hand, no matter how dull they may become. As with the bricklayer who patiently lays one brick at a time until the structure is completed, so must you also produce. The reward comes in worthwhile accomplishment, though the effort may be considerable. Take pride in all you do, be thorough, conscientious, and dependable. You'll not only progress, you'll earn respect as a person who gets the job done.

5—It's time to throw off all limitations. Let go of anything that holds you back, and get ready to go. Find a way to incorporate the activities of your destiny with travel, change, and variety. Selling is indicated—whether products, services, or ideas and beliefs. Don't let responsibilities keep you from going where you need to go and being what you need to be. Adapt so that you can get the most out of situations and people. Look into all that comes along thoroughly to see if there is value in it for you. Keep mentally and physically active, and don't repress your curiosity—it could lead you to the discovery of many beneficial things. Make the world your fireside, deal with people wherever you go, and seek a variety of experiences in order to understand life and human nature better. Don't condemn anything because it's different. Check it out. The opposite sex also plays a big part in getting you where you're going, as does good character analysis, so cultivate the influence of both. Don't try to be routine or traditional in what you do; look for new, flexible methods and ideas. When you find something that's worthwhile, let others know about it. Use your personality and persuasiveness to further your cause. Keep things moving swiftly, seek any changes that you feel would be good, and give yourself and others a new row to hoe.

6—For you there's no escaping responsibility—it's your tool for building better things for yourself and others. When you get involved in anything, you must realize that you can't just ignore the duties, the problems, and the caring that are a part of becoming concerned. Almost any situation and relationship can be bettered, and it's for you to seek out ways of bettering things and bringing about results. Your own stable nature can bring harmony, and your advice can help others to understand. Whatever your destiny tells you to do, you need to include caring for others, tending to responsibilities, making improvements, advising people, and solving problems. Make sure you bring love, patience, compassion, understanding, and sympathy to every situation. There are many weak souls who could use your help—it could mean the difference between a miserable existence or a full and happy life for them. When people come to you in need, let your generosity take over to give them the protection, guidance, and strength they lack. Be certain you are sincere, for people sense falseness. Many may come to depend on you. Be patient and tender. Teach them to stand on their own two feet—and then send them off stronger and wiser for your help. Don't allow them to become so dependent on you that they do not learn to manage for themselves.

7—The ability to see all aspects of any situation is always beneficial, and it is this that you must learn to do. When this ability is coupled with knowledge, it is a powerful force that can give truer understanding of all experiences. Analysis and examination are the keys; study and deep thought are the methods. Through the development of your inner abilities your purpose will be brought ever nearer to fulfillment. In an emotionally oriented society, objectivity is not the norm, but it can be achieved with practice. Seek the fundamentals, formulas, theories, and basic principles, and work with them. Above all, develop an attitude of faith—particularly in your intuitive powers. Realize that the only thing to fear is fear. Although you may dislike being alone at times, you need to overcome that feeling and learn to work well on your own. Never settle for less than the best—especially in the things you do. Your slogan should be "Quality, not quantity," and it will help take you far. Cultivate an air of dignity and poise. Don't speak out authoritatively unless you're sure of your ground. Gain all the knowledge you can, so that when you do speak it will be worth listening to. Because others don't bother to try to see all sides of things, it is up to you to help them do so—and in this way make yourself something of a counselor. You would do well to consider a field like science or teaching where you deal primarily with facts and formulas.

8—Business and commercial activity is the area for you to apply your talents and put them to use in positions of leadership and authority. Study the things indicated by your destiny and realize that they should always be uppermost in your thoughts in all situations where finances are involved. Your path could lead you to great successes with this vibration as your direction, and the primary key is efficiency. Be thorough and careful in all you do; never limit yourself or your plans. Planning should be made a way of life, but plans are useless unless followed with determined action. Take control and manage anything that comes along. Don't be bossy—be authoritative. People always listen to those who can offer practical courses of action. Only concern yourself with minute details if there is no one else to attend to them. Overseeing others is more the field of action for you. Take an interest in community affairs and develop an image that earns respect through dignity, pride, and efficiency. Whatever you do, strive to do it to the best of your ability.

9—Personal glory and wealth are definitely not what you should strive for. If you should decide to, the chances are you'll never reach your goal. If you put thoughts of self completely aside, almost anything could come your way. To achieve your destiny develop the qualities of a humanitarian. There is a need for you to look upon everyone as your brother or sister. Keep the Golden Rule foremost in your mind. The virtues of compassion, generosity, and humility can take you far and enrich not only others' lives but yours as well. Artistic endeavors are favored, as they can be a great gift to your fellowman. Make yourself aware of beauty wherever you go—in places, things, and people. Let your heart lead you. Learn to give love on a grand scale and expect nothing in return. Be satisfied with giving in any way you can. This is the vibration of completion, so guard against possessiveness and unwillingness to see anything come to an end. Having many friends can help you achieve your purpose, and they can learn much from you if you practice tolerance and patience. Ask little and give much, and be whatever they need you to be. This influence truly is not always easy, as it seems somewhat one-sided, but those who fall under it should remember that the giver *always* receives the greater reward. The degree of our selflessness determines our place in the realm we go to after this physical existence.

11—Master numbers always indicate service to mankind—those presently incarnated in the physical realm and those in spirit realms as well. Master numbers also indicate spirituality and this is a major key for you. Areas that could prove very beneficial are those of the psychic and metaphysical—areas that for ages have been labeled mystical should for you become realistic and everyday. If you seek fame and fortune, the power of this number is very apt to turn on you, but unsought, the strong magnetism of this influence can well bring both to you. Seek illumination, develop human understanding and tolerance, and strive to make everything practical and useful. Go forth with fire and enthusiasm in thoughts, words, and actions, and light the flame within others. Share your beliefs and wisdom with others, but leave them free to choose their own path. Realize that all cannot go the same way. Invention could be your avenue of accomplishment. Cultivate people who stimulate you intellectually, and practice being alert, making quick decisions, and using your mentality to the fullest. Spreading ideas and beliefs of any sort is part of the field of activity indicated for you.

22—Building is the message of this direction and your destiny can tell you much about the type of construction you should concern yourself with. The key is never letting the slightest thought of limitation enter your mind—be it from your own thoughts or from those of others. Shed all doubt and fear, and proceed with assurance, determination, and large plans. Keep your vision broad but practical, and be sure your activities are aimed at aiding others. This number says build for mankind, preferably things of lasting value. The larger the concern the better, for the power of this influence is great and shouldn't be wasted on small-scale things. Develop the ability to produce a practical plan of action for the visions you conceive. Learn to tune in to the blueprints for truly great construction being sent forth from the higher realms. This is the number of the master builder who can achieve almost anything if he or she believes it possible and is willing to put in effort and concerns himself or herself with service to others. How far-reaching will be the effect of your creation is up to you—this vibration truly knows no limits. Give forth an air of courageous determination and soon you'll have many followers to help you achieve your goals. The world is in great need of those who are brave enough to try to make their dreams reality.

33—This, the highest of all the vibrations, is that of the teacher who instructs through example. Whatever your faith, your beliefs, your morals, you are meant to be an example to others. That in itself makes this influence difficult at times, for all too often we do not practice what we preach or say we believe. Those who master the ability to do so are true lights unto the world. Your path is service and the need for spirituality is strongly indicated. Seek truth, and when you've found it, share it. But beware of the snare that traps all too many— failure to grow, because they believe they have found the ultimate truths and so do not perceive the greater expressions of it when they encounter them. This path is lined with people who must be met with understanding and love. Do not try to separate yourself from your fellowmen or their problems and pains. Give them a shoulder to cry on, a helping hand, a kind word, a new outlook, and share with them your strength and counsel. Remember that a teacher must always be a student as well, or soon his ability to teach will be nonexistent because his students will have acquired all his knowledge and have gone on to be taught by those who continued to learn. The purpose of life is perpetual learning. From the student the teacher can learn much. Make life and mankind your teacher. Shirk no task, however unpleasant, but be willing to do the most menial of jobs if necessary. Humility is the only virtue which brings true greatness. Strive to learn who and what you really are and make good use of the power that knowledge gives you. Then seek to help others come to the same realization.

Seven

THE HEART SELF

While the inner self tells about what the best in you or your soul wants you to be, the heart self tells what you desire to be. People talk about their "heart's desire" and this is truly what the heart self deals with—the type of person we want to be and what we want to do. When we are attuned strongly to this vibration it has a considerable effect upon our personality, and if we are more in tune with this number than with our other major numbers it is our personality. Usually, however, our personality is a composite. In the majority of people personality can be found in the combination of the outer self and the heart self. In some the inner self will show an influence also, and in some rare cases the heart self may not be involved in the personality at all. Consider your personality traits and then the characteristics of these numbers in your chart, and somewhere among the three you should find your personality.

When considering the explanations given for the numbers of the heart self, keep in mind that it's impossible to tell everyone exactly what they want to be like because people are individuals. Therefore the descriptions given are generalized, and so your number should fit you in a general sense. Not all of the things said about your number will relate to you—some of them should be the you that you would like to be.

The heart self is found in the total of the consonants of the full birth name. This influence does not change with a change of name; only the birth name is used to determine the heart self. For example,

```
D O Y L E      E D W A R D      W A L K E R
4     3         4 5   9 4       5   3 11  9
    7      +        22       +      28/10     = 30
```

In this example the heart self that we have to work with is a 3. Figure your own heart self in this manner; then look up your number under the numbers of the heart self.

THE NUMBERS OF THE HEART SELF

1—You would like to be a leader—showing others the way, making the plans, starting new ventures—a leader in all things. You want to create, to invent, to be progressive. You desire independence and want to be different from others, setting the styles, not following them. You admire strength, courage, and determination in others and want to possess these qualities yourself. You would like to explore, be a pioneer, see the unseen, and do the untried. You want to be the master of any situation you find yourself in.

2—You want to be loved by family, friends, and associates. You want people around so that you can do things for them and thus gain their appreciation and even their dependence upon you. You want to bring peace to all situations in quiet ways, as you have no desire to call attention to yourself. You like a life of comfort and ease and want others to take care of you, and you'll do what you can for them. You care about what others think of you because you want everyone to like you.

3—To be popular, have many friends, be good-looking and well dressed—these are all aspirations of yours. You would like to have a good sense of humor and be able to say things that will make you sought after as entertaining company. You would like to be the wit of the group—the one who keeps everyone laughing and the whole thing going. You would like to create something that others would enjoy, such as a good painting or a worthwhile book. You want to make others happy and desire a carefree life filled with many social events.

4—You'd like to be the rock that others lean on, to be thought of as dependable, reliable, the one who holds all together. You want to organize, establish system and routine, and make sure that all the details are attended to. You like all things to be properly and thoroughly done and you do not want to be rushed. You want to live conservatively, working and accomplishing, with your world carefully in order and nothing upsetting it. You are patriotic and love your country, although you see its weaknesses. You want to serve it in any way you can. You want to be respected in your community.

5—You like adventure and would like to travel extensively, meeting new people, seeing strange places, learning how others live and think. You would like to be free of responsibilities that would hold you to any place or to any situation. You want your life to be full of change, excitement, and stimulation. You want to face frequent challenges to prove to yourself that you can meet them and be the victor. You want to try to experience everything you can. You want people around who can keep life from being dull and will give you opportunities to use your charm and intellect. You would like each day to be different so you wouldn't be bored.

6—You want a home and family to be the center of your life because you can do so much to make your home a happy, comfortable place to be. You want your surroundings decorative and your life in balance and full of love. You want a mate to go through life with and children to adore you as a devoted parent. You want to open your home to others. You want to be looked to for advice and guidance. You want to make all situations better and be respected for your efforts. You want the kinds of responsibilities that others run from and the duties many ignore. You would like to help others in any way you can.

7—You want to live in a quiet, peaceful atmosphere, preferably in the country, away from city noise and confusion. You would like to own many books, good works of art, and furniture that has been beautifully made. Sometimes you would like to be alone to study and meditate, to carefully investigate things. You tend to want privacy and contact with people in small groups. You prefer people around you who are intellectual. You would like to be sought for your wisdom, respected for your knowledge, asked for your advice, and known for your quality. You like perfection and mental stimulation. You tend to be spiritual; you are interested in the occult, in the powers of the mind, and in the inner world.

8—You would like to be the head of a large business or organization—managing and directing, working on a large scale, planning and supervising. You want to handle money, preferably great amounts belonging to yourself or your companies. You want to be successful in the material world. You want to accomplish big things, live and work in plush surroundings, and be a substantial and respected member of the community. You desire power, control, authority, and a position where you can put your ideas and judgment to use. You would like wealth and all that goes with it.

9—You would like to do things for others and be needed for the love, understanding and compassion you have to give. You would like to be in a position where you could truly help the unfortunate and bring enlightenment to those who have not yet found it. You want to advise and comfort, aid and protect. You would like to create something of artistic and possibly great merit. You desire personal love, security, and happiness—outlets for your emotional nature. You would like to help bring about world peace and to end suffering.

11—You would like to be a spiritual leader who fills people with faith, understanding, spiritual zeal, and great holiness. You want to be spiritually enlightened so that you can share it with others. You would like to see your ideas become realities, to invent great things, to be a truly great leader in some way. You tend to be interested in the occult or mystical and would like to be a well-known psychic, possibly a prophet who could predict national and world happenings. You would like to be an inspiration to others and might even like being famous.

22—You would like to devise more productive methods of farming, more efficient means of transportation, ways to produce better products, build better buildings, improve working conditions—any improvement that would benefit mankind. You would like to build large and worthwhile things and do things on a large scale. You would like to be a statesman or diplomat in order to bring about peace and better relations among countries. You would like in some way to reach the people in other countries and become friends.

33—You desire to be truly spiritual and want to see the world become a spiritual place. You would like to help bring about the end of religious conflicts and competition, to the end that all would become united. You want to know and really understand spiritual truths. You would like people to listen to you so that you could explain your beliefs, your understanding of life, your philosophy. You want to live in your own quiet way and dislike the ways of the materialistic world. You want to be where things of nature and beauty abound, where you can enjoy the outdoors and can be at peace. You believe in freedom and want others to experience it too.

Eight

CHART OF THE MAJOR NUMBERS WITH THEIR SYMBOLS

Having learned about the major numbers and how to calculate them, you are ready to prepare your own chart. Each of the major numbers has its own symbol to help us readily identify it:

inner self	○
outer self	△
heart self	□
destiny	〰
direction	➜

Below is an example of a basic chart, using the major numbers, to show you how to begin setting up your own chart or someone else's. Graph paper with 4 squares to the inch is very helpful when preparing a chart.

```
    18/9      +      6       +      6      = 21/③
  9      9          1   5          1   5
  N I K K I      K A R E N      C A B E       9-4-11  △6
  5 9 11111 9    11 1 9 5 5     3 1 2 5
    45/9      +     31/4     +      11     = 24/6
  5    1111       11   9  5       3   2
    27/9      +     25/7     +      5      = 21/③
```

APRIL 16 1942   ARIES   NIKKI P I T T

$$4 \; + 7 + \; 7 \; = 18/9 \text{〰} + 1 = \quad 1 \text{➜} 9 + \frac{7\ 9\ 2\ 2}{2Ø} = \triangle 11 \text{ present}$$

In the example we find that

The inner self is a   ③
The outer self is a   ⑥
The heart self is a   ③
The destiny is a   9 ⟳
The direction is a   1 ⤳

We have calculated the present self in the example, even though it is not a major number. It is one of the secondary numbers, and this should be kept in mind.

Notice that when we do both the outer self and the present self we take the sums of the three names, or the name presently used, and list them ahead of the final total: 9–4–11⑥. The reason is that they go to make up the outer or present self, and as you get further into numerology you will see that they have some influence on the characteristics of the total. Anyone who decides to get deeply involved in numerology must learn to look at the numbers behind the various totals.

Before you go any further, study what you have learned about yourself so far. What vibrations are you in tune with? Which vibrations are not showing much influence in your life at present? Are you following your destiny and learning its lessons? Are you headed in the direction that you should be? Are you using your talents and abilities, or do you need to work at developing them? Does your job make the best use of your capabilities? Consider your outer self and your destiny together and see what you can learn about how you should be proceeding on your path. Then consider your destiny and direction together and see if you have combined them into constructive progress in the area you should be working in. What your inner self tells you is of great importance. Are you neglecting this aspect of yourself? Looking at yourself and your life, what changes do you need to make in order to be in tune with all of your major numbers?

When you have examined your chart carefully and have considered these questions, you are ready to learn about the secondary numbers, which are discussed in Part Two.

II

THE SECONDARY NUMBERS

Nine

THE DAY OF BIRTH

The vibration of the day of your birth has an effect upon your whole life and can tell you a great deal about yourself. It has its greatest influence during the middle years of life, the years when we are the most productive.

As you follow your destiny, this number will make its influence felt in your progress and development. Therefore it should be considered along with your destiny. Also consider the effect it will have on you from your late twenties to your late fifties, the period when you exhibit the strongest characteristics it describes.

When looking up your day of birth, look up the unreduced number, that is, the calendar day. The month and year are not considered here. If you were born on July 29, check number 29. If the day of your birth is February 17, then you must look up 17.

THE DAYS OF BIRTH

1st—It is doubtful that you have put all of your power to use. You must take care not to use it only for yourself because you are inclined to be somewhat self-centered anyway. Interested mainly in your own development, you are independent, forceful, and strong-willed. You are a planner rather than a builder and are better at diagnosing than treating. You prefer mental activity to manual labor, although you keep busy physically because of all your energy. You rarely express your emotions because that would indicate weakness, which you hate. You like to be an individual.

2nd—You have a talent for words and music—you like harmony in all things. Put your talent to use. Not very ambitious, you may not strive for the style of living you would enjoy. Unless you are careful, you can be moody and easily depressed. You are happiest when with loved ones and friends because you need the emotional security they can give you. In addition, they give you a chance to do things for them. You have a deep need for love, understanding, and a peaceful life. It is also part of your nature to be forgetful, sensitive, friendly, warm-hearted, nervous, and desirous of attention.

3rd—On the go, with many irons in the fire, you can be a social butterfly one day and a quiet, hard-working artist the next. Your many facets are part of what makes you interesting and entertaining. You are rarely depressed or sick for long or upset by the problems of life. You bounce back quickly, and you set a good example. Very artistic, you need to find an outlet for your talents and imagination—something outside your work or home. You need people and friends to give your love to, so you like to entertain and keep your schedule full of group activities. It is necessary for those close to you to understand your frequent tears—of both sadness and joy. You are a very emotional person.

4th—If you're not careful, you'll make your life nothing but work and routine, to the point of being very dull. Then you could become dull too and ill as well. Take up a hobby of an artistic nature, make a point of including social events in your schedule, and plan outings that provide a change of scenery. Don't spend your vacation at home. You feel deeply about your home, family, country, and your duties and are actually inclined to be serious about everything. A good and efficient worker, you like doing things with your head and hands—preferably both. A nature lover, you'd grow a great garden or run a good farm. You are apt to repress your feelings because of your tendency to overdiscipline, and others may not give their love to you because they feel it's unwanted.

5th—A born traveler—if it's not from place to place, then it will be from experience to experience, for you are never stationary. Marriage would be good for you, but make sure that the mate you pick is understanding and knows well your need to be active and unrestricted and your dislike for handling responsibilities. Keep your life full and varied. Although you are inclined to brag and exaggerate, still you are a great addition to any group because of your versatile and outgoing personality. You love people and life and fit in well anywhere. You are apt to be a flirt and may have a very active love life.

6th—A natural home-body because it means so much to you, you want others to enjoy and respect your home too. Your greatest need is love and you'll keep looking until you find it —no matter how many affairs and disappointments you have to endure. Your fear of poverty may make you very cautious about spending, and you feel best when you have the security of a nest egg. Very attached to your personal possessions, you care for them well. You like mental things if they aren't too deep and desire praise, attention, and protection.

7th—You know what you think is right and others aren't likely to change your mind. Looking at things mentally and in great depth, you like to read, study, and learn. You have great intuitive powers that you need to use, and you have good judgment and insight. You are reserved and refined, and others are rarely drawn to you for emotional reasons. You need to become a specialist in something. Your inborn spirituality makes you a lover of nature and beauty, a seeker of answers, a believer in meditation. You need time alone on a regular basis and plenty of rest and peace. You would be happiest away from city life, in a quiet, well-ordered atmosphere that allows enough time for your books, your thoughts, and the enjoyment of the finer things of life, like good music. You like quality in everything.

8th—Wherever you go you're inclined to step in and start managing, but at least you're usually good at it. You take great pride in what you have and in all that you do and can be counted on to achieve and do things well. You dislike waste and aren't one to be rushed or controlled in any way. You're not inclined to be extravagant, but you're extremely generous. You are usually fair and need to be sure to make honesty a part of whatever you do. You care for your home and family well and insist upon respect and organization. You'll be the most successful and satisfied in the business world. You probably won't want a partnership unless you hold the controlling interest and deal with finances.

9th—Don't let others make decisions for you, or you'll never be happy. You need to run your own life. In fact, you'd be good at running others' lives, or helping them in some way. You're artistic and like most artistic people, you are emotional and prone to great highs and lows. Very loving and generous, you like to do things for people and spend time with them. Spiritual and perhaps metaphysical matters are apt to appeal to you, and even the occult and psychic. You desire personal love, but it won't come to you easily. When it does, it may be short-lived though very deep. Try to learn to let impersonal love be sufficient for your happiness, because that is the kind you're most likely to get.

10th—A creator who starts many things, you need to see to their completion as well. With your strong will you need to use your mental ability to help you be less set in your ways. You can promote nearly anything and by determination make a way where there was none. If you don't receive help, it's because it appears you never need it. To others you seem a tower of strength and so they rely on you. You're interested in a variety of things, active in many, and do all of them well. You like people but spend a lot of time alone. You're not very domestic.

11th—You don't need a reason to do anything—you act on impulse, doing all with great energy. You may be hard to understand and live with—you may even have trouble living with yourself because of excess nervousness. Whatever you do is done with force and determination, but your interests are apt to change in midstream. If not controlled, your emotions can get out of balance and so can your desire to make others do things your way. You have the ability to stimulate others intellectually and spiritually. Intuitive, you make quick decisions and act accordingly. Sometimes you're too fast for others to keep up with.

12th—Using your ability with words and your convincing manner to establish peace and lead people in progressive directions, you're useful to have around. Imaginative, dynamic, and intellectual, you can really go places if you don't let your emotional nature hold you back. Your artistic nature and fondness for details should make you good at designing. Decide upon a purpose in life, stick with it, and don't allow yourself to be sidetracked. Your love life may include a number of involvements, not always for love but for companionship, enjoyment, entertainment, or plain ego-boosting. You have a good mind and enjoy using it.

13th—There may be some conflict in your life—or even in you—because of the force of opposites active here. You may be inclined to outbursts of temper, largely out of frustration at not knowing which way to go, from being misunderstood, or because you can't express yourself as you'd like to. On the one hand you are progressive, inventive, and like to be on the move, while on the other hand you are set in your ways and bound to routine and discipline. It is hard for you to change even though you want to. You love your home and nature. You feel deeply but rarely show it and tend to be spiritual but usually in a very conventional way. Unless you receive help from the other vibrations in your chart, you are likely to have trouble harmonizing the differences present here.

14th—You are the link between the material and spiritual worlds and something of both should be found in you. Your mind functions well in both areas and you delve into each energetically. You like variety and taking chances. You may also feel inclined to gamble. You should use your intuition and judgment to decide what is right for you. You have a very strong, feeling nature and can be reached through it. The physical appetites hold a strong attraction for you—too strong if you don't exercise your discipline and control. Forceful in a reserved way, you generally proceed with care, but there are times when you act impulsively.

15th—You love your home and family and will give greatly of yourself for them, but they will not be your whole life, nor will you allow them to control you. You enjoy doing things for others and are very generous but are mindful of your own needs and desires in the process. You like to stay active and keep yourself busy along both scientific and artistic lines. You believe in progress and are interested in new ideas and in innovation. You act like a magnet, drawing things to you—among them harmony and success. You like to have people around you and have little difficulty getting along with them or adjusting to any differences that may exist.

16th—You have a keen mind, which can benefit you in business affairs if you don't let your tendency to procrastinate keep you from using it. Because of your nervous nature, you are not always patient or tolerant. You can make mountains out of molehills and cause yourself needless grief. Often withdrawn and reflective and not one to do much to receive love, your family may find you difficult to understand and relate to. While you need them and care a lot about them, you also need your own private world with no one upsetting your plans or thoughts. When problems, confusion, or noise bother you, take time to go out into the country to regain your composure and enjoy nature and beauty.

17th—Your vibration is strongly inclined to business and shows good judgment and success in that area—whether it be managing your money or someone else's. You like to have things proven to you, as you are very technical-minded. You are ruled by your head even though you feel things deeply. You tend to be proud, set in your ways, and something of a loner. In some ways you are composed of opposites—you either accumulate lots or collect nothing, spend lavishly or pinch pennies, discard or cling to conventions. You seek knowledge, are adventurous, and may feel a tendency to write nonfiction. You can be stubborn and are very determined.

18th—Self-sufficient, capable, and determined, you'll succeed if only because you won't give up. You are an intellectual with a strong liking for discussion and debate, but too strong-minded to be swayed from your view. You may respond emotionally but your head will usually rule in the end. Because of your love, efficiency, and strength, you may gain the care of others—if not by choice, then by chance or circumstance. You like travel, variety, and a busy life. You are also careful with money but generous and conscientious. Much is generally expected of you by others. Not one to need guidance, you manage well on your own and prefer to.

19th—Knowing the extremes of emotional highs and lows, you feel for others in similar circumstances and are sympathetic and understanding. You are determined and practical; you reason things out and do things in your own way. Your public and private lives may vary greatly. Versatile and adaptable, you can be very artistic or very intellectual. You take your responsibilities seriously and do not give up easily, for you believe in finishing what you begin. You tend to cling to things and ideas simply because they are yours. You are talented and expressive and can be very inventive and ingenious.

20th—You're happiest when others are making the plans and

you're carrying them out. However, don't put yourself in the position of doing manual labor because you're not well fitted for that. You'll say what you want better if you write it, so use the mails rather than the phone. You enjoy working with others and do best when you're not too burdened by responsibilities. You like friendly surroundings, for you have a very feeling nature. You like to give and receive affection and sympathy, feel strongly for those you care about, and enjoy life away from the city. You enjoy detail work and accumulating almost anything.

21st—You value education and knowledge, things and people, and anything artistic or beautiful. You have an emotional and very nervous nature that you should try to control. You are able to receive love better than you can give it, and people are more likely to be drawn to you because of your magnetism rather than your lovingness. You possess a good voice and should find a way to put it to use. You have the ability to write and with your imagination could do well with fiction. If you're not careful, your imagination will cause you to dream up situations that don't exist. You need to guard against depression and unwarranted fears and dislikes.

22nd—A master number and so there is much energy here —if you're not careful, it will wear you out. It is fine to be active as long as you also get enough rest. You are likely to be quite nervous, so you need time alone to restore your balance and composure. Try to keep your aspirations impersonal; consider first the good of others. Keep your activities legal or they're bound to be discovered—the negative aspects of master numbers can be quite destructive. Trust your hunches, as your intuition is very strong and sound. Don't let your head interfere, for reason isn't always right. You can be successful in many fields if you don't get carried away by thoughts of self-gain or glory.

23rd—Popular, with an outgoing personality, you like people and social occasions. You get along well with others and make a good companion and friend. You feel things strongly, like to help others, and understand their needs and feelings. You are a builder, a creator, and also you are good at repairing and could make a fine doctor or spiritual healer. You prefer to stand on your own because you know you are capable of handling things. You like to be going places and doing things and are never a wallflower. You are intellectual and practical, often quite physical, and should take care that the physical attractions of others don't lure you into hot water.

24th—You're not inclined to be punctual because time really doesn't mean much to you; you can also be as careless about money and could end up with problems if you don't discipline yourself. You have a lot of energy and should stay busy. Keep your interests and activities varied. You can keep at a job until it's done, which is important. You love your home and your family and work hard for them. You should not have any trouble putting your talents to use because you know that you are capable of doing well. Be careful not to exaggerate situations out of proportion and cause yourself to become fearful, moody, jealous, or a worrier.

25th—You should decide upon a goal and then try to see it through—something you are not inclined to do. Pick some aspect of the occult, study it and become an authority. You should be good in this area. You're already intuitive and possibly psychic, and you should learn to use these gifts. Don't allow yourself to be lazy; practice what you preach. Cultivate your mental abilities and make them work for you. Stop trying to hide your feelings and your affectionate nature—be yourself. Artistic, you also have a good voice and the ability to play a musical instrument. If you discipline yourself, you'll be successful in any endeavor.

26th—Generous, domestic, and loving, you make a good marriage partner and should find enjoyment in the union. Extremely particular about the things that belong to you, you should take excellent care of those you love as well as what you have. You can be very artistic and successful if you apply yourself. The trouble is you're inclined to start things and never finish them. Don't concentrate on the past; learn to live for today and if you must look somewhere else, make it *tomorrow*. You'd benefit from a good education because you'd put it to practical use, as you do all things. Come out of your own little world and discover the great big one.

27th—You do not like to answer for your actions, but prefer that others mind their own business and let you do as you please. Somewhat inclined to be materialistic, you are yet still spiritual in an unorthodox sort of way, as you have your own beliefs. All of these things add to your desire for leadership, your determination, and your strong will. Marriage may not be what you hope for, but you're inclined to it. Your feelings run deep and yet you can be inconstant. You like books and learning and can be very artistic. You are versatile and can do a number of things well. You care a lot about others and like to do things for them, but you need time of your own to collect your thoughts and restore your values to their proper perspectives.

28th—You are very ambitious and will go to great lengths to reach your goals and be successful, but you should take care not to be led astray. You should continue to pursue your goals and not rush off to some new thing, or else nothing will ever be accomplished. Satisfaction for you lies in achievement. You have a strong will and want to control situations, but at the same time you are very loving and generous and will break rules and go out of your way for others. You tend to value things out of proportion to their real worth, and you need to learn to control this aspect of your nature. You dislike restrictions and appreciate having the freedom to be yourself and to do the things you believe in. You are full of energy, but laziness is something to guard against.

29th—All things in extremes for you—you are either very happy or very sad, love deeply or dislike greatly. You are equally as extreme in your opinions and beliefs. Usually spiritual and always intuitive, you are inclined to inspiring others, as well as seeking revelation for yourself. You'll never be happy without a home, but those who share it with you may find that you're hard to get along with. One reason is that your nervousness can make you irritable, short-tempered, and impatient. You also tend to live in a world of your own and therefore may not think about others as much as you should. This is something that you need to watch out for. Keep yourself busy with planned and constructive activities that will use the power of your vibration to good advantage. Use your loving nature to help you get along with others.

30th—You have a mind of your own and are fairly well convinced that your way of looking at things is right. Try not to push your beliefs off on others. You need to find ways to use your energy and vitality. You like people and are very friendly; sometimes you even flirt. You need to guard against nervousness. Imaginative and a very good director, you can be of help to those who are in need of someone like you. You do not like actual work very much and avoid it when you can. Learn to trust your intuition, and don't look for too much praise for what you do.

31st—You may find yourself interested in the psychic, but don't treat it lightly or you'll get burned. If you investigate it, do it seriously. Not one to be alone or to live alone, you will probably seek responsibilities to give your life purpose. You must learn not to hold grudges. Extravagance is something else you should guard against. Make certain that your goals are reachable because you tend to be unrealistic in setting them. You are intellectually and artistically inclined and love travel, people, and nature. Discipline yourself to concentrate, and learn to accept the value of routine and system.

Ten

THE FOUNDATION

Your foundation has the strongest influence on the material plane rather than on the spiritual. It helps to determine your outlook on life and has a lot to do with your natural tendencies. You were built upon this vibration and its influence can be balancing, energizing, and enhancing, or it can be restricting and retarding.

The foundation is the number value of the first letter of the first name given at birth. For example, my given name is *Kathleen.* My foundation is an 11, or the numerical value of the *K.* A quick look at your name will tell you what your foundation is, and then by looking up that number in the table given, you can determine what you were founded upon.

This is the first vibration that affects a child, especially if the child's name is picked before birth. Along with the birth date, it strongly influences the child from just before until shortly after birth. Many of the growth and behavior patterns of the small child are determined by its foundation.

When contemplating a full name change, the foundation must be considered. Part of the purpose of the foundation is to give strength to the outer self, though in some cases it restricts, which may actually be what the person needs. Therefore you have to consider the foundation and outer self together when doing a chart to determine whether its influence aids or hinders expression of the qualities that are desirable.

THE NUMBERS OF THE FOUNDATION

1—You were built upon the qualities of individuality, independence, creativeness, progressiveness, leadership, invention, stimulation, mental and physical activity, strong will, determination, originality, and courage. You may tend to be stubborn and egotistical if not careful.

2—Founded upon a loving, cooperative nature, you are a follower who is diplomatic, generous, agreeable, receptive, analytical, patient, friendly, considerate, sensitive, studious, and emotional. You can be careless, oversensitive, overemotional, shy and inclined to a bad temper and pouting unless you watch yourself.

3—Your foundation is that of happiness, laughter, imagination, artistry, charm, love, friendliness, intellect, being carefree, talkativeness, emotionalism, and self-expression. There is an inclination to be critical, vain, whining, jealous, and intolerant. These things must be guarded against.

4—Founded on qualities of patience, practicality, dependability, endurance, organization, logic, devotion, concentrational ability, and energy, you are a worker who likes routine, system, and building. You may tend to be repressed, dull, unfeeling, and narrow-minded unless you are cautious.

5—Built upon a desire for change and variety with the qualities of mental curiosity, adventurousness, friendliness, adaptability, understanding, progressiveness, good judgment, persuasiveness, and rejuvenation, you can be irresponsible, self-indulgent, thoughtless, inconsistent, and a procrastinator if you're not careful.

6—Your foundation is that of responsibility, devotion, firmness, harmony and balance, understanding, sympathy, justice, domesticity, love, service, and the ability to counsel. You tend to be worrisome, interfering, smug, jealous, and easily despondent unless you work at being otherwise.

7—Your foundation is built upon mental analysis, introspection, perseverance, poise, spirituality, quality, intuition, perfection, faith, sensitivity, secretiveness, a need to be alone, and a dislike of confusion. You are apt to be melancholy, aloof, critical, sarcastic, and repressed if not cautious.

8—You are founded on qualities of efficiency, leadership, practicality, judgment, self-reliance, dependability, intelligence, power, management and control, determination, and a businesslike attitude. Unless careful, you can be materialistic, scheming, careless, bullying, and demanding of attention.

9—You are based upon love, compassion, sympathy, generosity, understanding, romance, emotionalism, artistic talent, magnetism, a broad viewpoint, and charity. You can be overly emotional, impractical, fickle, uncaring, and an aimless dreamer if you don't watch yourself.

11—Your foundation is built upon spirituality, idealism, mysticism, intuition, inventiveness, nervous energy, insight, capacity for leadership, appreciation of beauty, inspiration, and power. If not cautious, you can be impractical, shiftless, miserly, dishonest, and falsely superior.

22—Your foundation is that of great power, large ideas, human understanding, uplift, organization, intuition, skill, tact, friendliness, coordination, accomplishment, diplomacy, and practicality. There is a danger of becoming scheming, self-promoting, greedy, indifferent, and suffering from an inferiority complex.

Eleven

YOUR KEY

Your key number is just that; it is your key to accomplishment and it will open the doors of life. You must understand, however, that even though we use our key, not all doors will open because some are locked from the other side. Keep in mind that when we have used our key we know that we have done all we can do, and if it is meant for us to go through the door, the latch will be lifted from the other side and we will be able to pass. We are never helped until we have done all that we can do for ourselves—that is one of the universal laws.

The key is also one of the first vibrations to influence a child and it is of importance all through life. When considered with the destiny, it gives valuable information about how we can accomplish our purpose. Looked at along with the outer self, we can see how to put our abilities to better use and make greater headway in our chosen vocation. Our key can truly unlock experiences if we learn what it is and then put it to use.

The key number is the sum of all of the numbers indicated by the letters of the first name given at birth. Our key is only as good as we make it. It is a tool, and much like a hammer, it can be used to build or to break apart. Consider your key carefully and how best to put it to work for you. For example, if your first name (at birth) is Jim, then your key would be a

5. Add up all of the letters of your first name at birth to determine your key, and then consult the chart of key numbers to see how best to put it to use. Remember to consider it along with your destiny and outer self to get a better picture of how it can work for you.

THE KEY NUMBERS

1—Accomplishment comes through faith in yourself and your ideas, in courage, creativity, strong will, determination, progressiveness, pioneering, and in inventive and individualistic behavior. Experiences should be met with force, independence, originality, activity, intelligence, and positiveness.

2—Accomplishment comes through giving service and being receptive, adaptable, agreeable, charming, friendly, and analytical; by putting to use your ability with details and your liking for rhythm and music. Experiences should be met with cooperation, diplomacy, patience, consideration, and love.

3—Accomplishment comes through using words well and being imaginative, friendly, talented, happy, clever, intellectual, intuitive, artistic, and inspired. Experiences should be met with optimism, kindness, a sense of humor, and love and with freedom from worry and a joy of living.

4—Accomplishment comes through work and being punctual, dependable, economical, organized, conservative, conscientious, energetic, loyal, mentally and physically active, accurate, precise, and trustworthy. Experiences should be met with practicality, concentration, devotion, and patience and with proportion and perspective.

5—Accomplishment comes through mental curiosity, good assessment of human nature, cleverness, versatility, adaptability, travel, change, progression, and experiencing all aspects of life. Experiences should be met with understanding, an adventurous spirit, friendliness, interest, discarding the outdated for the new, perception, energy, and vitality.

6—Accomplishment comes through accepting responsibility and being protective, helpful, balanced, conscientious, devoted, and harmonious; giving service and advice. Experiences should be met with love, sympathy, understanding, patience, poise, ideals, justice, domesticity, concern, and a willingness to bear burdens for others.

7—Accomplishment comes through analysis, research, inner guidance, spirituality, perseverance, refinement, wisdom, a desire for perfection and quality, study, meditation, intuition, and knowledge. Experiences should be met with inner peace, sensitivity, faith, poise, and wisdom.

8—Accomplishment comes through management, organization, efficiency, executive ability, good financial judgment, leadership, achievement, power, intelligence, and zeal. Experiences should be met with practicality, self-reliance, control, good judgment, tact, authority, ability, and dependability.

9—Accomplishment comes through helping others, artistic talent, love, leadership, magnetism, self-sufficiency, reliability, honesty, cooperation, sociability, intuition, and spirituality. Experiences should be met with selfless service, understanding, compassion, generosity, sympathy, a broad outlook, and concern.

11—Accomplishment comes through energy, inventiveness, intuition, penetration, insight, intellect, inspiration, illumination, service, spirituality, power, leadership, zeal, quick decisions, and mental activity. Experiences should be met with immateriality, intuition, love of beauty, ideals, mysticism, and human understanding and concern.

22—Accomplishment comes through power in all areas, direction, skill, organization, uplift, the ability to analyze, coordination, practicality, application, travel, people, large duties and plans, and service to others. Experiences should be met with intuition, tact, diplomacy, understanding, friendliness, helpfulness, and a desire for improvement.

33—Accomplishment comes through revelation, spiritual understanding, loving service, insight, perception, ability, leadership, instruction and guidance, demonstration of knowledge and truth, wisdom, counseling, power, and love of nature and beauty. Experiences should be met with spirituality, love, faith, patience, tolerance, inner peace, optimism, and an understanding of the laws that govern life.

Twelve

THE SUBCONSCIOUS SELF—THE INCLUSION TABLE

To delve further into numerology we are going to have to go "behind the scenes." We will begin by setting up an Inclusion Table from the birth name. This table will be used to determine several things, which will be discussed in this and in other chapters.

To set up an Inclusion Table we consider the value of each letter of the birth name and how often that number appears in the name. For example,

```
N I K K I        K A R E N        C A B E
5 9 1 1 1 1 9    1 1 1 9 5 5      3 1 2 5

              2.....1s
              4.....2s(3–11s)
              1.....3
              0.........4s
              4.....5s
              0.........6s
              0.........7s
              0.........8s
              3.....9s
                          _____
       Total   14
```

Notice that although the 11s are counted with the 2s, we do not lose sight of them but make a note beside the number how many times they appear. Although reduced they are 2s and are counted with the 2s, their appearance adds the qualities and power of the 11 to the person's makeup and should always be considered.

Studying the amount of times each number value appears can tell us much about a person. The absence or weakness of numbers tells us a lot also, and this will be discussed in later chapters.

In the example given we find more 5s than anything else. (Remember that the 2s are a combination of 2s and 11s.) Five is the number of man and so is the number that most often occurs. To get a true picture from the Inclusion Table we must subtract 2 from the number of 5s that appear. That leaves two 5s, so therefore there are more 9s and 11s.

We shall consider the effect of the numbers in the Inclusion Table. In our example the strength of the 9s gives this person a great love of her fellowman, a desire to be of service, a romantic nature, and psychic and spiritual leanings. The 11s also show psychic and spiritual inclinations and so these influences should be strong in her life. The 11s also add power, energy, and idealism, and both 9 and 11 are quite intuitive and are lovers of beauty. The 11s should help balance the emotional nature of the 9s, while the 9s should lend human understanding that the 11s tend to lack. The 5s and 1s should make her progressive, active, mentally inclined, and a leader. From the 1s should come a desire for independence; from the 5s a desire for freedom and variety. There are not enough 1s to create much danger of self-promotion, or enough 5s to make irresponsibility much of a problem.

THE SUBCONSCIOUS SELF

To determine the subconscious self we must consider the number of vibrations missing and subtract this number from 9. In this case we find there are 4 vibrations missing, and in subtracting 4 from 9 we find that the subconscious self is a 5. The symbol for the subconscious is used in the example.

```
2. . . . .1
4. . . . .2(3–11s)
1. . . . .3
0. . . . . . . . .4
4. . . . .5
0. . . . . . . . .6        ^5
0. . . . . . . . .7         ≡
0. . . . . . . . .8
3. . . . .9
```

Total   14

If we find an Inclusion Table where no vibrations are missing, then the subconscious self would be a 9. The lowest subconscious self to be found is a 3, and that is extremely rare. The higher subconscious numbers are becoming more common than they used to be, and where a 9 used to be rare it is found far more frequently now. We will go into this further in Chapter Thirteen, The Karmic Lessons.

The subconscious self tells how you respond to situations and relationships. It deals totally with emotions and shows the reactions when there is no time to refer to the brain for guidance, as in an emergency or crisis. It does not influence us consciously at all and could therefore be called the "unconscious self." It has no desires, no abilities, and does not urge us in any direction; it merely is the part of us that takes over and functions when the conscious does not. Otherwise it is inactive.

When you have set up your Inclusion Table and have calculated your subconscious self as shown, then consult the numbers of the subconscious to see how you are inclined to react when your conscious mind has had no time to step in and assert its influence and control.

THE NUMBERS OF THE SUBCONSCIOUS

3—You are bound to find life very hard and are apt to rebel strongly at what comes your way. You are nervous, flighty, and interested only in the pleasant aspects of life. You insist upon self-expression and if hindered, opposed, or restricted will generally lose control of yourself. You have great difficulty concentrating and tend to be emotional to the point of imbalance. In an emergency you would be of use to no one and might even break down, possibly endangering yourself and others. You might become so nervous that you could not produce a constructive thought or action to help the situation.

4—You are held back by your own slow-moving pace and are so bound by detail and routine that progress would be impossible. You cannot see the whole picture because you concentrate on unimportant details. You look at everything only from a practical point of view and see only the little things that are right under your nose. In a crisis you would see only the details and the need to work on them and would never see the really important things that need to be done. To you the only way out of any situation is unending hard work.

5—You are never satisfied, demand variety, and have a point of view that is totally material and physical. Concerned with your own pleasure, you are restless, trivial, and self-indulgent. You are flighty and seek too much change. You scatter your thoughts and energies in too many directions. In a crisis you would be nervous, irresponsible, and overly talkative and would think of many different things to do at once and get none of them done. If you lose your self-control, you are completely lost and may end up screaming or just crying and shaking—accomplishing nothing.

6—Your first concern is always for those you care about the most, and the center of your life is your home. You try to comfort, serve, care for, and give love to everyone, whatever the situation. No matter what happens, you feel that you have the answer to everyone's problems, and your goal is to make things better for people if you can. In times of crisis you would create problems for others because you would feel the need to protect all of your prized possessions, family, and loved ones and to make sure that they were with you if you saw any way to manage this.

7—You react to situations with seeming indifference. You may appear unemotional, aloof, and almost uncaring, but underneath you are sensitive, feel deeply, sympathize, and care very much. You analyze everything and usually sees all sides; in addition you're secretive, well-balanced, and often technical in your approach to things. If you are negative, there is a good possibility that you will turn to drink. In emergency situations your response is to pray.

8—Viewing things with a very businesslike outlook, you usually handle situations with efficiency, taking control and reasoning all things out. You believe that all effort should bring gain. Dependable, firm, authoritative, you may be somewhat cold and factual because of a lack of emotional involvement. You can be diplomatic, conservative, and logical. In an emergency you will organize things very well and will see to it that everyone has a specific task to perform.

9—Having experienced most of life already, you tend to be bored by it. You are often impersonal in your behavior and may seem unfeeling and uncaring, but it is because you have your own way of viewing things. You can even see good in what appears to be bad. You are often unsure of your opinion and do not like to argue. You have a slight interest in many things but probably no strong interest in any one thing. You tend to generalize and to be critical. You are emotional but because you function on a different level from most people, you may not understand the things that bother them. In an emergency you are resigned and usually believe in fate and that good comes from all situations.

If you possess the lower subconscious numbers, you may find the effects softened by other numbers in your chart, but generally it is advisable to consider changing your name. If a name change is contemplated, you should take care that it has some of the vibrations that are missing from your original name and if it can be managed, all the vibrations that are included as well. This will to some degree lessen the effect that the birth name has in this area, although nothing will negate it completely. A conscious effort to balance negative traits will in time have a constructive effect also.

Thirteen

THE KARMIC LESSONS

Karmic lessons are situations and experiences that we have failed to meet and cope with or that we have met and misused in past lifetimes. A lesson is not Karmic until we have failed to learn it. At this stage of human evolvement all souls have experienced each lesson at least once, and so our lessons are now Karmic. It is universal law that each soul must learn all of the lessons and that until we do certain situations and conditions will continue to present themselves to give us the opportunities needed for learning.

Once we bécome aware of just what our Karmic lessons are we know what to work on, what to expect in life, and how to train ourselves to respond. Thus learning becomes easier. Once a lesson is learned and learned well it does not have to be repeated, and we are then free of the circumstances we were once bound to. When we are free of circumstances that often are unpleasant, life becomes better, easier, and more rewarding. Sometimes there are experiences that keep coming to us even after we have learned their lessons, but once we have learned to handle a situation it no longer poses problems for us and so does not make our life miserable anymore. How many times have you wondered why the same circumstances constantly seem to appear in your life? The answer may well lie in your Karmic lessons.

With numerology we can not only determine how many Karmic lessons we have, but we can tell exactly what they are and what kinds of situations they will bring to us. We can also get an idea of what we have neglected or abused in the past so that we don't repeat our mistakes.

To find the Karmic lessons we must again look at the Inclusion Table. The Karmic lessons are shown by the missing numbers. Consulting the example given in the last chapter, we see that the missing numbers are 4, 6, 7, and 8. This shows us that there are four Karmic lessons. To find out exactly what they mean in relationship to our experiences we must look them up under the numbers of the Karmic lessons. Life's lessons are contained in the numbers 1 through 9. Although we count the 11s and 22s when setting up an Inclusion Table, we do not count them when determining Karmic lessons.

In the last chapter I mentioned that at the present time far more people have a 9 subconscious than was common in the past. This indicates that they have no Karmic lessons. People with no lessons have gone through life's experiences and have learned what we all must learn. When a soul has learned all of the lessons, it does not have to incarnate on the earth plane anymore. These souls have chosen to come back to give service and in some cases to perfect their learning to an even greater degree. At the end of one age and at the beginning of a new one, such advanced souls always incarnate in greater numbers to assist their fellowmen and to prepare for the coming of the Christ to earth again. This is even more true now when the souls of the earth are being prepared for a spiritual awakening such as they have never known, and the earth is about to undergo the greatest changes since the sinking of Atlantis. I find the greatest number of these souls when doing the charts of children and babies.

Speaking of children, I would like to say something to parents at this time. Determining what your children's lessons are and then helping them to begin working on them at a young age gives them a great start in life. You can aid them in building the habits and traits necessary for adult life and they can complete their learning processes much sooner. For this reason I have tried to keep children in mind when discussing the Karmic lessons.

Knowing about anything in advance lessens the impact it has upon us, and so it is with the lessons. You can remain the victim of their circumstances, or you can arm yourself with knowledge to fight them. Often we find that we have been working at learning these things even though we had no idea that they were our lessons. The reason is that because we dislike the experiences they bring, we chose to learn or saw a need within ourselves. Learning our lessons is really a matter of strengthening our weak spots. Regardless of how the learning comes about, we must always remember balance; we must take care not to be overzealous and thus tip the scales in the opposite direction. One thing is certain, we can only run from learning our lessons just so long and then life will somehow force us into doing what we avoid—in one lifetime or another. In the beginning, life is fairly gentle as it tries to persuade us to attend to our neglected lessons and tries to show us that we need to learn them now. If we rebel, then the experiences given us become continually harder, to the point of being extremely harsh. It is all done for our own good and progress, although it may not seem so at the time.

When you look over your chart, you may find that the numbers you lack in your inclusion often turn up somewhere else. This indicates several things. One, it indicates that you're being given an extra push to learn, and at the same time you are being given help in learning because you carry the vibration elsewhere. If it shows up in the numbers of the birth date or in later calculations made from the birth date, then it shows a time in your life when you will really need to concentrate on learning that lesson in particular, and that if you learn the lesson before that time, life will be considerably easier for you.

THE NUMBERS OF THE KARMIC LESSONS

1—In the past you have failed to learn the value of independence; you avoided making decisions and have been afraid to be a leader. You chose to follow quietly. Fear and overcaution kept you from using your talents and abilities. You failed to face things, ran from anything new, and molded yourself totally after others, so that the real you was lost in a maze of imitation.

In this lifetime you will have to conquer these fears and find the real you. Life will force you into situations in which you will have to rely upon your judgment and abilities. You will be made to lead, to accept progress, to make your own decisions, to develop your individuality, and to acquire courage and strength. You will have to depend upon your own will and form your own opinions, and often you will be required to look after others and fight for your place in life.

A child with this lesson should not be unduly repressed; it needs to be encouraged toward independence, individuality, and striking out alone at a young age. It needs to be allowed to grow up to be an individual, so try not to set unnecessary patterns for it to follow.

2—You have avoided cooperating with others and failed to learn the value and need for tact, patience, and consideration of others' feelings. You have neglected the lessons to be learned from service, detail, the small things of life, and obedience. You have been careless about time and the acquisition of small things. You have been too concerned with yourself to give much thought or love to others.

Life will present you with opportunities to help you realize the need to be sensitive to others' thoughts and feelings, to make sacrifices for the sake of getting along well, to learn the importance of attending to small things. You will not accomplish anything worthwhile unless you learn patience, attend to the details, and give service to others. You will need to be friendly, loyal, diplomatic, and a peacemaker to learn this lesson. You have a tendency to collect things—be careful that you don't become a hoarder or a kleptomaniac. Don't repress the urge altogether, or you'll find yourself unable to hold on to anything. Any 11s in the chart may tend to soften the effect of this lesson, but the very fact that the 11 is a higher vibration is what keeps it from negating the lesson.

A child with this lesson needs to be encouraged to associate with others and to work at getting along with them. It needs to learn how to share. Help it to think about how other people feel, and insist that it do all aspects of anything—especially the little details that a child is not even apt to be aware of. Help it form a habit of seeing and attending to these things.

3—You have failed to learn to express yourself and have tried to withdraw into your own little shell. Often this desire to hide causes poor posture, such as round shoulders, or a tendency to keep your arms folded across your chest. This indicates that you are trying to shut yourself off from the world. You have tried to conceal your personality because you lack confidence in yourself. You have allowed others to repress and stifle your expression and have become intimidated and something of a recluse. You fear being noticed and having contact with people.

Situations will be such in this lifetime that you will be called upon to speak your mind, to participate in social events, and to deal with the public. You may be forced into a position in which you must sell—what will not matter. You will be forced to learn to use words in an effort to bring yourself out of hiding. As long as you continue to underestimate yourself, you will achieve little or nothing. You must develop your personality and overcome your fear of people and of yourself and your tendency to apologize for being what you are.

The child with this lesson needs contact with people outside its own family circle. It must not be allowed to spend too much time alone, and it should be encouraged to do artistic things to give it an added outlet for self-expression. Ask its opinion; get it to talk about its feelings and beliefs. Praise it so that it feels worthwhile and that it can do things to be proud of. Give it a lot of love and help it see that it can love itself as well.

4—In the past you have disliked work—the slow, building, manual kind of labor. You have avoided it by choosing life situations where it was not necessary. Work to you represented physical strain with little to show for it and a mentality that made laborers fit for nothing else. You have been inclined to do things hastily, taking shortcuts and putting forth as little effort as possible. You have failed to learn self-discipline or organization and routine.

In this lifetime you will be forced to see that little of value is accomplished without work or effort. You will have to learn to discipline yourself, establish system and routine in your life, and discard haste and shortcuts for patience and accuracy. You will be forced to work to achieve anything—to help you realize that work can be rewarding. You will learn that doing good work requires intelligence and that labor can gain you self-respect and dignity. You are no less a person and possibly a better one for working hard. You will have to be patient and adopt a slow and careful way of doing things, keeping in mind that quality is better than quantity.

The child with this lesson should be given definite chores to do, starting when it is young, and be made to work as a contribution to its home and family. Impress upon it that poor work —at home, at school, or anywhere—is unacceptable. Show it how to do things in a well-ordered way, and insist that it keep its own room neat and well organized. It should be given opportunities to earn the things it wants so that it will see the benefit of work. Do not make the mistake of just handing everything to this child.

5—You have run from life in the past and consequently
failed to acquire an understanding of people and of life's experiences. You have of course encountered both many times, but
have gained little from them because you chose to remain blind
to their lessons. You neglected to learn to be sociable, tolerant,
agreeable, progressive, or versatile. You have a fear of change,
of the unknown, of anything strange or different. You have
avoided situations where you could learn about what was going
on in the world in favor of familiar, secure situations.

In this lifetime you will be forced to accept change: new
ideas, people, places, and things. You will encounter experiences and emergencies wherever you go until you decide to
meet them head on, to deal with them and learn from them.
You will have to learn about life and your fellowman and
acquire tolerance. You will be faced with a variety of situations
and will have to discover what life is all about. You may find
it hard to have and to keep a home or a place of your own, and
you may not be allowed any relationship for long until this
lesson is learned.

The child with this lesson must be helped to see why change
is necessary and good, and then should be aided in adapting to
it. Do not shelter it from life, but encourage it to experience life
and understand it. Help it to see life as an exciting adventure.
Put as much variety into its life as you can.

6—You have been overly concerned with yourself and so
have refused to accept responsibility, burdens, and obligations.
You have not bothered to finish whatever you have begun and
have wanted no part of unions, partnerships, or close association with others. You know nothing of giving service or devotion. You have failed to learn to share or to put balance in your
life.

Until you learn to accept responsibility, and to do so willingly, life will be frustrating because obligations will be forced
upon you at every turn. You will be placed in positions where
you must care for and provide for others, often creating a

hardship. You will have to learn to bear distress and to do your duty well and with love. You will need to learn the value of a home and family and of creating an atmosphere of harmony. If you fail to learn the lesson of being a good mate, the union will most likely end, leaving you feeling guilty and unhappy. Others will expect a great deal from you, even require it, and you will receive little in return. You will have to learn how to solve problems for yourself and others, and learn the value of lending a helping hand. You should also be sure to finish the things you start.

The child with this lesson must be helped to appreciate its home and loved ones. It should be taught to do things for others, and with no thought of reward. It should also be taught to accept responsibility. For example, get it a pet that it must feed and care for. Ask it to help watch and care for younger children in the family or in your neighborhood. When it has a problem to solve, try to help the child help itself.

7—Fear is one of the big problems of this lesson. It is one of the most frequently found lessons in adult charts at this time. The age that we have just passed through has been one in which a great deal of the preachings of most churches concerned themselves with hell, purgatory, and eternal damnation. Salvation lay in living a spiritual life. At the same time, living a spiritual life all too often meant poverty, being shut off from the world, fasting, penance, great discipline, and abstaining from most of the pleasanter things in the world. Those who were considered truly spiritual were removed in almost all ways from ordinary life, for example, monks, hermits, nuns, and lamas. Many people had a great fear of not being religious enough. This lesson also indicates that you've neglected to develop your ability to analyze—to really examine things and think them through well. Both of these are aspects of the unseen worlds— the mental and the spiritual—which you have failed to see in their true perspective. In addition you have failed to develop these parts of yourself to their full extent.

In this life there will be many opportunities for you to see things properly and so release your fears in favor of faith. You will have to learn to see what is important and to rely on your own resources. You must learn to become comfortable in your use of the unseen worlds and must learn to make them a part of your everyday life. You must gain an understanding of what spirituality really is and see the beauty in it. You will need to make time in your everyday schedule to be alone with your thoughts, so you can face your fears, look closely at all things, and search for truth. You may well find this a life in which you will do without until you learn true faith.

The child with this lesson needs to be helped to see that the Creator is total love and not to be feared. Never add to its fear with talk of hell or Divine punishment. Teach it about Karma and reincarnation so that it will gain true understanding. Aid it in its search for understanding in all areas. Encourage the child to think things out for itself and help it to see all aspects of a thing. Help it to see the impermanence of material things and to put in perspective the true value of objects and possessions. Encourage it to spend a reasonable amount of time alone in reading, studying, and thinking. Help it to see through its fears and to establish faith in its life.

8—You have run away from making decisions, handling matters involving money, and managing your own affairs—especially those of a business nature. You have used poor judgment and have tried to avoid the material and physical aspects of life. You have wanted nothing to do with the commercial world or authority and know little about achieving and acquiring because you've been afraid to try. You have refused to learn about the laws governing money and success and have therefore missed the lessons that can be learned from the power that goes with them.

Life will be such that you will be forced to learn how to handle money, make decisions, and assume authority. You must learn to manage things yourself and learn to use good judgment. The big lesson to remember is never to use money, success, power, or anything solely for self-advancement. If you do, there will be consequences. Often the penalty is loss of health, happiness, or contentment. Until you learn how to manage well for yourself, you may be striving hard to achieve without satisfaction—with many disappointments and failures the result. Money could be very hard for you to come by and when it does come it could almost seem to vanish into thin air —it goes so quickly. Then you will be made to feel the absence of funds keenly. Once this lesson is learned well you stand at the door of success.

The child with this lesson can be helped by being given money to spend and then by being taught how to spend it wisely. Assist it in managing things for itself—push it in this direction but always with supervision. If there is any way of making this child into a young businessman, it could benefit greatly from the experience. Insist that some portion of its money be saved—just so it has the security of having some put aside. Planning is important for this child, for the future as well as for today.

9—You have failed to learn about your own emotional nature and that of others. In the past you have kept your emotions too well controlled—to the extent that you know nothing about them. To feel is to be human and you have little understanding of what that really means. Because you've refused to feel, you have not experienced suffering, hurt, or heartache. You felt that if you kept others at arm's length—never really loving or allowing yourself to be loved—you couldn't be hurt. The result has been thoughts mainly about yourself.

This lifetime is intended to teach you how to feel—mainly through being hurt and suffering. You will be made to be less selfish and to do without for the sake of others. You are going to be taught to really live. You must acquire sympathy, compassion, love, generosity, and understanding. You will have to dispose of your personal desires and be satisfied to give without

expecting reward, for you will not receive anything truly satisfying until this lesson is fully learned. You may long for a
lasting personal relationship, but it is doubtful that it will be
yours until you can really love and give selflessly.

The child with this lesson must be made to think about others
and to try to understand their feelings. In no way should its
emotional nature ever be repressed; it should be *encouraged*.
There is nothing wrong with tears—not even in men and boys
—tears are not a sign of weakness but rather of the ability to
feel. The same is true of displays of affection. Help it to use its
hurts to better understand the hurts of others. Stress the beauty
and satisfaction in giving, and minimize receiving. Help it to see
how to really love so it can be loved. The best way to teach is
through example—when the child sees your loving, sympathetic, and understanding nature in action, it will realize faster
its benefits and the desirability of developing these qualities.

Fourteen

THE MAJOR LIFE CYCLES

There are two kinds of life cycles, the major and the minor. In this chapter we will be dealing with the major cycles, although there will be some mention of the minor cycles because of their influence upon the major ones. We will go into the minor cycles in detail in the next chapter because they are part of the general numbers of the chart.

Everyone's life is divided into three major cycles that we will refer to simply as life cycles, or cycles, from now on. When speaking of the minor cycles, we will refer to them as the personal years so there won't be any confusion as to which kind of cycle we are talking about. The life cycles have the greatest influence on our life and on our approach to life. They also have a great deal to do with our destiny.

The cycles are each approximately twenty-eight years in length. In this area astrology and numerology work together. The change from the first cycle to the second cycle is determined by when the progressed moon in the astrological chart has completed its first revolution. This actually takes about twenty-eight years and four months to complete. We refer to numerology to see when this change will be fully realized. This is determined by the personal year.

The personal years follow in succession from 1 to 9, with the

1 years the beginnings and the 9 years the completions. The full effect of a change of cycle will be realized about the time of the 1 personal year nearest the change, whether before or after, as this is a time of beginning. The effects of the cycle that you are passing out of will begin to diminish noticeably in the 9 year closest to the change. As the change of cycles comes approximately every twenty-eight years, we leave the first and enter the second in the 1 personal year nearest our twenty-eighth birthday, and we go from the second to the third in the 1 personal year closest to our fifty-sixth birthday.

The vibratory influence of the cycles is determined by the three numbers that make up the destiny, or in other words, the reduced numbers of the month, day, and year of birth. The month indicates the first cycle, the day the second cycle, the year the third cycle. Our first cycle is the growth period, and by the time of the second cycle we should be fully matured and adult. The second cycle is the productive period of life when we generally accomplish the most, and it is a time to prepare for the last cycle, which is primarily a rest cycle. During the last cycle we also have a chance to look at the life that we have led and see what can yet be done to further fulfill the destiny.

The change from one cycle to another can be a very easy, almost unnoticeable thing, or a very drastic change that may completely alter one's life-style. The change is generally determined by two things. First to be considered is the vibratory influence of the two cycles; if they are what you could call harmonious or somewhat alike, the change is most apt to be one that will not make a great difference, although the differences can be seen and felt if aware of the cycle changes. If the cycles are at odds or two vibrations that have little in common or may even be the opposite of each other, then the change can truly alter nearly every aspect of the life-style. This is why some people feel the need, for instance, to wait to marry until close to their twenty-eighth year; for many others marriages end at about this time. Many feel the urge to change jobs close to this age or make other big changes in their lives. Older people quite frequently begin to think of retirement about the age of fifty-six, or they want to travel or change their way of life in some way or another. We tend to give these things little thought and often are not even aware of the changes in ourselves at these times because we do not know about or think about the life cycles and their influences.

When considering the cycles, it must be remembered that they are a part of the total of life, or the destiny. They have an influence of their own which goes hand in hand with the destiny. They tell us how best to proceed toward our purpose during that particular period of our life. The cycles should always be thought of along with the destiny; no matter how we may proceed in life we must always keep the end, or destination, in mind. The cycles give us information about the experiences we will meet, the situations we should look for and make use of, the tendencies we will feel, and the things that we need to make a part of our life and learn about as we travel toward our goal.

It is an advantage to know about our cycles so that we can prepare for them in advance. When we are prepared for an event, it loses much of its terror, and also we can begin to acquire the qualities we will need at that time. In addition we can start to make the situations that will be best for us a part of our life before they are really needed and can, so to speak, get things set up and ready to go. It gives us time to contemplate how best to put that period of our life to use, and this is one of the greatest helps of all. Again, remember to consider the cycle and destiny together and to expect the full influence of the cycle in the 1 year nearest to the time of change. The following will tell you how to calculate the personal years.

THE LIFE CYCLES

1—This cycle is intended to be a period of independence and a time for you to develop your individuality. You must strive toward your goal courageously, putting aside all doubts and fears, and never limiting your thoughts of what you can do. During this time you are to do what you feel is right, listening to others for what they may say of value, but never allowing them to sway you from your own opinions if they are well-founded. You must use your talents and abilities to their fullest, never depending upon others but going ahead on your own. Develop your strength and determination so that others will look to you for assistance and so that you will need to look to no one. Be a leader and set out with force to realize your purpose.

As a first cycle this can be a very difficult vibration because a child is not capable of handling the independence it feels driven to try for. It is apt to feel frustrated because its elders seem to be continually trying to stand in its way, to do things it feels capable of doing. Many times the elders are right, but not always. Thought should be given to the areas in which it can safely assert its independence, because it really should be encouraged and not repressed. This child tends to be strong-willed and dominant, to enjoy doing things alone, and to be the leader or instigator. It may not adapt well to the patterns you set because it needs to exert its individuality. This is one of the hardest first cycles.

As a middle cycle this vibration is best and can be a very productive and satisfying period. These are the years in which it is usually the easiest to be independent and to develop the self to the fullest degree. This is a cycle of activity, but one in which you will be most comfortable when functioning on your own or in a position of control. It is a good time for going into business by yourself, or for striking out to get a job as a boss or manager. Marriage or any partnership during this time can be a strain for you and consequently for others unless this vibration is understood and kept in mind.

As a last cycle there can again be some frustration involved if either independence or activity becomes a problem. This vibration is conducive to mental and physical activity, so the activity aspect is not a problem nearly as often as that of being independent. The lessening of physical activity often increases mental activity, so the creative and inventive qualities of this vibration can be more fully realized as a last cycle if they are put to use. This gives a feeling of productivity and progressiveness that is needed. It can be a good time for writing and for devising new plans and ideas that are very innovative.

2—During this cycle you are to progress toward your goal by cooperating with others. It is a time when you must be diplomatic, thoughtful, sensitive to others' feelings, and willing to do whatever is necessary to keep peace. You will need to pay attention to details, collect all that you can, particularly knowledge, look for opportunity in the small aspects of life as well as in the large. Never try to assert yourself too strongly. Be willing to take a back seat to others. Be patient, give loving service whenever you can, and learn obedience. Be receptive, easygoing, and gentle. Work at studying and analyzing all things, for this is a period when learning is important and easy to acquire.

The child with this cycle is often overly sensitive, consequently it can be very emotional. Its tears may come easily and frequently and for what to others seem like trivial reasons. A desire to please makes this child easy to get along with, and it wants things to be peaceful and happy. An atmosphere of disharmony will upset and depress it and can create emotional problems that will evidence themselves in school work or social behavior. The child is usually quiet and studious and has a great need to both give and receive love. It likes to do things for others and needs to know its efforts are appreciated. If aided in

keeping its emotions in check and it is given a pleasant atmosphere to grow up in, the time can be a beautiful period for
everyone involved.

With this influence as a middle cycle you could do well in any
job where you can practice your ability to create harmony. You
might consider politics, diplomatic work, or being a personnel
manager or marriage counselor. Check your destiny and the
rest of your chart to see what is indicated. The inclination to
attend to details and the need to work and cooperate with
others must be developed. Collect knowledge that will help you
with your destiny. Be sensitive to others' needs and feelings.
This is a time for giving service, often in small ways, so don't
overlook them. You will need to be adaptable to many situations, putting thoughts of yourself second. Always keep your
purpose in mind so you will know what area to work in. This
is a good vibration for marriage and partnerships, and either
should flourish during this time.

This is usually a quiet third cycle when you will want to
acquire things—anything from objects to increased knowledge.
You would do well to use this time to study, to analyze life and
people, and to aid others. You must strive to make life pleasant
for all those around you, especially since this will help assure
you of the companionship you will feel a great need for. Get
involved with other people if you're not already involved, and
stay involved. You could find club activities very rewarding.
You'd probably enjoy being an antique dealer and would do
well at it if your desire to collect didn't make it hard for you
to part with things. You would get a lot of satisfaction out of
collecting almost anything. You might find getting involved in
politics to your liking. This is usually a very peaceful vibration
to carry as a last cycle.

3—This cycle is concerned with the pleasant and beautiful
things of life and should be predominantly free of care. It is a
time for self-expression: artistically, with painting, sculpting,
writing; musically, with singing, playing an instrument, danc-

ing; with words, acting, lecturing, entertaining, or just talking. It is not usually a good cycle for learning; it is too concerned with outward expression rather than inward accumulation. During this period you should entertain a lot, build friendships, develop your personality, and enjoy life. You must learn to open up to others, saying what you think and believe; give of yourself and your affections. Whatever your destiny, you will progress toward it during these years by self-expression and by associating with people.

The child carrying this vibration may be inclined to be overly expressive—some children have a way of going to extremes. There is a tendency in adults to suppress children's attempts at expression—to keep them seen and not heard. Feeling pushed to speak its mind or be noticed, this child may be quieted just so long, and then in a rebellious way will try to be heard. It would be better if some form of expression were allowed so that it would be quieter and there would be no built-up frustration. Give this child all the opportunities for social contacts that you can. It is inclined to be outgoing, talkative, active, possibly a poor student, and very unconcerned with anything but having a good time. Unless given outlets for expression, this child could be unruly and something of a problem.

This influence as a second cycle points to enjoying life. You will only meet with frustration if you try to concentrate solely on work and the mundane aspects of life. You can't forget them altogether, but you should include social activities in your schedule—time for friends and fun. Take up an artistic hobby if your work doesn't provide such an outlet or if you aren't already doing something of that nature. Develop the ability to use words well. During this period, make people a big part of your life—you could do well at a job like selling if there is any indication of this in your destiny or in your other major numbers. This should be a good time for any sort of union, and hopefully your mate or companion will enjoy socializing too. Make beauty a part of your life—art, music, nature—whatever appeals to you. Remember that this part of your path deals with self-expression.

This is one of the most enjoyable vibrations for a last cycle. It is a time of friendship, pleasantness, socializing, laughter, and all the things you may not have had much time for until now. It's a good time for artistic activity and one form to be sure to consider is writing—especially if you develop your sense of humor and imagination. Often these can be put to use with your life experience to make enjoyable and successful reading material. You might like to travel—both to visit friends or family, or just to see the beauties of various places. You can continue to fulfill your purpose by contact with new people and old friends and by helping them to enjoy life too. Whatever you do, make sure it includes the important aspects of this vibration.

4—There is one word which sums up most of the meaning of this vibration: *work.* This is the number of the builder who with great care erects a sound structure for the future. Much of this cycle is concerned with creating for the future, preparing both within and without. This is a time of productivity—far more so than for most vibrations. Pick definite goals and jobs and work toward them patiently and surely. Be practical, systematic, and economical. Do everything thoroughly, making certain that each task is completed before you go on to another. Give whatever service you can to others. Establish routine in your life and things will go better for you. Realize that all things can be used in one way or another, so make everything of service to you. This can be a good vibration for close associations, although with personal ones you might find yourself having some difficulty in showing your feelings unless other aspects of your chart are strongly emotional and expressive.

For a child this vibration can present problems because it is the opposite influence of the natural tendencies of children, who usually want life to be all fun and play. The child may have some difficulty in showing feelings or in talking about the things that matter to it. It will be more comfortable in an atmosphere of routine and where it has regular duties or chores to attend to. It needs to be encouraged to complete whatever it starts and to do all things well. It may not respond much to affection, but it needs a lot of it just the same, although at times it may have to be given subtly. It needs to be kept busy at constructive activities and encouraged to develop manual dexterity. Find some way to show that work is rewarding and not just hard or dull. Give praise generously for all things that are well done. This influence can also indicate that this may be a time of financial disability and repression.

This is a great vibration for a middle cycle because it can be so productive. The danger lies in going to the extreme, becoming so work-minded that life becomes dull. Life needs balance, with time allowed for all things, and you must set up your routine with this in mind. You are preparing for the future, so build well. Whatever your destiny, your path is that of work, service, discipline, and organization during these years. To proceed with your purpose you must put forth mental and physical effort. Do nothing in haste, taking care with all, and never be wasteful. Make the practical a part of your life. Financial matters need watching especially. Marriage during these years can be very enjoyable and satisfying because you enjoy doing things for others. However, your partner and family should not expect you to be too social or too affectionate.

As a last cycle this vibration can be limiting unless you have prepared for it. There is the work aspect, but this doesn't have to be a problem if you've found work you enjoy. You will want to make your life as well-ordered as possible, but this is usually easier in later years anyway. You need to be concerned with producing, and if money is not a problem, you can still do a lot that will be beneficial and give you a feeling of satisfaction and usefulness. You could be of considerable service to your community during these years—possibly through politics or church affairs. Whatever, you will need to stay busy, and it would be best if you picked definite things to turn your efforts to.

5—This is the vibration of someone who adapts to any situation and who thrives on variety. During this cycle, don't try to settle too securely in any one place because you probably won't be there long—whether it's a job, a town, or a home. The influence is one of change, variety, travel, experiences—and all at a fast-moving pace. Stay on the go and learn to adjust to whatever comes along. Look for new and different things and learn all that you can about them. Meet all the people you can and see what they can teach you. Unions are apt to be hard to keep intact while under this influence because you need to be free of responsibility and free to go when it is time. Few can understand this need fully unless they have experienced it themselves. Always with this vibration there is the danger of abusing freedom through the physical senses and appetites. The physical passions are usually increased by this influence and must be guarded against.

This can be a very strong vibration for a child to cope with because of the inclination to freedom and the added physical stimulus. Generally it will have to learn about the world from its own experiences rather than from those of others. It will dislike responsibility and probably not see to it very well. Bored easily, very inquisitive, and with a keen mind, it will learn quickly and want to go on to new things rapidly. It will learn fast and yet could do poorly in school. It is apt to leave home at a young age but is resourceful enough to make a success of it. It will also be inclined to start trying all manner of things at an earlier age than most children, which may create problems for itself and others. You might as well resign yourself to the fact that this child will have to try almost everything to learn for itself, and all the protesting, cautioning, and worrying in the world won't deter it.

As a second cycle travel, change and varied experiences are indicated. This is not a time to take on restricting responsibilities. Keep your hat in your hand and a change of clothes in your suitcase. Your opportunities will be found in new and progressive things that are not a part of the normal routine. If something does not happen to provide change, then you must make the change happen yourself. Learn to let go of the old and familiar when it has served its purpose and go on to other things. Use your mental ability and your judgment of people to benefit you and help you toward your goal. Don't expect any relationship or situation to last too long, for very little will be permanent during these years. Learn to adapt to anything—no matter how strange or different from what you're used to. Keep yourself as free as you can and be a "happy wanderer." Variety of experience is the key to furthering your purpose.

When a third cycle, this vibration usually indicates that there will be variety, people, and usually travel and that there should be enjoyment of all. This should be a time free of cares so you can indulge in the pleasant things that you like. There is likely to be a desire for the intellectual in people and books, and you might even feel the urge to try your hand at writing or inventing. It's a good time for any kind of travel, but you'll especially enjoy going to other countries and learning about their people and ways of life. If you feel the need of something to do, look for things that would put you in contact with people or variety, or you will find little satisfaction otherwise.

6—This cycle involves responsibility and serving others, and generally is concerned with the domestic scene. It is to some degree a restricted cycle; you will not experience much freedom because of the duties you have to tend to. You may feel heavily burdened at times, but the burden must be carried with all the strength and ability you have if you are to progress with your purpose. It is a time when much of your thoughts and energies must be directed toward home, family, and friends. During these years, you will probably be faced with solving numerous problems, making frequent adjustments, and helping those who are less fortunate than yourself. Although restrictive, this vibration is also one of harmony and all close associations should be enjoyable, pleasant, and probably lasting. You should be surrounded by love and protection during these years, possibly even devotion. Although you must give a lot under this influence, it should be a time of happiness and satisfaction for you if you willingly accept the duties that come your way.

The child with this cycle may feel restricted because it will draw protection strongly and may feel too guarded. It could be given too much responsibility, which would sit heavily on small shoulders. It is usually very attached to home and loved ones and is not one to leave home at a young age. In fact, leaving home could be hard unless it has another to go to. It will be miserable unless those around it are getting along well with each other. It is apt to be a worrier and needs to feel secure and to know that it is loved and wanted. This vibration is very conventional and bound to tradition and that could frustrate it at times because children feel the need to be different. It may have problems shaking this influence. It is generally easy to get along with, likes being helpful, and may well have an artistic streak that needs to be encouraged.

As a middle cycle the tendency is usually toward marriage, responsibilities, putting down roots, and establishing a happy home life. Without most of these things, you won't do much toward accomplishing your purpose or feeling contented. Develop your ability to solve problems. This is a time of doing for others, of being dependable and strong, and of learning to be the one with the answers. Others will probably look to you for advice and guidance, which you need to give as best you can. Don't wait for others to do things for you because chances are they won't, and unless you learn to rely upon yourself, life will just put you in one poor situation after another. Use your artistic talent in some way. Be devoted to the people and things you care about and continually strive to make conditions better for everyone. Don't try to impose your ideals upon others—everyone needs to have his own.

As a final cycle the protection of this vibration can be comforting. It indicates that you must continue to look after the things that you began or were involved with earlier. There could be some problems in adjusting to the differences that may come your way and in bearing the burdens that may be thrust upon you. All anyone can ever do is the best he is capable of —no more than that is ever asked except by humans. So just do what you can. You should be blessed with family, friends, and a comfortable home if you have prepared for this cycle as you should. Wherever you are you make it home because you have this ability. If for some reason you are unmarried, you could find great enjoyment in a late marriage during these years. You are not likely to be very happy living alone unless you see a lot of people. You may travel, but you'll always be glad to get back home again, for that's where you are most at ease.

7—The vibration of this cycle is definitely mental and indicates a time for developing your intellect to the fullest. The influence is also that of the unseen worlds, so this vibration can be very spiritual. It is a time for gaining inner wisdom— through study and learning and through meditation and attunement to your inner guidance. Seek time alone during this cycle and don't go into business partnerships. Rely upon your intuition and develop all that you have to the greatest possible degree. The metaphysical meaning of this number is perfection, and you will need to do everything as well as you can. Do not strive for personal gain—your opportunity is in that which comes to you, not in that which you might go after. You must learn to adjust to things of the material world, as you strive for understanding of the unseen. Search for inner peace and hidden truths. Develop poise and refinement and become an authority on something. Concern yourself with the fundamentals; approach everything scientifically, analyzing every aspect carefully.

A child with this cycle is likely to be somewhat reserved and withdrawn, and therefore may be very misunderstood. Often it is thought of as abnormal because it lives in a world of its own. Its world is very much that of the unseen. This child is thoughtful and introspective, often listening for inner guidance and aware of much that adults have forgotten exists. It likes to be alone in an atmosphere of peace and quiet where it can read, study, think, and seek understanding of the worlds it lives in. It is so much a part of the unseen worlds that it is often hard for it to adapt to the physical world. It needs understanding and patience. It does not talk about its thoughts, worlds, and what it knows because most adults do not remember these things and often stifle what they feel is imagination. So at a very young age this child learns to keep things to itself. In addition this influence is one of secrecy and not very expressive. It would be better for all if this child's knowledge was sought and valued. This is usually one of the best vibrations for study and learning and it is one of the hardest first cycles.

As a middle cycle this points to a technical, studious nature that must know all about all things and see the reason for them. Analyze carefully whatever you become involved in—books, situations, jobs. You are apt to be very introspective during this period, but much of value can be learned about yourself if you are honest in your self-analysis. Take nothing at face value; look for what is real within all things. Spend time alone and use it for meditation. Don't run after things; let them come to you and you will receive what's best for you. Marriage during this time will require a very understanding mate because your inclination is to be alone. Unless other vibrations in the chart show much expressiveness, you are apt to repress your emotions and be unresponsive. You could be considered cold, aloof, and unfeeling—which really is only a shell covering your very sensitive nature.

This vibration as a last cycle indicates a quiet time of life concerned with the gaining of knowledge. Often the influence is toward the philosophical and the spiritual. Study of such matters could interest you and you could become very knowledgeable if you listened to your inner guidance. Although you feel the need to be by yourself, you are apt to feel lonely at the same time. You must learn not to be. Study and research those things which interest you and become an expert about them. You will probably be sought for your ability to advise, so work at seeing all sides of a situation in order to help people more. Develop your inner peace, for there lies your strength. Never feel that life ends with the end of the physical aspect; use this time as a preparation for that which is to come. Have faith in the unseen worlds and put your trust there.

8—This vibration is concerned with the material world, especially the business, commercial, and financial aspects of it. It should be remembered and understood that all things are governed by spiritual or universal laws, and the material world is no exception. This is a time when attention should be directed toward affairs of business and finance and other practical matters. This is where your opportunity lies. Develop your ability to lead and direct, to manage and organize. You should succeed in any partnership or union as long as you are in control. Although your concern should be mainly material, do not allow it to become overly important or it will consume you. Take care not to become too involved with thoughts of self-gain. This vibration carries much power and the influence of success if used correctly.

A child may find the power of this cycle hard to handle. It could cause the child problems in later life unless carefully directed and assisted in the earlier years. The tendency is to financial freedom while the judgment is undeveloped. Consequently mistakes could be made that could cause it to have serious doubts about its ability to make decisions. Therefore cowardice is something to guard against. It needs supervision in all matters and patient explanations about the good sense of decisions. Help it develop good judgment and an economical nature because it is very generous and could be rashly foolish.

It is generally interested in learning and learns most by doing. It likes to direct but may shy away from real work. Encourage it to think about others, for it could be inclined to think only of furthering its own ends.

As a second cycle this vibration indicates a time of accumulation, when achieving and success in business matters are featured. You should concern yourself with the practical side of things and make sure that all is done efficiently. The first step is always to have a good plan and then put it into effect. You then have the drive and determination needed to see it to a successful completion. You will find a sense of satisfaction during this time in a well-run home, in a family that you can take pride in, and in living in a community that you can be an active part of. Develop diplomacy, friendliness, and a way of looking at things realistically and logically; these qualities are helpful in any world, but especially in the commercial world. Don't limit yourself—look to big things and have faith in your power to achieve them. Manage your finances well and be thorough in all you do. Take control—don't leave it to others.

This can be a very constructive third cycle and a time of considerable achievement if you put your abilities to use. You won't really be happy or successful though unless you stay active in business or in some position where you can manage and direct. Should you decide to retire from work, get involved in community affairs, politics, or club activities. Keep in tune with what is going on in the world around you. Your greatest opportunity lies in forming plans and seeing that they are put to use efficiently and are successfully completed. Whatever you begin, see it through to the end. If you don't put your energies to constructive use, you will find yourself very discontent, for this vibration carries a lot of energy. There is always a place for someone who can organize and direct things well and who has insight, so stay active. Make sure that you manage your own affairs—you probably have the ability to do so better than others.

9—This vibration is largely concerned with selflessness. This is meant to be a time when all aspects are devoted to others: energies, desires, belongings, love, concerns, goals, affections, and sympathies. You must learn to think of others first and to concern yourself with their welfare if you are to achieve anything toward your goal during this cycle. Develop your understanding, compassion, and sympathy and be willing to give selflessly. This is not an easy cycle because it does require putting aside all personal goals and desires. It is a completion cycle and you are likely to find many things "finishing" in your life. It is not a particularly good time for marriage or partnerships because of this influence. Love may be hard to come by and it may be short-lived.

For a child the influence of this cycle is probably the hardest of all. It generally feels alone, confused, frightened, and frustrated. For everyone, the early years are a time of self-development, and the influence of this vibration conflicts with this situation. This is also an emotional vibration; consequently the child's feelings and emotions are likely to be very close to the surface. This is something it may not understand and may fight to control, causing greater conflict. It needs tremendous understanding and patience. The vibration is artistic and the child should be encouraged in any artistic endeavors, as this will aid in some degree of harmony with the cycle. Try to help it understand that thinking about others and caring for them does develop its character, but understandably this is hard for a child to grasp. It is apt to suffer frequent upsets because its personal desires are rarely realized and also many situations pass from its life when it would like them to remain—owing to the completion aspect of this number. Part of the problem lies in the power of the higher numbers, which put a strain on a child who is really not able to cope with them well.

As a second cycle the concern is meant to be totally selfless. You will never reach any degree of success if you desire gain or personal achievement. You must take a back seat to the good of others. It is not a time to strive for personal love; if you do, you are bound to be disappointed. Learn to content yourself with the rewards of loving others on a grand scale. Don't accept limitations or restrictions and try to understand all of life. Watch so that your emotions don't get out of hand. Cultivate any artistic talent you're already aware of, or try to discover one that hasn't surfaced yet. Be tolerant and a humanitarian. You are liable to experience losses during this time because of the completion aspect of this cycle. You will need to learn how to accept and adjust to these losses. Remember that little in this cycle is likely to be permanant.

As a final cycle this is truly a time of completion and many things will pass from your life. Lessons begun before will be finished during this time, consequently many situations will no longer be needed in your life. Concern yourself with providing service to others, for continuing on the path for you means doing things to aid others' welfare. Give unselfishly, knowing that you will always be provided for. Do anything artistic that appeals to you, for you need to cultivate this aspect of yourself. Seek association with artistic and emotional people. You will find them enjoyable and beneficial, and they will be far more likely to understand you. Give your love to all that you meet and you will be surprised how much you will receive in return. Make this time of your life a contribution to others and your reward is assured, and you will be happy.

11—The power of a master number is present in this vibration and this should be continually kept in mind. As with all master vibrations, the power can be of great benefit or it can be your undoing, depending upon how it is used. This number carries with it the possibility of fame and great success; chances are that neither will be gained in the business world. If success does come, you'd do well to hire someone to manage your business affairs for you. The influence is that of revelation, intuition, inspiration, and inventiveness. There is the ability for leadership here, but make sure that you lead well. Often there is a tendency to nervousness because of the great amount of energy which needs channeling. Interests may run to the spiritual or occult, but whatever you do, don't try to force your beliefs on others.

The child under the influence of this cycle is inclined to feel divided because it lives in two worlds. Often it possesses or receives knowledge it doesn't know how to communicate. Generally this is because the knowledge differs from the things it usually hears talked about, and so it feels the need for caution. Perhaps it doesn't even understand the knowledge itself. It is apt to be nervous and very full of energy. At other times it may be very quiet and even introspective, trying to understand its own thoughts and the things it's aware of. It needs to be helped to gain an understanding of human nature and to show compassion for others. It could tend to be somewhat self-centered. Most often a young child will suppress the true nature of this vibration and express its other side. But it may still be very inspired at times and great wisdom could quietly fall from its lips. It generally learns quickly and the older it gets, the more help it needs in bringing forth the higher aspect of this cycle.

When this vibration is in the position of a second cycle, there is truly the chance of great inspiration and accomplishment, especially if you stay out of the business world. The influence is meant for the nonmaterial world and you won't get far in usual, practical matters. Learn to rely on your intuition. If you've never tried meditation, this could be the perfect time to begin. Chances are that great revelations could come your way. Develop your inventiveness. Consider teaching something. Specialize in whatever interests you. You are capable of inspiring others and should strive to do so. Partnerships of any kind could go either way during this time—it depends on you. Encourage your artistic nature. Don't seek fame, but prepare yourself to handle it if it comes. Pick some aspect of the occult and study it. You may find yourself more interested than you expected and may even become successful in this area.

As a final cycle there is still ever present the chance of fame, especially if you begin preparing for this vibration in advance. You may find yourself inclined toward spirituality more so during these years. Don't be upset if your beliefs aren't quite orthodox. The influence of this number may well lead you to perceive truths that others aren't aware of. Work at increasing your understanding of people and life. Have something artistic in your life if only as a hobby. Stay as active as you can, for there is great energy in this cycle and it needs an outlet. Otherwise you could become irritable and bad-tempered. Cultivate your inventive ability and friendships with artistic, intellectual, and emotional people. If physical activity becomes a problem, then stay mentally active. Pick something to become really good at and preferably something that will put your mind to use. Don't give way to becoming impatient or intolerant with others. Your beliefs are fine for you, but they may not be right for others, so don't expect them to look at things as you do. Concentrate on your goals and make sure that they are clearly defined so that you always know where you are headed.

22—This vibration is strongly that of leadership—nothing should be undertaken on a small scale. There is tremendous power here and you must be very careful that it is always used for good. The only limitations of this influence are those you make. If you begin restricting your thoughts and ideas about what is possible, you are undoubtedly going to reduce the vibration to a 4, which you don't want to do. Think big and have faith in yourself. Partnerships can do well under this influence if you remember that you are a leader and don't put yourself in the position of being controlled. If you do, you won't be happy for long and you'll want to "get out." There is no first cycle for this vibration, which is a good thing. A child couldn't possibly handle its power, and in fact, many adults find it difficult.

As a middle cycle the power needs to be recognized and coped with well. Find a place in life where you can lead and proceed to do so quickly. You can be successful in any area, so the other vibrations of your chart should be considered for direction. Under this influence, you are apt to experience nervous strain because of the great amount of power given you—channel this energy into constructive activities. Do the big things and let others handle the small aspects. Find ways to put your ideas to practical use. You are capable of managing and directing your own affairs and those of others as well. You can realize almost any dream or goal if you will only have faith in your ability and go forward strongly. Unions during this time can be enjoyable and rewarding if you don't expect others to keep up with your pace, for few are capable of doing so. Remember that nothing is too big for the power of this vibration to undertake and complete successfully. It is often called the influence of the master builder and that describes the scope of its power very well. You will find yourself far more successful if you keep your interests and energies directed toward things that affect the many and not just a few. The power is intended for the good of mankind.

As a last cycle the energy and power of this vibration could tax you because of the activity it needs for an outlet. Keep busy so that you keep the energy flowing and a build-up doesn't result. Don't take a back seat; stay in the lead and be well informed about what's going on. Find a job which will enable you to direct activities in a big way. Your ability to manage should make you an asset anywhere and so keeping active should be no problem. You can conceive large plans and follow through on them, and you should put this talent to use. Don't set limits for yourself or allow others to, because you really shouldn't have any. This can be a very productive, successful, and rewarding time of life for you if you put the power at your disposal to work.

33—This influence is found only as a last cycle and it's probably just as well; few people have gained sufficient understanding of life and people to handle it well before this. Hopefully life's experiences have taught you that you never receive without giving and that the measure of what you receive is determined by how much and the way in which you give. Unless we give with love and no desire of reward we aren't really giving at all. This is to be a time when your only thoughts should be of others. There is great power here, but it can never be used selfishly or great unhappiness will result. Responsibility always accompanies power and you will have to learn to accept all that comes your way gladly, and discharge your duties well. There is the opportunity for discovering great truths about yourself and others if you listen to your inner guidance. Humility needs to be developed while keeping sight of your inner strength. Concern yourself with the welfare of others and be of service in any way that you can. Learn to express the knowledge you've gained, for knowledge is something to be shared. You should derive great pleasure from things of beauty and could well create some yourself. You are to inspire others during these years, largely by your example, and so should give great thought to the things you do. Always listen for the inner voice, for when heard clearly, its guidance is sure and its wisdom unfailing and true. Seek inner peace and place your faith in the Creator. Let your calmness and poise give strength to everyone. Whatever you do, make sure you don't shut yourself off from people, for they are your key to opportunity and to progressing toward your goal and fulfilling your destiny. Don't concern yourself with material things; trust in your Father to provide what you need.

III

THE GENERAL NUMBERS

Fifteen

THE PERSONAL YEARS—THE MINOR LIFE CYCLES

Our personal year is the vibration that influences our life for any given year. It gives us some guidelines about what years are best for certain activities, and it also helps to show us when it would be best to avoid doing some things. By making ourselves aware of these yearly influences, we can aid ourselves in becoming more successful, happier, and less inclined to meet with disappointment and frustration.

Often, by looking back at our personal years, we can see how they form a pattern in our life. This is because our personal years go to make up the lesser cycles of our life. They follow each other in succession from 1 to 9, except that some 2 years are 11s, some 4 years are 22s, and some 6 years are 33s. The lesser cycles, then, are nine years in length, with the 1 years the beginnings and the 9 years the completions.

Although the personal years follow in succession, they do not necessarily begin with 1 because our first personal year is the total of our birth date, or the same as our destiny. Therefore, we know what our first year was already. To find our personal year for any other year we add the month and day of birth to the year in question. For example, someone born on July 29, 1941 would have a first personal year of 6, or the same as the destiny. That means that 1942 was a 7 personal year for this person because the years follow in succession. To find the personal year for 1948 we add the month and day of birth to the year 1948.

$$\begin{array}{cccc} \text{July} & 29 & 1948 \\ 7 & + \; 11 \; + & 22 & = 4 \end{array}$$

We see that 1948 was a 4 personal year. To find the personal year for 1957 we use the same method.

$$\begin{array}{cccc} \text{July} & 29 & 1957 \\ 7 & + \; 11 \; + & 4 & = 22 \end{array}$$

For this person, 1957 was a 22 personal year and therefore one of the exceptions to the rule of succession.

Once you have established your personal year vibration for any given year, you have only to consult the numbers of the personal years to know what the influence was, is, or will be. We come under this influence at the beginning of the year but usually find it increased once we have passed our birthday that year, for then it comes into its fullest power, and its influence may exert itself slightly until the next birthday even though we move into another year.

As mentioned in the last chapter, the personal years also determine when we will come into the full influence of a change in major cycles by the 1 year closest to the approximate time of change.

We are also influenced by personal months and days and by universal years, months, and days, which will be discussed later in the book. Of all of these the influence of our personal years is the greatest, which is why it requires a chapter of its own. Its greater effect upon our lives is the reason it is classified as one of the general numbers, while their minor influence makes them members of the fourth part of the vibrations in a chart.

1 Personal Year—This is a year for beginnings—new starts, new ideas, new anything. Develop a plan for what you want in the next nine years and begin to work on it now. What is begun this year can truly have an effect on the eight that are to follow.

Be yourself and go your own way. After you are sure that you are right, take a stand. Don't let others sway you. Push forward with determination. It's a time when you should make any changes you've been considering and feel are good. Things begun now may not come to fruition for a while, but don't let that stop you.

Unions are best not entered into now, for the influence is too strongly that of independence and self-promotion. You can lay the groundwork for a union, but wait to complete it in a year when partnerships are more favored. If you decide to go ahead anyway, you will have to suppress some of your independent tendencies. You need to stay busy and keep things moving at a brisk pace. Don't repress your pioneering spirit—this is a perfect time for exploration.

2 Personal Year—After a very busy year you are entitled to some rest and quiet, and this year you should make it part of your schedule. Now is the time to study and acquire all the knowledge you can to help you with the plans you conceived last year. Companionship and association with others is featured, so this can be a good time for establishing unions. This is a time of growth, which may not be seen right away because you are still in a preparation period. Attend to details, be patient and calm, wait for opportunity to come to you, and look for the useful and collect it. Build friendships and stay in harmony with everyone. Proceed quietly on the path you've chosen and be content to wait until later for results—before the plant appears the roots have to form. Think about your ideas and plans of last year and prepare for the year ahead.

3 Personal Year—This is a year when the things you have begun and worked toward should begin to make their presence felt. The influence is social and artistic—a time for friends and doing the things you enjoy. Entertain all you can and go when you're invited. Be active, but keep it on the light side; remember that we must always keep things in balance. It's a good time for a vacation or a short holiday. Try to attend plays or musicals and try an artistic hobby if you don't already have one. However, don't try to do too much. You'll have to watch that you complete what you've started before you begin something else. You should be primarily concerned with enjoyment, but don't lose sight of your goals and purposes. It should be a fairly carefree time when responsibilities won't weigh too heavily upon you.

4 Personal Year—After a year of fun it's time to knuckle down and get back to really working. This is a year for being productive and organized. It's a time to be busy and to follow a schedule. Get everything in order and see to the smallest details. Make self-discipline a rule and avoid all tendencies to loaf or be lazy. You are building for the future this year, and if you want to be successful, you'll have to make sure that all is well constructed. The more effort, the greater the benefits and rewards. Correct any errors of the past and give your plans a thorough going-over to be sure they're well made. When everything is in order, things run smoother and problems are avoided. If you have any problems, now is the time to solve them so you can be free to do other things.

5 Personal Year—This is the time for a real vacation and for changes. Let go of the routine you're used to and try something different. Look at things from new angles, discard old ideas, do something new and maybe even unusual. You'll find opportunity in variety and in new scenery—be it places, people, things, or situations. Get out and experience life. Whatever you do, it should be useful—keep that in mind. Consider making changes—in yourself, your business, your home, your life-style. See all the people you can and keep your mind and your body active. Don't become too restless; channel your energies into good uses. The key word is *change.*

6 Personal Year—This is a year when home and family are highlighted. Make them the center of your life and attend to all of your responsibilities. This is the personal influence that is concerned with all that belongs to you, so look after those things and people this year. Finish whatever you start and do everything well. This is not a time for halfway jobs. Take things as they come, establishing a rhythm and harmony in your life. Avoid haste and rushing about. Plan time for your loved ones and for maintenance of your possessions. This would be a good time to spend your weekends with your family and friends, put in time with clubs or groups, and paint the house. Spend a good deal of your time at home, and if you feel the desire to see other people, try to arrange it so that you are the host. Adjust differences, solve problems—your own and others'—counsel, guide, and give assistance when needed. Make time to do things for those who can't manage themselves. Give of yourself, for that's where much of your opportunity lies this year.

7 Personal Year—This is what you could call an inner year —a time of reflection, study, development of resources, and self-analysis. Plan to spend time alone and use it constructively, even if it's merely to look over the past with the idea of learning from it. Analyze your thoughts and actions, take stock of your capabilities, and decide how to increase them and put them to good use. It is a growth and preparation year when the inner you should be developed to the fullest. Look over your life and decide what really is of value. Pursue studies which interest you and become well versed in them. If you'll let things come to you —not reaching for anything—much will come your way, including money. The influence may be very spiritual—one of deep introspection and searching. Don't concern yourself with business and material matters any more than is absolutely necessary. Leave your social life for some other year and don't make changes or start anything new except in the area of thoughts and beliefs. Sit back and relax and look at everything closely.

8 Personal Year—This is the year for business, for all material matters, and one you can be very successful in. Through effort and activity you can achieve great things. Take the lead, be forceful and determined, and go after what you want. Deal with everyone fairly. Get your affairs in order, including finances, and keep everything well organized. Work at being a good manager and do everything efficiently. This can be a year when you can accomplish big things. Form a good plan of action and then see it through to completion. Don't let little things stand in your way. Be dependable and thorough. You can have whatever you want if you've got the nerve to go after it.

9 Personal Year—Time to start "spring cleaning" in preparation for a new lesser cycle—and don't forget the attic and basement. Get rid of all that is finished and no longer of use to you. Also, things are likely to just pass out of your life now. It's a year which should be full of love, friendship, and happiness as long as you don't try to make it too personal—or go to the other extreme either. Artistic activities are featured. Take time to do things for others. Get your whole life in order and make any changes that are indicated. Be patient, especially with others. Enjoy the out-of-doors and surround yourself with all the beauty you can, particularly the natural kind. It's not a time for beginnings but endings—and they shouldn't be sorrowful ones. Realize that you're going on to new and better things.

11 Personal Year—The influence is that of inner growth, a time of evaluation and reflection when much illumination can be gained. The power of this vibration is intended for checking our motives and ethics and for setting new standards where needed. Interests are likely to involve the spiritual or metaphysical, which includes the psychic and occult, and study in these areas can be beneficial. Take inventory and make sure your personal "books" are in order. Take stock of your methods and motives in all areas of life. See if you're living up to your ideals, and adjust them (or your life) if you have to. Business matters aren't favored and may have their ups and downs, though you can come up with a lot of good ideas for later use. Opportunity comes to you—don't go in search of it.

22 Personal Year—Now is the time to find a way to put your ideas into action, unless they're purely personal. Anything that is solely for yourself is apt to be very unsuccessful. If your main motives are the good of others, then charge ahead because you will have power behind you. Don't limit your goals or your thoughts of success—you can accomplish almost anything. Go after your dreams. Think big and then follow through with determined action and positive thoughts—expect successful results. Make what you want a reality, but be sure you are building something worthwhile. Stay active and put all your mental and physical energies to work for you. Take charge of the show and it's bound to be a hit. Just keep others in mind, or the power of this vibration will work against you.

33 Personal Year—Best forget yourself completely this year, for it truly doesn't belong to you. Direct all your energies toward the benefit of others. Think only of what you can do for them and expect no compensation. Don't even look for gratitude or appreciation. Learn to lose yourself in thoughts of others. The influence is also spiritual—this is a time to seek truth, understanding, inner peace, and illumination, and then share it. Make contact with people a part of your life, but spend time alone as well. Get in tune with nature. In business affairs put others first and success will be drawn to you. Materiality must be put aside and seen for its true value. Strive to gain the proper perspective about everything. Give love and understanding to all. Be tolerant, patient, sympathetic, and a source of strength. This can be a beautiful year if you work to make it that way for others.

It should be kept in mind that there is a rhythmical pattern to the personal years. When we realize and understand this pattern, it is easier to attune ourselves to the influences because we see their purpose. The lesser cycles are meant to be cycles of growth, with each new cycle carrying us to greater heights when used correctly.

Beginning with the 1 year, we find it an outer year when growth is concerned with the development of the self through outward activities. The 2 year is a year of inward growth, but still concerned largely with the material—a time when self-development comes through working on the inner self. The 3 years are again outward and considerably material, and 4 years are a repeat of the inner-material growth. With the 5 years, we're back to outward and material, but the discarding of the old is in preparation for a change in the rhythm and growth pattern. The 6 years are both inner and outer while still very material, but they give us a taste of what is to come, for growth is always gradual. The 7 years are not only totally inner years, but for the first time the concern is with the nonmaterial, though still personal. During 7 years it is to be hoped that we will grow enough to learn to use the very material influence of 8 years unselfishly so that we can reap their full harvest. The 9 year is a chance to see how we've progressed, for it is inner and outer while also being nonpersonal and nonmaterial. It combines the best aspects of all of the other years. The idea is that with each new lesser cycle we will use the influences more as they're meant to be used and so increase our growth.

The master vibrations are somewhat test years when we are given extra power that can benefit us greatly if we learn how to put it to use properly. Proper use of 11 years is for great inner growth and should not be concerned with the material world. The 22 years give us a chance to really use our inner growth in the material world in nonpersonal ways. The 33 years are opportunities to see whether we can really be nonpersonal and nonmaterial in a material world and to see whether we're really learning to live by spiritual laws and truths. The extra power can help us make great strides forward, or it can quickly point out where we've neglected our lessons.

All of the vibrations give us a chance to demonstrate the knowledge we've gained along life's path, and if you will read all of them you will see that they are aimed at developing us fully. Their spiral is intended to carry us upward, not just around in circles. While many of the influences are the same, each vibration has its own individual characteristics that are intended to aid in our growth. The more we grow the more we become in tune with the higher aspects of each influence and so bring forth finer fruits. The ultimate goal of everyone is to learn the value of service and this goal is depicted in the succession of the personal years. When we begin to see and understand this and work consciously toward that goal, then life becomes a smoother path to walk and we progress much faster.

Sixteen

THE CHALLENGES

The challenges show us weak links in our nature that need to be strengthened. Much like the Karmic lessons, they bring certain influences to bear in an effort to get us to realize that we need to work at reinforcing certain aspects of ourselves. Their influence is very subtle though, so they are not as easily recognized, but because they directly affect our destiny they are of considerable importance.

Until they are dealt with, the challenges form rough spots on the path to achieving our destiny and can hinder our success and accomplishment. They are concerned with material matters and outward relationships, and dealing with them requires inner growth as well as external effort. When neglected they can only present us with problems that generally appear unexpectedly and we are often unaware of their importance at first.

Any chain is as strong as its weakest link, consequently the challenges should be given great consideration no matter how minor their effect upon your life thus far. Overcoming them is an indication of considerable progress and it insures you a smoother and more rewarding journey.

Through numerology we can determine what the challenges are, when they are likely to exert their greatest influence, and when we will need to work on them the hardest. There are three challenges which are derived from the major life cycles. The first challenge will make its influence felt during the first cycle, and this is when it should be concentrated on and overcome. If ignored or not overcome, its influence will continue to be felt beyond the first cycle, and possibly throughout your entire life. The second challenge is primarily concerned with the second cycle, although it can show up earlier. If neglected, it will do as the first challenge and continue to make problems until it is attended to. Lastly there is the main challenge, which makes its presence felt throughout the entire life, although it is strongest during the third, or last, cycle.

Challenges can be worked on in advance. Just because the second challenge doesn't appear until the second cycle doesn't mean that you must wait until then to begin strengthening this aspect of yourself. In fact, the sooner all the weak spots are reinforced the better. It does mean you may have to work a little harder when the challenge comes into full power, but by starting early you will be way ahead of the game. Also, we find a similarity between the challenges and cycles in that both begin to exert their greatest influence in the 1 personal year nearest to the time of the change.

Because the challenges interrelate with the cycles and the destiny, they should be considered together so we can get a clearer picture of our specific weaknesses and how best to correct them. Let's assume that in someone's chart we find a 6 ≈ destiny, a middle cycle of 4, and a second challenge of 1. The cycle tells us this is a period of work and production, and because of the 6 ≈ destiny we know that it must be directed toward home, family, responsibilities, and service to others to make progress. The 1 challenge indicates a need for independence, individuality, and creativity, but they must be used in our work and to discharge our responsibilities. This is very basic but should give you an idea of how the three influences need to be understood. By considering them alone, we do not really understand any of them fully.

Part of the challenge of a challenge is striving to achieve balance. It should be remembered that there are two aspects to every vibration. We must guard against going to either extreme because then we will accomplish nothing. What we are striving for is the center—the balance between the two, where the best qualities are found. For instance, if we are dealing with an 8 challenge, we must learn to efficiently manage material affairs without either becoming totally materialistic or becoming neglectful of material matters. Either extreme would definitely create problems in our life. The key word here is *balance*.

The formula for determining the challenges is a method of subtraction, using the month, day, and year of birth, or the numbers of the major cycles.

1. We take the numbers of the first and second cycles and subtract the smaller number from the larger. The remainder is the number of the first challenge.

2. We take the numbers of the second and third cycles and again subtract the smaller from the larger. The remainder is the second challenge.

3. We take the numbers of the first and second challenges and subtract the smaller from the larger. The remainder is the third or main challenge.

The following example shows how we do this in a chart:

From this example we can see that

1. Subtracting the 7 first cycle from the 11 second cycle gives a first challenge of 4.

2. Subtracting the 6 third cycle from the 11 second cycle gives a second challenge of 5.

3. Subtracting the 4 first challenge from the 5 second challenge gives a main challenge of 1.

There are times when the remainder will be a 0 (zero). The meaning of this vibration can be found at the end of the list of numbers of the challenges.

THE NUMBERS OF THE CHALLENGES

1—The Challenge of Independence and Individuality

You must learn to stand on your own two feet, but without stepping on others' toes to do it. Others may try to get you to do what they want, and you must consider carefully what is best for you and all concerned. If their method does not seem right, you must strengthen your will and proceed your own way despite their protests. Be yourself and develop your talents and capabilities. Don't depend upon others; let them learn instead that they can rely upon you. Be strong. Be confident. Be courageous. Learn to rely upon your own inner strength, for the more you use it the greater will be your awareness of your own true value and abilities. Look beyond what you think you are, because concepts falsely gained from yourself and others may have blinded you to the truth. See yourself as you really are, and what you can really do. Don't limit yourself. This is the time to discover and perfect the real you.

2—The Challenge of Cooperation and Sensitivity

You need to consider the feelings and welfare of others, without losing yourself in the process. Don't become so sensitive that you are hurt by every little thing—even imagined things. Learn the value of diplomacy and tact. Be thoughtful, devoted, obedient, and generous. Work at cooperating and getting along well with others. Keep the peace, but don't let others take advantage of you either. It is great to give, but true balance allows us to see that we don't have to be treated as worthless just to make others happy. Treat others with respect and concern. Give service in this way and show by your example how people should treat one another. Don't overlook the small things because they can add up to something of importance.

3—The Challenge of Expression and Optimism

Expression can take many forms and you should work at developing as many of them as you can. Don't allow others to stifle your means of self-expression. Say what you think; talk about your beliefs and opinions. Develop your sense of humor. Don't be a wallflower. Try painting, acting, dancing, writing—any form of self-expression that appeals to you. Keep a bright but realistic outlook. Don't allow worry and depression to enter your life. Realize that life must have its ups and downs or it would lose its teaching value. See the "downs" as opportunities to gain strength and as the lower swing of the "ups." Nothing stays down permanently, and with this in mind keep a cheerful attitude. Develop a philosophy that sees life as it really is; this makes it easy to look toward better times when things seem bad. See the value in every situation.

4—The Challenge of Self-Discipline in Its Various Aspects

One of these aspects is work. You must learn to see the value of putting forth effort to achieve your goals, without letting life become a bore. Learn patience and tolerance and to pay attention to detail. Establish system and routine, but realize that life must have flexibility as well. Life must also have purpose; we must set goals for ourselves. Without these goals and the discipline that helps us reach them, life becomes meaningless. Make yourself do the necessary. Be thorough. Keep busy at constructive activities, and see to it that laziness and self-indulgence are not part of your life. Don't make excuses for sparing yourself the efforts that are needed for achievement. Push yourself when needed and be determined to reach the goals you have set. Don't let yourself stand in your own way.

5—The Challenge of Learning the Value and Meaning of Freedom

The danger is the abuse of freedom. True freedom allows us to do that which is good and lets us progress to the new and beneficial. Freedom does not mean doing whatever we please— we must realize that we have responsibilities to others and ourselves to live within certain laws—universal laws as well as social ones. It is a time to learn to use our freedom correctly. We must not overindulge in physical pleasures and desires. True freedom comes to us because of competent and thorough handling of our duties and responsibilities. During this time, however, it is generally not advisable to take on a lot of burdens. You'll have enough to handle with those that come along anyway. Learn to adjust to change easily and to discard that which is no longer useful in your life.

6—The Challenge of Responsibility and Service

The key to meeting this challenge is *willingness*. It is the time to learn the value of giving willing service to all those in need and willingly attending to what may well be burdens that need our attention. You must see the benefit that all gain from your cheerful acceptance of responsibilities and your taking care of them efficiently. Don't allow yourself to become so carried away that you take from others those responsibilities that they should handle themselves in order to learn needed lessons. This is where you will have to learn to be discerning. Also don't try to impose your beliefs on others. Everyone cannot follow the same path, nor should everyone try to. There are as many paths as there are people, and each must be left free to go his or her own way. Live your own life and let others do the same—just be willing to give aid when you know that it's needed.

7—The Challenge of Analysis and Inner Guidance

This is a time when you must look at all things comprehensively, searching things out and seeking that which is not readily apparent. Learn to think scientifically. Once things are seen thoroughly, the challenge is then to listen for and heed your inner guidance. Inner guidance is often called "intuition" or "hunches"—but whatever name we give it, it is a part of ourselves that we need to learn to attune ourselves to. The more we listen, the surer the guidance and the clearer it becomes. This is a time for developing your inner resources. Don't take the advice of others without considering it carefully. Always do what you feel is best. Don't feel that you must answer to others for actions that don't concern or affect them. Use your inner guidance and reasoning ability in all affairs, and where there is a conflict between the two, trust your guidance. Maintain your calm, poise, and dignity and keep peace in your life. Make self-analysis and introspection part of your daily routine. Don't stifle your spiritual nature; encourage it instead.

8—The Challenge of Judgment, Efficiency, and Organization

To meet this challenge you will need to put all your affairs in proper order, handle things thoroughly and well, and exercise good judgment in all matters. It is a time to learn to manage your finances well, spending carefully and avoiding extravagance. Don't settle for doing a halfway job of anything. Manage things yourself—don't turn control over to others. Make your time and efforts count. Stay busy—constructively. Meet business matters head on and make sure that they are taken care of. Above all, keep your head about you; whatever you do should be guided by reason. Although this is a time for handling material matters, you must take care that they don't become the dominant factor in your life. Remember that even material things are governed by spiritual laws, for in truth all things are spiritual. Learn to see all things in their proper perspective.

9—The Challenge of Human Understanding and Compassion

Human understanding requires an understanding of life, and this cannot be gained without effort. You must learn to look at people, situations, and experiences closely to perceive the reasons for their being what they are. Try to understand and not to judge. You will have to strive to place yourself in others' shoes, to search out their feelings and motives, and to look beyond the present and the visible. At all times you should try to give sympathy, love, and help, genuinely and sincerely. The thought, "There but for the grace of God go I," can be a great help to someone with this challenge. Always remember that you only have to answer for your actions; the law requires this and no more. This releases us from the need to judge, for we are all judged according to our own deeds and thoughts. Knowing this also helps us give sympathy, but never give pity—that helps no one.

0—The Challenge of Choice and All Challenges

It shows that first you need to study all nine challenges and work on them. Second, after studying the challenges you should decide which areas are your weakest and then work hard on them until you are at least equally strong in all aspects. The 0 challenge indicates that you have reached a point where you can decide for yourself what you should be working on, with the help of discernment and intuition. This matter of choice is a challenge in itself—to see if you really can choose correctly. Working on all of the challenges at once is a challenge that not everyone is equipped to handle. So, although the 0 challenge indicates a need for greater effort, it also shows you are capable of meeting the extra challenge. It is an indication of progress and growth to the point of being ready for new things. It also tells us that in most cases all of the challenges have been worked on sufficiently. You could say it is a time of smoothing out the rough edges—even the best of gems need polishing for their real beauty to be seen.

Seventeen

THE PINNACLES

The pinnacles, like the challenges, are also determined from the birth date, but where the challenges indicate stumbling blocks or pitfalls, the pinnacles show us how we may smooth out the path. If used correctly they can aid us in achieving greater successes in life, especially if they are used as guides toward the fulfillment of our destiny.

The pinnacles can be prepared for in advance, and in fact, it is an advantage to do so. The influence of the pinnacles is quiet and subtle but nevertheless deep and sure. They may be the reason we become dissatisfied with a certain kind of work or way of life; they may cause us to feel the need to make changes in our job, home, locality, friends, life-styles, or in ourselves. They can affect our thinking or feeling natures, create new interests, and bring new situations and people into our life. If we understand them and learn to use their influence, they can increase our successes and accomplishments and make our life more rewarding. Consequently, the pinnacles need to be given a considerable amount of thought in order to make them benefit us.

From the pinnacles we can learn:

1. The general kinds of situations, events, and associations that may present themselves. These usually prove beneficial to

us if used correctly, and you may find it helpful to seek them out instead of waiting for them to appear.

2. Qualities, abilities, and tendencies that should aid you if you will work at developing them and using them.

3. Attitudes, outlooks, and responses to situations and people that should be cultivated and made a natural part of your reactions. This information is not meant to suggest hard and fast rules but rather guidelines, which you should apply as you wish.

To determine the pinnacles we use the following formula:

1. Add the month and day of birth together to get the number of the first pinnacle.

2. Add the day and year together to get the number of the second pinnacle.

3. Add the first and second pinnacle together to get the number of the third pinnacle.

4. Add the month and year of birth together to get the number of the fourth pinnacle.

Next we must determine the years that each pinnacle covers. This is the formula for calculating the years:

5. Subtract the number of the destiny from the number 36. If the destiny is a 22 or a 33, we use the reduced number of 4 or 6. The number that we have left will be the ending of the first pinnacle.

6. To the end of the first pinnacle we add nine years. This gives us the period of time that the second pinnacle will cover.

7. To the end of the second pinnacle we add nine years. This gives us the period of time that the third pinnacle will cover.

8. The last pinnacle is from the end of the third pinnacle through the rest of our life.

We now have an eight-step formula for determining the vibrations of the pinnacles and the years in which they will exert their influence. It should also be remembered that while the pinnacles come into effect at the precise times determined, their strength will reach its peak in the 1 personal year that falls within the period of time covered. With the first pinnacle its strongest point will be the 1 personal year nearest the end of the pinnacle. With the last pinnacle the strongest point is usually the 1 personal year nearest the beginning of the pinnacle. With both the first and last pinnacles it is very possible for the influence to remain at full strength for the nine-year cycle before or after the 1 personal year mentioned.

To further clarify the formula for the pinnacles, let's take a look at the following example:

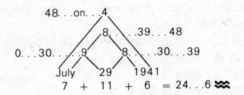

From this example we can see that

1. Adding the 7 of the month to the 11 of the day gives us a first pinnacle of 9.

2. Adding the 11 of the day and the 6 of the year gives us a second pinnacle of 8.

3. Adding the 9 of the first pinnacle to the 8 of the second pinnacle gives us a third pinnacle of 8.

4. Adding the 7 of the month to the 6 of the year gives us a fourth pinnacle of 4.

5. Subtracting the 6 of the destiny from the number 36 shows us that the first pinnacle will cover the years from birth to age 30.

6. Adding 9 years to 30, or the ending of the first pinnacle, tells us that the second pinnacle will last from age 30 to age 39.

7. Adding 9 years to 39, or the ending of the second pinnacle,

tells us that the third pinnacle will cover the period from age 39 to age 48.

8. Because the third pinnacle ends at age 48 we know that the last or fourth pinnacle will cover the period from age 48 to the end of the life.

For maximum benefit, the pinnacles should be considered along with the destiny and the cycle or cycles in which they fall. It should also be noted that the pinnacles will increase in power and in their capacity to aid success once the challenge they fall in is met and overcome. Because of all the influences that assert themselves on the pinnacles, they can only be covered in a very general way here. To understand more about their specific influence in your life and how best to interpret them and make them work for you, you will have to consider them with the other numbers already mentioned. Because they are covered only basically, do not underestimate the importance of considering their effect upon life and their ability to aid you in accomplishing your purpose.

We should also notice whether any of the numbers of the pinnacles are the same as some of the other numbers of the chart. For instance, if a pinnacle number is the same as a Karmic lesson, it indicates a time when the effects of the lesson will be strongly felt, when the situations it can bring to bear will most surely present themselves. It also shows us the time when we will need to work harder than ever to learn the lesson or suffer the consequences of not learning. If a pinnacle number is the same as the inner self, we will feel more driven during those years to do what our soul, or best self, desires for us, and it should be easy to attune ourselves to this vibration at this time. When a pinnacle and the outer self are alike, we will find during those years our best opportunities for really developing our natural talents and abilities and making them work for us. If a pinnacle and the heart self are the same vibration, those years will be the easiest time to realize our heart's desires and to be like we want to be. When the destiny is the same as a pinnacle, the indication is a period when we'll be blessed with more success as we work at fulfilling our purpose in life, and during those years we should concentrate on doing whatever we can to achieve our destiny.

Using the formula, calculate your own pinnacles and then check the table of numbers given to determine their general influences. Following the table, you will find an illustration that is designed to help you to see how the various vibrations interrelate and influence each other. This should help you to understand how your own vibrations affect one another.

THE NUMBERS OF THE PINNACLES

1—This is an active period when situations should be new and changing and providing you with chances to explore, to use your pioneering spirit and initiative. Events should provide situations where you can work alone or as a leader and make use of your mental ability.

Develop creativity, individuality, inventiveness, and independence, a capacity for leadership, and the ability to get things done.

Your outlook should leave no room for thoughts of limitation or repression. Be strong, even forceful, independent, courageous, determined. Keep yourself active, particularly your mind, and stay on the alert for good new ideas.

2—Situations should be such that you are in contact with people and in positions where you can help keep peace and harmony. Be of service and do things for others. Associations and events should provide opportunities for you to demonstrate cooperation and diplomacy.

Develop tact, diplomacy, the ability to handle details and to take orders well, a peaceful nature, and carefulness.

Respond to situations with a willingness to give of yourself freely and a desire to make life easier and happier for others.

Become sensitive to others' feelings and needs.

3—Situations should include social events and contacts, pleasant, cheerful activities, artistic stimulation, emotional associations, things on the light and beautiful side of life, and chances to let people know how you think and feel.

Develop any artistic talents, your ability to talk and socialize well, a sense of humor, creativity, your ability to entertain and be a good host, a pleasant personality and cheerfulness.

Your outlook should be happy, free from worry, optimistic, with a desire to put sunshine in others' lives. Learn to enjoy people, things of beauty, the outdoors, animals and children, and giving of your affections freely in the proper manner and circumstances.

4—Situations should require your effort and labors. Generally you'll work with others and not in a position of authority. Give service, submit to routine, attend to details, be constructive and productive. These things will require exactitude and thoroughness. Associations should be such that you can be of help to others.

Develop determination, perseverance, accuracy, tolerance, manual dexterity, carefulness, a liking for detail and system, a willingness to work.

Respond to situations by being dependable, loyal, patient, and tolerant. Do things as well as you can, seeing to every detail and not allowing yourself to be rushed or wasteful. Your attitude should be that effort pays off in accomplishment and achievement; you should take pride in all you do.

5—Situations should provide variety, change, travel, intellectual stimulation, social contacts, comparative freedom from responsibility, and new experiences. Associations should provide mental challenges and should not be limiting or binding.

Develop your ability to handle and deal with people. Inventiveness, a keen mentality, adaptability, perception, an inquiring nature—all should be goals.

Respond to situations by being progressive, mentally curious, aware of life and seeking a greater understanding of it, adjusting easily to the strange and different, readily discarding the old in favor of the new and better. Your attitude should refuse limitation and restrictions.

6—Situations should center around family, friends, and home, the welfare and care of others, community concerns, responsibilities and burdens, giving of advice, solving problems, bettering conditions. Associations should provide opportunities for you to use your talents for the benefit of others.

Develop your ability as a counselor or adviser, peacemaker, and problem-solver. Foster your musical, artistic, and decorative talents.

Respond to situations by providing harmony, looking for ways to improve conditions, making a home wherever you find yourself, making others comfortable and "at home," being protective, loyal, devoted, sympathetic, concerned, and understanding. Your attitude should be a desire to discharge all responsibilities well.

7—Situations should be intellectual, where mental and not manual effort is needed; they should be refined and quiet, providing an atmosphere that allows study and meditation, opportunities for learning, spiritual stimulation, and enjoyment of nature. Associations should be pleasant and intellectually inclined.

Develop poise, intellectual capabilities, intuitiveness, your ability to advise and to see all sides of situations, a peacefulness and inner calm.

Respond to situations and people by seeking understanding and truth. Learn to share your knowledge. Introspection and a spiritual outlook are also important.

8—Situations should be concerned with business, finances, and things of a material nature, large plans and operations, constructive activities, positions of leadership and control, reaching goals, community matters. Associations should put you in positions of leadership.

Develop efficiency, dependability, strength, diplomacy, executive abilities, and determination.

Respond to situations with loyalty, perseverance, hard work, definite goals, thoroughness, an exacting and uncompromising nature, big plans and faith in your ability to achieve them, good judgment. Your attitude should be purposeful and you should expect to be successful.

9—Situations should involve others and should be non-material, social, emotional, entertaining, and pleasant. They should increase your understanding of life and human nature and provide opportunities to enjoy things of beauty. Associations should be such that others look to you for help.

Develop your artistic talents, a pleasant personality, intuitiveness, perception, broadmindedness, understanding, and a willingness to give selfless service.

Respond to situations with a lack of personal desires, sympathy, compassion, a desire to be of help in any way needed, a willingness to make personal sacrifices for the good of others. You should also be understanding, spiritual, and nonmaterial.

11—Situations should be intellectual, spiritual, nonmaterial, and nonpersonal, providing chances to lead and to deal with others and possibly may involve fame. Associations should be inspiring and concerned with gaining an understanding of human nature and enjoyment of life's beauties.

Develop intuition, inventiveness, ideals, perception, spirituality, psychic abilities, the ability to inspire and illuminate, and constructive outlets for your energies.

Respond to situations with practicality, understanding, constructive ideas, positive actions and plans, spirituality, and tolerance. Avoid nervous tension and giving up your ideals.

22—Situations should concern large-scale material matters, community, national or international affairs, bettering conditions, giving service, positions of authority and power, working with others for their benefit, constructive activities.

Develop your ability to conceive ideas, especially large ones; to achieve results and goals, to organize, plan, lead, and accomplish.

Respond to situations with understanding; desire goals that are unselfish and beneficial to others. Have a broad, nonmaterialistic outlook and faith in your ability to achieve whatever you go after. Your attitude should be spiritual, with a desire for increased consciousness.

33—Situations should involve others and put you in positions of giving service, sharing knowledge, advising, gaining understanding, and teaching. Associations should give you the chance to demonstrate the truths you have learned and to live what you believe.

Develop your love of beauty, compassion, and sympathy and your ability to do whatever needs to be done, to give advice, solve problems, to keep peace and harmony.

Respond to situations with understanding, seeing only the good in all things and people. Be free from worry, be unconcerned with personal or material gain, and seek truth. Your attitude should be a desire for greater consciousness, spiritual awareness, and illumination.

HOW THE DESTINY, CYCLES, CHALLENGES, AND PINNACLES AFFECT EACH OTHER

To explain how all of the influences derived from the birth date interact, we will use the following example as an illustration:

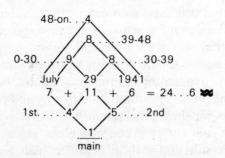

Using the formulas described elsewhere, we have arrived at the following information:

a destiny of 6 ♒
a first cycle of 7, a second cycle of 11, a third cycle of 6
a first challenge of 4, a second challenge of 5, a third challenge of 1
pinnacles: 0 to 30 years: 9   30 to 39 years: 8   39 to 48 years: 8
48 years on: 4

In discussing the vibrations we will be dealing primarily with basics, but remember that all the influences should be considered in their more complex aspects to get a complete understanding. We must also remember that to be aware of when the influences will come into full effect we will have to determine the 1 personal year nearest to the time in question, or in the case of the pinnacles, the 1 personal year falling within the period of time that they cover.

First—We see that the destiny indicates that the path is one of responsibility and of giving service, and is largely concerned with home and loved ones.

Second—The first cycle is one of development of the inner resources or thought processes. Family and responsibilities should be used to aid in this development, and to progress with the destiny these resources will need to be used in these areas also. The challenge of 4 shows that this person will have to put forth considerable effort and learn the value of routine and detail, using them hand in hand with the inner growth and responsibility. It also tells us that this person will have to develop a great deal of self-discipline in order to accomplish anything. During this time there is the need for an attitude of love and service, situations involving others, and development of the emotional and artistic natures, which is indicated by the first pinnacle of 9.

Third—The second cycle of 11 tells us that the middle years are a time for spiritual development and could be a time of fame if the duties of the destiny are accepted. The challenge of 5 indicates that a balance between freedom and responsibility must be sought, and the spiritual growth will depend largely upon the ability to discard the old for the new. Approximately the first two years are still under the influence of the pinnacle of selfless service. Then begins the second pinnacle of business and financial concerns. During these years (and those of the third pinnacle also, in this case) good judgment, organization, and material matters are the key to furthering the purpose. It will be necessary to put them to use in the home and even in spiritual matters. If put to use well, the fame indicated could easily become reality.

Fourth—The last few years of the second cycle are influenced by the fourth pinnacle, which shows the need for work, routine, and attention to details. If fame has been achieved, it needs to be directed toward helping others. Whatever has been achieved must be made a part of the life-style. They are also necessary for further progress, but the challenge now is not to let irresponsibility and a desire for change deter this person from necessary work or from proceeding with the destiny.

Fifth—As we come to the third cycle we see that it is the same vibration as the destiny. This indicates that great strides can be made in these years toward fulfilling the purpose, but it also shows that these years will be heavy with responsibility that must not be ignored. What has been gained and begun before now needs to be carefully taken care of. It also tells of a time of protection and the possibility of being sought out for advice. The challenge is to be independent and progressive in discharging responsibilities, giving advice, and doing work. Everything is to be done with individuality and creativity. It says to be careful not to succumb to repression and limitation. The fourth pinnacle is still in effect and will continue to be, showing that further progress will only come through work and keeping all things in order, providing service, accepting routine, and being dependable.

Briefly, we will also take a look at the other vibrations that

are either strongly affected by these numbers or that have a
strong effect upon them:

inner self   4
outer self   7
heart self   3
Karmic lessons   6 and 7

The first challenge of 4 shows a time when the inner self is
striving to force its influence upon the life and to promote its
development. Overcoming the challenge will do much to aid in
the development of the inner self, and if the challenge is met as
it should be the inner self will be attuned more strongly. Whenever we attune ourselves to our inner self, we find there is far
less frustration in the life, for then our soul is much more
content. We are working together with it.

The last pinnacle of 4 indicates a time when the inner self
should find its expression the easiest, when the soul should
definitely be attuned. Consequently, there should be greater
harmony in the life.

The fact that the 7 of the first cycle is the same as the outer
self shows that during the first cycle the development of the
natural talents and abilities should be easiest and should really
be achieved without a lot of striving. This person should feel
drawn to develop these attributes during this time, and doing
so should provide quite a sense of satisfaction.

There is no time when development of the heart self is
stressed or aided, and this aspect will have to be concentrated
on totally through a conscious effort for full development.

The first cycle will also be a time when the effects of the 7
Karmic lesson are bound to be strongly felt, and to soften the
situations indicated a great deal of effort at learning the lesson
will be necessary. Because so much of this time is in childhood,
the effects are most likely to present themselves and just be
suffered through unless the child is fortunate enough to have
informed parents who propel it toward overcoming the weaknesses it has not previously eliminated.

The last cycle will be a time of strong influence from the 6 Karmic lesson unless the lesson is worked on and learned before then. Because the destiny is also a 6, there is strong indication that there will be little or no accomplishment made until the lesson is learned—a fact which could well force the learning well before the last cycle, even if there is no actual awareness of the fact that there is such a lesson.

Reading a chart is a complex matter that requires time and care. It is simplified only by the use of step-by-step methods of interrelating and considering the various aspects one at a time. When done in this manner, a truer, clearer picture is obtained, and thus numerology becomes a great help in understanding ourselves, others, situations, and experiences. We really begin to see things more clearly when we learn to compile a work-up from the chart we have prepared, which will be discussed in Chapter Twenty-seven.

Eighteen

THE METHOD OF APPROACH

Everyone has his or her own method of approaching events, experiences, and situations. The approach tells us a great deal about ourselves and also what is natural for us. In many cases we will find that the natural tendencies have been suppressed. It is important to be aware of our natural tendencies and to avoid repressing them. If we don't, then we are being other than our real self. This repression can lead to frustration and dissatisfaction with what we are and how we are living our life. All too often we have no idea why we are unhappy or displeased.

When we consider our approach, we take a look at how we approach or should approach the situations life brings us. The approach is found by simply adding the number of the day of birth to the key.

```
J O H N          Born: May 4, 1953
1 6 8 5
  20
```

In this example we add the key of 2 to the 4 day of birth and find that the approach is a 6.

When we know someone else's approach, we have a fair idea how they'll react to situations, and we gain insight about how to present them with experiences and information and what we can expect from them. You could say that knowing another's method of approach helps us know how to approach him or her.

The most natural tendency of approach and the one most often used is that of the key of the first name at birth and the day of birth. It is possible though, if someone has changed his or her first name, or uses another name or a nickname, for the natural approach to be replaced by the key of the name used plus the day of birth. For example, if John changed his name to Alan

$$\begin{array}{cccc} A & L & A & N \\ \underline{1} & \underline{3} & \underline{1} & \underline{5} \\ & 1\emptyset & & \end{array}$$

he could replace his natural approach of 6 with the 1 key of Alan plus his 4 birth date to get an approach of 5. If you know someone who does not use his or her natural approach, then consider this possibility and you may find the answer and a greater understanding of the person. If you yourself have by chance done this, keep in mind that attuning ourselves to our natural tendencies is always best, unless they happen to conflict strongly with other aspects of our chart.

To the general characteristics of our vibration we all add our own individuality. Often we can tell something about the individuality we will add by looking behind the sum or approach at the two influences that go to create it. We are apt to find that we add some of their tendencies to those of the sum to change it somewhat, perhaps in a very subtle yet detectable way. In many cases in our chart the numbers that go to make up our final vibrations are apt to exert their subtle influences upon the totals. All of our numbers work together to create an individual who is different from any other soul.

THE NUMBERS OF THE APPROACH

1—You approach situations with a forceful, determined attitude and a strong will. You have your own way of handling things and are not likely to be deterred by the opinions or methods of others. If opposed you are not inclined to back down, but respond with strength and courage. You look at things in a creative way and do not mind proceeding on your own. In fact, you may prefer to. You tend to lead, and running the show comes naturally to you. You are the one to go out and grab the bull by the horns—fear is usually not part of your approach. Unless you watch yourself, you could become thoughtless because you are too concerned with your own desires and goals.

2—You approach situations with an attitude of keeping the peace and providing whatever service you can. You feel that if everyone will just work together the outcome can be achieved smoothly. While others are concerned with end results and large problems, you show concern for the details. You prefer to have others make the decisions and tell you what to do. Your easygoing nature makes you agreeable and your thoughts are usually for the feelings and needs of others. If not careful, you can be petty and lose sight of the goal for worrying about the small things along the way.

3—You approach situations with an optimistic, cheerful attitude and generally with a lack of worry. You are likely to want to do the less pleasant things hastily in order to get on with the more enjoyable ones. You become emotionally involved easily and tend to see things from that standpoint. You like to see a smile on everyone's face, and therefore you try to bring humor into all situations. If you allow worry or depression to overtake you, you sink to the very depths—although you may not stay there for long. You feel that almost anything can be resolved by talk, and you can usually talk yourself out of many a tight spot. Avoid being careless and unconcerned—this can create problems for you.

4—You approach situations with the attitude that constructive effort can get anything done. You tend to dig right in and go to work, staying busy until you've accomplished the desired results. You like to see things done in a systematic and orderly manner. You may plod along and although it may take you a while, you are sure to reach your goal and possibly more lasting results because of your careful methods. You may be so set in your ways that you won't accept new ideas that could be better than the ones you're used to. You are also inclined to be intolerant of those who don't do things your way.

5—Your approach to situations is progressive and often different because you favor looking for new ways. You may become easily bored and therefore want things to move quickly and provide excitement. You tend to try handling people and can usually sell them on your way of doing things. If that doesn't work, you may very well try to outsmart them in order to get your own way. You don't like responsibilities and may shirk them—work at overcoming this. You enjoy the challenge of trying to figure out new ways of handling situations, often to the frustration of others.

6—Your approach to situations is generally to step in and assume the responsibilities, often with the attitude that you know best how to solve the problems. You often give advice which is usually well meant and intended only to be helpful. You want to change conditions for the better and so look for ways to do so. If not careful you can overdo in your tendency to take on duties and thereby tax your energies. You try to be of service; your concern is usually for the welfare of others. You like things to be fair and to see that justice is done.

7—Your approach to situations is with an attitude that they need to be carefully studied and understood. You tend to stand back and look things over thoroughly, withholding comment or action until you have formed an opinion as to the best means of progressing. This may make you seem uncaring and cold to others, but when you do venture forth it is generally with wisdom and you are usually right. You remain dignified, and calm—at least on the surface. You are apt to see things in a spiritual or philosophical light, which others may not understand. Don't be so slow to act that you end up missing the boat. Also, don't be such a perfectionist that you're never satisfied. You may appear very unemotional, but it is something you affect to hide the truth.

8—Your approach to situations is with the attitude that everything can be handled best in a businesslike way. You are inclined to charge in and begin organizing and directing, but you generally do so efficiently. You look at things with logic and reason and so your judgment is usually good. You are a planner with broad vision and the determination to accomplish what you set in motion. You expect a lot of others and yourself. You believe in loyalty, honesty, and dependability. You see constructive activity as the answer to most problems. You are apt to be overly materialistic and too concerned with making everything pay. Don't let acquiring money and material things be your downfall—greed has ruined many a good person.

9—Your approach to situations is with an emotional attitude that relates all things to feelings. This can result in not seeing things clearly. You empathize with people, and so try to do all you can to ease their burdens and make them happy. You are apt to spread yourself very thin trying to do everything at once and being all things to all people. Your outlook is broad and you are very understanding. You are usually willing to give whatever is needed, especially affection, and you may be inclined to think of yourself as "The Great Lover." Approach situations freely and expect no personal gain or you're likely to be disappointed.

11—Your approach to situations is with far-seeing vision that must be tempered with practicality to be really worthwhile.

You have the ideas, but you need to find ways of putting them to use. You can be energetic to the point of nervous exhaustion if you aren't careful. Because you want to be respected, you strive for it. You tend to be guided by intuition and your spiritual nature, which is good. You may even search for answers through psychic means. You tend to look at things differently from others and may try to impose your ideals and morals on them. You should recognize inspiration and revelations when they come your way.

22—Your approach to situations is with an attitude of getting things done. You rarely see a problem that you feel is too big to be coped with and don't understand why others do. You proceed with a definite plan, determined to be successful, and you usually are. Your primary concern is often with the material aspects of a situation. Although you can be emotional, you don't generally allow your emotions to get in your way. You tend to look for ways to improve almost everything, and at times your ideas may be more than the average person can visualize. Don't let others' lack of vision cause you to limit yourself or to become intolerant or indifferent.

33—Your approach to situations is generally with a philosophical attitude that may make you appear unconcerned and uncaring, which could even irritate others. People often respond with anger to things they don't understand. You tend to remain calm and quiet, even when those around you fret with nervousness and worry. Your understanding and acceptance of conditions is admirable only if it is not an excuse for laziness and inaction. You are usually perceptive and a stabilizing influence, someone who is willing to do whatever needs to be done to resolve a situation. Most often you are a help to others because you try to make them see things as they really are.

Nineteen

THE RULING TENDENCY

From what you have learned about the numbers of the chart thus far you can see why certain hobbies, interests, and activities appeal to you. We now have a greater understanding of why we are what we are and why we do the things we do. We also have a clearer picture of *how* we do things. Despite all of this information, there still may be aspects of ourselves that are unaccounted for.

The ruling tendency is the vibration in our chart that can tell us about *what* we enjoy doing. It's not concerned with our progress, development, or achievement, but rather with the things we do simply for enjoyment. It can also have a considerable effect on our actions and can influence our personality. From the tendency we can gain insight into the reasons why we choose our interests and hobbies, and can see why some "passions" rule us and others don't.

To determine the ruling tendency we must go back and look at the Inclusion Table we set up before. The ruling tendency is that number which is strongest in the table, that is, the number which appears most often in the full birth name. It is very possible that more than one number will appear often. In such cases the numbers share equally the position of ruling tendency. Two numbers are not at all unusual, and generally three are the most to be found sharing the tendency.

It should be noted that 5 is the "number of man" and is often called the "natural" number. It is inclined to be dominant in the inclusion. For this reason we follow a rule of subtracting 2 from the number of 5s found, otherwise our deductions about the tendency are apt to be inaccurate. When we have subtracted 2 from the 5s and find that 5 is still the predominant number, or shares the position, then we know that the 5 is truly the ruling tendency or a part of it.

In other words, if we look at an Inclusion Table and find four 9s and 3, 2, 1, or 0 of all the other numbers, we know 9 is the ruling tendency. If after subtracting the 2 from the 5s we find three 5s and three 7s and 2, 1, or 0 of all the other numbers, we know the ruling tendency is shared by the numbers 5 and 7. We must also consider the effect of the numbers 11 and 22 if they appear. In the inclusion we list the 11s and 22s separately alongside the 2s and 4s, for the reason that if these numbers are not vibrated to in their higher aspects they will then be reduced to 2s or 4s. If we find in an Inclusion Table four 9s, for instance, and also one 2 and three 11s, we must consider the chance that the 11s will be reduced to 2s. If this is the case, the ruling tendency would be a combination of 9 and 2. Then we would list the 9 as the tendency, while keeping in mind that the influence of the 2 could also be evident. We must always take these possibilities into consideration. If you should run into such a situation, list it in the chart as follows:

ruling tendency. . .9. . .(2?)

As we look at the Inclusion Table we should also note something else that can influence. To continue with the example above, let's say we find four 9s, three 11s and 2, 1, or 0 of all the other numbers. The appearance of the 11s in strength, compared with the other numbers, has an importance that should not be overlooked. If we find four 1s in a table, three 5s and three 6s and 2, 1, or 0 of all the other numbers, then we should consider the influence of the 5s and 6s as well as that of the ruling tendency of 1. Therefore, in the numbers of the ruling tendency you will also find the influences of "many" listed. Generally these aspects are not readily apparent in our lives unless they happen to be the same as stronger numbers in the chart, but they do indicate qualities that can be developed if desired. It shows us that if we decide to develop the qualities indicated, we have some backing for our efforts.

THE NUMBERS OF THE RULING TENDENCY

1—You tend to be ruled by a desire for independence and to be different from others. You lean toward creative and progressive activities, often preferring to do things by yourself. You enjoy being active.

Many 1s—Leadership, bravery, strong will, energy, creativity, a pioneering nature. You may be domineering and self-centered.

2—You tend to be ruled by a desire for peaceful conditions. You like group activities and being with others and things that require detail work and manual dexterity. Your hobbies will probably include collecting almost anything. You are interested in the quieter things and not a lot of physical activity.

Many 2s—Sensitivity, thoughtfulness, rhythm and a fondness for music, friendliness, grace, appreciation of small things. Guard against being petty.

3—You tend to be ruled by a desire to enjoy all the pleasant things of life. You like music, the arts, and things of beauty. You enjoy talking, creating things, being with people, entertaining, children and animals.

Many 3s—Imagination, sense of humor, fun-loving attitude, creativity, artistic ability, optimism. Watch out for being frivolous and impractical.

4—You tend to be ruled by a desire to have everything

orderly and neat. You like activities that call for physical effort, detail work, and the use of the hands as well as the brain. You enjoy being with others, but in a fairly quiet atmosphere.

Many 4s—Dependability, productivity, self-discipline, conscientiousness, strong morals, accuracy, thoroughness. You can be repressive and restrictive.

5—You tend to be ruled by a desire to be unfettered. You enjoy travel, new sights and experiences, books and mental stimulation, and being active and progressive. You like people, variety, the outdoors, challenges, and hobbies that provide activity. You have a passion for freedom.

Many 5s—Varied interests, adaptability, friendliness. You like change, publicity and attention and are intellectually curious. You can be too irresponsible, nervous, and flighty.

6—You tend to be ruled by a desire to look after and protect everyone and everything. You like activities that involve your home, community or improving conditions for others. You enjoy artistic, creative and musical things, children and pets, and events that include family and friends.

Many 6s—Acceptance of burdens and duties, musical ability, domestic talents, caring for others, harmonious nature. You can be stubborn, overprotective and possessive.

7—You tend to be ruled by a desire for perfection, quiet, and analysis. You enjoy books, nature, antiques, the classical and refined, searching for answers. You like doing things alone and enjoy collecting and acquiring knowledge.

Many 7s—Analytical nature, an appreciation of beauty, dignity, poise, well informed, artistic appreciation, peacefulness, mental ability. Guard against being secretive and conniving and an inclination toward alcohol.

8—You tend to be ruled by a desire for organization, control, and achieving material successes. You like to plan, direct, and handle financial matters. You enjoy people, community activities, and social events and take pride in your home, family, and possessions.

Many 8s—Efficiency, a power for making money and being successful, executive personality, good judgment, planning ability. Guard against being materialistic and overly concerned with money and its powers.

9—You tend to be ruled by a desire for romance, pleasure, and being with others. You like artistic activities and anything that provides outlets for your emotional nature and love of beauty. You enjoy helping others, being needed and wanted, life's pleasures, social events, creating and dreaming.

Many 9s—Artistic talent, compassion, willingness to give of yourself, understanding, thoughtfulness, sensitivity, grace, and charm. You are apt to be overemotional and moody.

11—You tend to be ruled by a desire to lead and to gain respect and recognition. You like activities involving people, mental stimulation, ideals, invention, and possibly things of a spiritual nature. You enjoy the psychic or the occult and being the center of attention, expounding your beliefs.

Many 11s—Inventiveness, leadership ability, energy, strong opinions and convictions, helpfulness, inspiration. You are apt to be nervous and impractical.

22—You tend to be ruled by a desire for accomplishment and improvement. You enjoy activities that call for broad vision, determination, organization, and a progressive and successful attitude. You like being with and doing things for others, seeing your plans reach completion, being in control. Matters of national or world concern also interest you.

Many 22s—Successful outlook, practicality, magnetic personality, power to achieve, unlimited thinking, desire to better things. Guard against dishonesty and too great a desire for personal gain.

IV

THE REST OF A CHART

Twenty

THE TESTS

The tests are concerned with Karma, but unlike the Karmic lessons, they are not merely an indication of something we need to learn, they are a debt we have to pay. Our lives are governed by the law of Karma—whether we believe in it or not, whether we like it or not, whether we are even aware of its existence or not. The law of Karma is simply that for every action there is an appropriate reaction, or as we sow we reap. Whether our actions are good or bad, we reap their harvest. The term "Karmic debt" is used to mean the need for payment for actions that were unjust to others; anything foolish, abusive, overindulgent —actions that could be called bad. These are the kinds of debts that the tests deal with.

The tests bring into our life certain circumstances that give us opportunities to pay off the debts we owe. If these situations are met with resentment and bitterness, we not only slow our rate of payment and limit our ability to pay, we run the chance of creating further debt. If we ignore the need to pay our debt we also are apt to increase our Karma, because it multiplies. Therefore once we are aware that our own past actions have created the debts, we can meet them with an attitude of acceptance, which will speed the payment. Being aware of our debts also gives us another advantage; it is not enough to pay a debt if we keep making the same mistakes again. We will only re-earn the same Karma. So our tests point out pitfalls for us to avoid, and if we study all of the tests, we can further reduce our chance of earning unpleasant future Karma.

When we find a test number in our chart we can usually find evidence of it in our life. This is not always the case, however. Sometimes the number indicates a debt that is as yet unsatisfied and whose evidence will appear at some later time. That is, unless we heed the warning and make certain that we do not repeat the mistake. We must strengthen ourselves in this area. With effort it is possible to pay the debt before it actually becomes due and thereby avoid or soften the unpleasantness.

There are four test numbers: 13, 14, 16, and 19, and they are test numbers only if connected with the inner self, the outer self, the destiny, or the heart self. If they appear in some other area of the chart, they can be ignored. In the specified areas they apply only if they appear as subtotals. For instance, if the day of birth is the nineteenth, it does not indicate a debt, but if the total of the month, day, and year of birth is a 16/7≈ then the 16, being a subtotal, is a test number. When we find a test number in the chart, it is a good idea to underline it twice (16/7≈), so that when we look at the chart the tests are readily apparent.

THE TEST NUMBERS

13—This could be called the mildest of the tests. The negative power of this vibration has been increased because of superstition until it has become to many a number to be feared. That this number is "bad" or undesirable is a myth man created. It has made people fearful—even to this day. There are no bad numbers. In fact, before the time of Jesus the Christ, the number 13 was largely considered a good omen and a positive power. Negative feelings about the number rose because of the

Last Supper, where thirteen were present.

The sum of 13 is 4, and it shows former insistence (the 1) upon the frivolous (the 3) to the point of avoiding work, necessities, and everything the 4 stands for and shows concern for nothing but pleasure. Regardless of which of the four major numbers the 13 is a subtotal of, it indicates that the test is to attend to work in material matters, to be constructive and productive, and to avoid laziness and overindulgence in physical pleasures. If this number appears in your chart, study and practice the constructive qualities of the 4 which are given in Chapter 2, Basic Characteristics of the Numbers. Also study the negative aspects of the 1 and 3 and be sure to avoid them.

14—Because the sum of 14 is 5, which is the number of physical man, the 14 indicates former abuse of physical passions and sensations. It can be an indication of overindulgence in food, drink, sex, or any of the physical appetites. Since it is concerned with the physical senses, it generally has to do with physical situations: sickness, material losses, deformities or handicaps, sudden death. It warns of the danger of being overly concerned with physical appetites and shows a need for self-discipline and even self-denial in this area.

If a subtotal of the inner self, the possibility is that in all emotional matters there will be setbacks and limited satisfaction.

If a subtotal of the outer self, there is the possibility that hopes and dreams will meet with disappointment and frustration.

If a subtotal of the destiny, there is the possibility of a delay in reaching goals, accomplishment, and success. It also indicates the need to learn to let go—that nothing can be possessed.

If a subtotal of the heart self, there is the possibility that affairs of the heart will be less than desired and may be of short duration. All desires could meet with hindrances and be limited.

16—Because the sum of 16 is 7, which is the number of

spiritual man, the indication is a former lack of faith, a neglect of the spiritual, and an attitude full of fear and doubt. We can take a lesson from the ordeal of Jesus on the cross and see that to attain the spiritual (the 7) there is the need for love (the 6) that surrenders or crucifies the self (the 1).

Only when the self has been put aside because of a love that transcends all can the spiritual part of man truly be born and come into its rightful place. It is said that the 16 can also be an indication of illegitimate love. If there is true love, if we feel no guilt and hurt no one by our actions, then there can be no Karmic debt incurred.

If a subtotal of the inner self, there is a possibility that friends and associations won't be what they seem and that unions will be unrewarding and hopes will go unrealized.

If a subtotal of the outer self, there is a possibility that whatever is gained will be lost—money, possessions, name, loved ones, position—all to teach us that we should not be overly concerned with material things and should lay up our treasures elsewhere.

If a subtotal of the destiny, there is a possibility that all of the hard lessons must be learned: loss of love, letting go of what we'd like to hold on to, and gaining success only to sink to the depths and lose all. Thus we learn of our inner strength and find the peace that only the spiritual can give.

If a subtotal of the heart self, there is a possibility that the pain of a broken heart may be suffered again and again until we learn to let the love of the minute be enough for a lifetime and realize that all things are temporary unless they are spiritual.

19—Because the sum of 19 is 1, which is the number of the self, the indication is that in the past power has been used for self-gain to the point of abuse and even injustice to others. There is the necessity for completion (the 9) of all things pertaining to the self (the 1); consequently debts must be paid off during our lifetime so that the law is met. It also shows the need for the unpersonal service and love (the 9) that puts others before the self (the 1), and so truly develops the self and brings lasting rewards. The test is usually to see how much we can stand. There has been the use of universal power, or the abuse of it, and payment must be made.

If a subtotal of the inner self, there is the possibility that we may have to go to the brink of death in order to see life for what it really is. Those things that you would like to keep secret are apt to be revealed. Life is largely concerned with seeing things realistically, which may not always be pleasant.

If a subtotal of the outer self, there is the possibility that despite great efforts, we may end up with nothing to show for all our endeavors. We will feel pushed to continue trying to reach our goals; we should, for sooner or later success could be ours.

If a subtotal of the destiny, there is the possibility that the burdens of the past will have to be carried. We will find limitations where freedom is hoped for and have to sacrifice whatever we thought of as ours.

If a subtotal of the heart self, there is the possibility of being used, mistreated, and badly hurt—all in the name of love. Also our personal hopes are likely not to see fulfillment. We must learn not to be bitter or to shut off our feelings, but to let impersonal love provide the needed satisfaction.

Twenty-one

THE FIRST VOWEL

Because the vowels deal with our inner self, or soul, and the soul is concerned with our more spiritual aspects, the first vowel of our first name at birth has a great influence on our spiritual outlook. Therefore, from our first vowel we can tell a lot about our general spiritual attitude. We can also gain some insight into the way we approach things of a spiritual nature. If we consider the influence of the first vowel and the number of our inner self together, we usually get an even clearer understanding of matters. If we were to give the influence of the first vowel a name, we could call it "our spirituality."

The vowels also help to make up the outer self, and for this reason our first vowel can also tell us something about first impressions—how we are likely to affect people. It is able to tell us something about the tendencies in ourself that are strongly developed.

Vowels fall into three categories: positive, receptive, and dual. The strength of the influence and characteristics of our first vowel is determined by which category it falls into. The criteria are simple. Positive and receptive vowels are defined by pronunciation. A positive vowel is a long vowel. A receptive vowel is a short vowel. Dual vowels are defined by the spelling. Dual vowels can be either a diphthong or require two sounds.

When it is positive, as with the *a* in *Jane,* the vibration is at its strongest, and always with a strong vibration there is the danger of letting the power get out of hand. When it is receptive, as with the *o* in *Donald,* the strength is weakened to a point where there is little danger of its being too strong, but there is a definite chance of being too receptive. When dual, or combined with another vowel, as with the name *Laura,* the power is divided between the two so that both vowels lend their influence. Often this results in vacillation or confusion.

When dealing with the vowels, numerology and astrology once again work together. The vowels are closely associated with health conditions, and because each vowel is under planetary as well as numerical influence, it is possible to determine the areas of the body that each vowel governs. If there are many of a certain vowel in the name, there is a strong possibility that if health problems arise they will be of the nature indicated by the vowel. These influences will be covered under the heading of each particular vowel.

THE VOWELS

a—Governed by the planet Mars, there is apt to be much static energy produced by its influence. If the first vowel is *a,* or if there are many *a*'s in the name, there is the indication of health problems having to do with the head, such as headaches. Many *a*'s also incline one toward being sarcastic, critical, intolerant, and cynical in outlook.

General Characteristics—Full of feeling and fire, you can be zealous and enthusiastic. Your convictions are strong and deep; you are open to new ideas but accept them only if they are better than your old ones. You really prefer to be the one who has a new idea. When someone has a better idea than you, it is apt to hurt your ego. You are going to go your own way, regardless of what others think, do, or say. You feel very safe in your ability to decide for yourself what is best for you. Going forward without a backward glance, you feel fairly sure that sooner or later others will follow your lead and see things your way. But if they never do, you'll just keep on going—you really don't care. You feel certain that if they don't follow your lead, it's their loss. Besides, if you forge ahead alone, you can't be slowed down by anyone, and you like a brisk pace.

Your first impression is most likely that of authority, ambition, activity, aspiration, strength, force, independence, and power. The feeling you generally give others is that of being a ruler or ringleader, one who knows just where he or she is going. Consequently you are often looked to to "run the show." People sense that you are sure of your capabilities and this gives them faith in you.

The Positive a as in *Amy, Grace, James, David*—you can be so set in your ways that you cannot accept anything new; you miss much of value and do not progress. You may also be inclined toward dominance and egotism if not careful.

The Receptive a as in *Anna, Alan, Patrick*—you can be scatter-brained, frustrated, and an idle dreamer. Often you accept new ideas too easily, without sufficient consideration.

The Dual a as in *Laura, Faith, Paul*—you may have no beliefs that are really your own. You can become false by trying to be what you aren't and dual by not being what you seem to be.

e—Governed by the planet Venus, which exerts its influence on the emotions with subtle power. If the first vowel is *e,* or if there are many *e*'s in the name, there is an indication of health problems with the throat, kidneys, or nerves of the stomach region, resulting in such things as indigestion and ulcers. Many *e*'s also incline one toward being unstable and nervous.

General Characteristics—Progressive and open to new and even strange ideas and beliefs, you seek to discover greater truth. You investigate whatever comes along and enjoy the challenge of trying to find something worthwhile. You strive to link the realms of the spiritual and physical, looking for answers in life's experiences. Change and variety are almost as necessary to you as food, and you put your intellect to use in any situation. You won't be bound by convention and don't mind being considered different. You have such a way of making your ideas sound interesting to others, they're inclined to feel they're missing something if they don't respond. You have difficulty sometimes because your spiritual and intellectual natures are so strong that you are pulled off balance by them. There rarely is middle ground for you—you go to one extreme or the other in all things. You have a tremendous amount of energy and feel the need to keep busy. When things slow down, you get bored quickly.

Your first impression is generally that of energy, excitement, and enthusiasm—versatility, perpetual motion, adaptability, and intellectual curiosity. To others you may seem restless and often bored—and you may just be. Looked to for your intellect, you are generally knowledgeable to some degree in all areas and take pride in this. Quieter people are not sure what to make of you.

The Positive e as in *Eve, Lena, Peter, Steve*—you can be a bundle of nervous tension and miss out on a lot because you are inclined to change too quickly. Sometimes your search for the new and unusual gets you involved in things that you later regret.

The Receptive e as in *Betty, Jenny, Fred, Edward*—you can search so hard that you fail to see what you find, which usually makes you even more frantic. You are inclined to lose control easily and be quite nervous and unstable.

The Dual e as in *Jean, Deanne, George, Sean*—you can be confused, frustrated, and suffer irritation of the soul. You are too flighty. You tend to rush from one thing to another, never taking time to stop.

i—Governed by the planet Saturn, which exerts strong control. If the first vowel is *i,* or if there are many *i*'s in the name, there is an indication of health problems involving the brain, heart, knees, teeth, bones, and inner ear. Many i's also incline one toward being overly sensitive, petty, and easily offended or hurt.

General Characteristics—Intensely emotional, you feel everything deeply, and so you suffer. Because of this, you can understand and sympathize with the sufferings of others. You have a broad, humanitarian outlook and see things on a large scale, disliking the petty and small-minded. With strong faith in your beliefs, you are still a searcher, with a great desire to understand human nature and to find a way to live the truths you've found. You tend to weigh new ideas with emotion rather than with reason—if they feel right, then they must be right. Often you are guided purely by intuition, and if properly listened to, it will lead you safely.

Impulsive and passionate in all things, when the feeling strikes you, you rush forward with great force and energy. Interested in the welfare of others, you can be generous to a fault, but material things really matter little to you anyway. You are usually aware of the law that says whatever we give returns to us tenfold. Loving and caring, you generally have many friends, and you need them. Usually spiritual, you may be inclined to the mystical or the occult or to unorthodox religious beliefs. What matters is that they fill your needs; don't mind what others think or believe.

Your first impression is usually that of intensity and immateriality—magnetic personality, abundant energy, love, forcefulness, compassion. You impress people as one who understands and will help in any way, and so you are often looked to for sympathy and aid. Others may seek you out for your ideas when they feel their vision is not great enough.

The Positive i as in Irene, Ida, Simon—you can achieve greatness in any area—both for good or "evil" and must guard against being cruel and selfish.

The Receptive i as in Vicky, Gina, Jim—can easily become

bored, selfish, indifferent, with emotions and reactions out of control unless logic and judgment are cultivated.

The Dual i as in *Diane, Viola, Lionel*—is apt to be double-natured—one time positive, the next negative, unless the positive nature is strengthened and maintained in force.

o—Governed by the planet Jupiter, which can produce explosive power. If the first vowel is *o,* or if there are many *o*'s in the name, there is an indication of health problems involving the blood and circulation. Many *o*'s incline one toward being stubborn, slow, and unable to make quick decisions.

General Characteristics—Being emotional but balanced makes you very responsible and helps you to see things in perspective. Set in your beliefs, which are inclined to be conventional and dogmatic, you tend to want others to see things your way. It's not that you are pushy; you believe that you're right, and what's right for you must be right for others. Strong-willed, you may never give in, but if you do you'll give completely. You like to counsel others, see justice done, play the gracious host, and get involved in community affairs—particularly betterment projects. You have hidden power and beauty that you must release for everyone's benefit. Don't let a desire for personal gain lessen your mental ability. Learn to relax and wait; what you want will usually come to you.

Your first impression is generally that of obedience to your beliefs—poise, reliability, sympathy, helpfulness. Others are aware of your strong moral values and sense of responsibility and know that you will attend to your duties well. They are inclined to trust you with a great deal. Your understanding manner should make you looked to for advice, and your good nature should put you in the position of settling differences for others.

The Positive o as in *Olivia, Roberta, Otis, Jonah*—you can be very gifted artistically and musically, but should guard against being dominant, selfish, unfair, and argumentative.

The Receptive o as in *Rhonda, Donna, Tom, Ronald*—you

can be emotional, enduring, and the recipient of much protection, but should take care not to create disharmony and unpleasantness, or give way to criticism or despondency.

The Dual o as in *Joanne, Joel, Louis*—you can possess tremendous understanding and tolerance but can have problems deciding how to practice them; how best to act, think, believe. Through indecision, nothing will be accomplished.

u—Governed by the moon, which has fluctuating and receptive influences. If the first vowel is *u,* or if there are many *u*'s in the name, there is an indication of health problems involving the nervous system, mental stability, asthma, and stomach illnesses. Many *u*'s in the name incline one toward being tenacious and clinging, often suffering what you fear most—loss.

General Characteristics—Very intuitive, your beliefs are inclined to be based on this aspect of your nature unless you let your receptivity get out of hand. In that case your inspirations will lose out to the continually changing ideas of others, which would be a truly great loss to you. Retain your openness; value highly the knowledge that comes to you from within, for this is the source of all true wisdom. Open to influences, you may well attract the unusual, which could be a strain on your generally conservative nature. Learning could come slowly because you tend not to ask questions for fear of what others would think or say. This fear also makes you inclined to keep your ideas and convictions to yourself and to present what you feel will be an acceptable front. Usually happy and talkative, even if you don't really say much, you are a joy to be around and often are colorful and entertaining. You are well liked and like people in return. You may find yourself very interested in the psychic world and could be active in some area of it because of your intuitive powers. If you cultivate this ability, you are very likely to find your spiritual outlook becoming less conventional. You are idealistic and must learn to accept certain limitations.

Your first impression could well suggest the unusual or uncanny because of your ability to perceive others' thoughts. Artistic, optimistic, peaceful, inspired, friendly—you are often sought for your bright outlook and love of beauty as well as for your fresh ideas and creative ability.

The Positive u as in *Judy, Ruth, Hugh*—you can teach and write well if insight is heeded. You need to keep your clannish and provincial nature and desire for accumulation in proportion.

The Receptive u as in *Duncan, Butch, Buster*—you can be a great power for uplift if not detracted by selfishness or a desire for secrecy, or by narrow-mindedness and too much conservatism in actions and ideas.

The Dual u as in *Quentin, Quincy*—you are torn between the extremes of being confused and indifferent or too carefree. You have to work at acquiring and maintaining balance.

y—Governed by the planet Mercury, which influences with duality and speed. If the first vowel is y, or if there are many *y*'s in the name, there is an indication of health problems involving the reproductive system, arms and hands, and lungs. There can be hard-to-diagnose illnesses caused by nervous tension or disorders of the nervous system. Many *y*'s can cause a person to be introverted and too decisive, which could cause problems.

General Characteristics—You have a two-sided nature and a depth others may not even be aware of. You may seem materialistic but are really very spiritual; you are also reflective and study things carefully. Intuition plays a strong part in your life. Your beliefs are likely to be very deep and ingrained because they have been carefully examined. You search for truth, but often when you find it you are uncertain about accepting it because of your cautious nature. Your guidance is surer and your ability to perceive inner wisdom is keener than you are aware of. You seem to always be faced by two paths to choose between. No one can make the decision for you—just be guided by your intuition. Inclined toward meditation and a quiet life, you seek knowledge and analyze everything. Others usually find you hard to understand and harder yet to really get to know because you value privacy. You share the knowledge you've gained only with those you feel can truly appreciate it, and you give your opinion or advice only to those you believe will heed it. To do otherwise would be wasteful to you. When you do decide to speak on a subject of importance, it would benefit others to listen, for you usually have something worthwhile to say.

Your first impression is usually that of being quiet, reserved, thoughtful, often with a touch of the mysterious—studious, refined, analytical or scientific, with a tendency to like form, theories, and even rituals. Others sense your great knowledge and they generally value your advice. You may appear unfeeling because of your reserved nature.

The Positive y as in *Byron, Tyrone, Myra*—you can be receptive if left to choose for yourself. If pushed, you become closed and stubborn.

The Receptive y as in *Yvonne, Lynn*—you cannot be guided but must be faced with logic and facts and shown great patience. Secrecy and introversion are your pitfalls.

The Dual y as in *Joy, Kay, Dwayne, Roy*—you are usually overruled by the stronger first vowel, which tends to add only uncertainty or indecision. The big problem is confusion.

w—is a vowel only when part of a diphthong, and then it is never a first vowel. It is always overpowered by the stronger first vowel but still has an effect.

General Characteristics—There is great power here but, as always, the direction of power is decided by the user. Power just is; the user decides whether it shall be used to bring forth good or bad. It is much easier to go down than up, but the power needed to reach the heights is here. There is the possibility of deep spirituality and freedom from limiting concepts and beliefs that could keep truth hidden. If negative, the resulting problems will be self-indulgence, conceit, egotism, and narrowmindedness. There is the chance of going to extremes, in either a positive or negative way. The qualities are apt to be explosive, fiery, and full of feeling. It is apt to make one changeable or unstable.

When dealing with dual vowels, the first vowel is always the stronger, but the effect of the second vowel should never be overlooked. With dual vowels, we are dealing with both singular numerical vibrations as well as the combination of the two. Brief explanations of the characteristics of the dual vowels follow:

ai—Ambition and inspiration can be combined to produce a personality that sees a great plan and sets about putting it in use. There is the possibility of great illumination. Care must be taken so that the emotions do not get out of hand. Lack of action through indecision may be a problem.

au—Aspiration that is apt to meet with unnerving confusion, which could result in frustration and inactivity. The key to handling the problem is intuition and inspiration, as these are strongly indicated. Care should be exercised so that the quality of forcefulness is not wasted in overindulgence or in search of pleasure. It should be used to develop the mental and creative abilities.

ay—Ambition that may be weakened by yielding to indecisiveness. The power for material accomplishment is indicated but is apt to be weakened because of indecision. The intuitional and mental aspects are strong, but faith in them may be lacking. Feelings of insecurity and inferiority may be masked, but they are still there and need to be acknowledged and overcome.

ea—Energy and ambition combine to give power for considerable progress and success if used correctly. All of the aspects are evident here: the mental, physical, emotional, spiritual, and inspirational. Not knowing which to listen to may result in confusion. Heed the inner voice that gives us all proper direction; don't let ego, reasoning, and feelings alter its guidance.

ee—Enthusiastic energy that could prove overpowering. Strongly ruled by physical desires and yet very spiritual, there is apt to be considerable conflict and frustration. Human understanding and perception are strong. The path to greater understanding is through life's experiences. The tendency is to move too quickly, so that full value is not obtained from situations, associations, ideas, and sources of learning.

ei—Energy and intensity combine to create agitation within the soul. This is apt to evidence itself through restlessness and compulsive searching. The problem may be just what to search for. The soul searches for truth and only that will bring peace. This seeking makes one desirous of change and contact with people, ideas, and experiences.

eo—Enthusiasm that is directed toward obedience or overindulgence. There is the possibility of great spirituality here, and illumination can provide the needed understanding. Conflict may result from the need for freedom and feelings of responsibility. Harmony should be striven for so that spiritual and inspirational aspects can be allowed to develop to their fullest.

ew—Energy combined with wonderment about what to do with it. Power, ambition, activity, enterprise—all are evident here, and also possibly agitation. The physical aspects are strong and if not controlled could get out of hand. There is a great need to understand life and human nature, to search and investigate, to sell ideas and beliefs to others.

ia—The qualities and tendencies of the *ai* combination are here, but with a greater need for perfection and stronger qualities of sympathy and understanding.

io—Intenseness and oversensitivity can be the problem. The emotions can be too strong and easily get out of control. Here there is great compassion, sympathy, understanding, and a desire to aid others. There is the possibility of being oversensitive to the extent that slights are imagined. The desire to give away and the desire to keep for oneself can create confusion and conflict. Artistic abilities are strongly indicated.

oa—Obtaining aspirations. The danger here is that the desire for personal gain and power could obscure hidden power and beauty. The will is extremely strong and has the power to obtain anything truly sought. The emotional nature is strong and may direct the spiritual and inspirational aspects, which is the reverse of the best method of direction.

oe—The qualities and tendencies are the same as those of the *eo* combination. Here though, the tendency toward convention and tradition is apt to be stronger.

oi—The qualities and tendencies of the *io* combination are here, though this influence is apt to make one more self-concerned. Artistic abilities tend more to those involving color and harmony.

ou—Obtaining understanding seems to be the quest. Love of beauty, especially music, is indicated. Strong feelings may inhibit the equally strong intuitional nature. There could be a problem controlling one's emotions and the tendency to be overly concerned with physical pleasures.

oy—Other-worldly or mystical. This influence is very spiritual, ethical, and idealistic. There is the ability to see things clearly through inspiration, but inactivity and indecision may result because of not choosing a plan of action and following it. The ability to advise others is in evidence and should be applied to oneself as well.

ow—Other-world wonderment—a desire to know about and understand the unseen worlds, which could prove a problem if sight is lost of the fact that we still must live in this world. Inspirational and spiritual qualities are combined with physical experience here to provide great human understanding. The abilities of counseling and working with others are strongly indicated. The responsible nature should be directed toward providing enlightenment for others.

ua—Uncanny activity that can lead to constructive and productive ideas and projects is the wealth of this influence. The uncanny activity is a very active intuition. The tendency is to be either cool and apart or to be too open and free. It is possible to get into a rut because of overconcern with pleasure and self-indulgence, conventionality that limits vision and progress, or forcefulness and compulsion that has little regard for others.

The emotional nature is strong and could override the intuition that tries to guide it.

ue—Unusual energy that should be directed into productive channels. The concerns are apt to be materialistic, though the underlying nature is spiritual. Suppression of the spiritual aspects creates conflict and confusion. Overindulgence in physical things can create guilt. Caution and control are needed. Beliefs are apt to be progressive and different, and there is a danger of not looking deeply enough into things.

ui—Unusual immateriality is the possibility of this influence. Pleasure-seeking may conflict with spiritual beliefs and moral values, and there may be a tendency to try and ignore them. Strongly ruled by feelings, the tendency is to be impulsive, which could create problems. There is a need to follow one's intuition and to govern one's emotions.

TRIPLE VOWELS

Triple vowels are defined by the spelling. In the case of triple vowels, as in *Louise* and *Louis,* all three influences and their total should be considered. The influence of the first of the three vowels is always the strongest. The effect is similar to that of dual vowels, in that there is likely to be some degree of confusion and frustration. With the combination *oui,* we have the three vibrations of the trinity—3–6–9—with the influence of the 6 the strongest because it is actually the first vowel. At the same time the 9 is quite strong because it is both one of the numbers of the vowels and is also the total of the three vibrations. In these three numbers there is great harmony and power if used correctly. The emotions are a strong force and need to be guided by the inspirational nature, which is equally as strong. Beliefs may tend toward the orthodox, and personal desires could limit the good intended for someone with this influence. Harmony, beauty, and other people are necessities. Generosity is indicated.

Twenty-two

THE ELEMENTS

Anyone with a basic knowledge of astrology is aware that the four elements—fire, earth, air, and water—play a part in that science. The elements also have their place in numerology, and to varying degrees they are contained in every individual. In astrology the elements are determined from the date and time of birth. In numerology their influence is determined from the name at birth; we consider the individual letters and also the total.

To fully understand the importance of the elements we must realize that each one has specific characteristics and areas of influence. Fire is feeling—earth is body—air is spirit—water is mind.

Fire represents the feeling or emotional nature. In its lesser aspects it can deal with the lower emotions and also with what are called surface emotions. Its true realm is the area of strong feelings: devotion, reverence, compassion—any sincere feelings that are felt to the depth of our being and that are prompted by spirit (or soul), not by physical sensations and ego.

Earth represents the body or physical world and is largely concerned with material aspects. Its realm is the everyday world in which we live and the things we do: accumulating, accomplishing, succeeding. To gain these ends the body is necessarily the means.

Air represents the spirit or the spiritual and inspired aspects of man. It deals with the inner being or the soul and is concerned with its development and its achievement. It progresses through inspiration and illumination, to discovery and understanding of truth.

Water is mind or the thinking, reasoning, intellectual aspects of man. It is concerned with logic, facts, knowledge, and education. It progresses through logic, reason, judgment, and analytical thinking.

To fully understand the elements one must understand the law of energy, or the way in which energy works. Everything is made up of energy, as scientists have proven with the atom. Energy is vibration, and the density of matter is determined by the rate of vibration of its energy. The slower energy vibrates the denser it becomes. The vibration of energy in matter is measured by machines. Most people, with a little practice, can sense the vibrations in certain things. The next time you're out where there are rocks, pick one up and hold it in one hand for a few minutes and then in the other. Do this with several rocks and you'll notice a difference in them. You will be feeling their energy patterns. All energy conforms to a natural law, that is, for energy to exist there must be vibration, motion, and friction. For friction to exist there must of necessity be opposite forces. For example, consider a battery. All batteries have positive and negative poles and the friction between the two creates energy. When one of the poles gets weak, so does the energy. When one goes dead, the battery is no longer a source of energy.

This principle works within all living matter and man is no exception. The electromagnetic field in man has been measured by scientific instruments and has even been photographed, as its vibrations extend beyond the body to some degree. To many this portion of the electromagnetic field outside the body is known as an aura. Thus, contained within man is what could be called both positive and negative energy. The term *negative* does not mean "bad," but merely the opposite of positive.

Within the four elements energy exists also, consequently there must be opposing forces that provide the friction necessary to generate energy. Fire is the positive pole of earth and through the qualities of fire the energy of earth is transmuted. Air is the positive pole of water and through the qualities of air the energy of water is transmuted. The higher aspects of our feeling nature, which fire represents, transmute the physical emotions of earth into those of devotion, reverence, idealism, and true love. The higher aspects of our spiritual nature, which air represents, transmute the mental or intellectual nature of water through revelation, inspiration, illumination, and intuition, and thus transform knowledge into wisdom.

Fire unlocks the energy of earth to give it greater, fuller expression, as does air with water. Earth cannot unlock water or vice versa, as they are both negative poles. The same is true of fire and air. The energy of the two negative poles can work together—the intellect tends to either control the emotions or to be controlled by them—but they cannot release the energy within one another. Our true feelings and our spiritual nature go hand in hand but cannot raise one another—the energy of the positive elements is released through transmuting that of the negative poles.

It is possible for fire to transmute water, as the two together create steam, which provides power. Air cannot unlock earth's qualities, as it takes heat to raise the vibrations of earth. Fire and air are compatible, as are earth and water, because they are somewhat alike. The negative elements need to be taught, while the positive are inspired to achievement. In man energy manifests itself as qualities, characteristics, and abilities. In numerology the realm of each element is classified by numbers:

fire—1-3-9   air—5-6-11
earth—4-6-8   water—2-7-22

The numbers within one element cannot transmute each other, but they do intensify the power each has by functioning in the same area. Within the elements each number has its own characteristics and its own area of influence. The first of each trinity of numbers is concerned with personal aspects and situations, the second with groups and community, and the third with large-scale or universal matters. The characteristics of the individual numerical vibrations in relation to the elements is as follows:

FIRE

1—Indicates self-development, personal relationships, activity and personal progress. Energy is used by the individual mainly for self-promotion.

3—Energy is used to express beauty, love, enlightenment, happiness, and an optimistic outlook to friends, family, and community.

9—Indicates the use of energy to love on a universal scale rather than on a personal level and to provide aid to others.

EARTH

4—Service and sure construction in personal areas make use of the energy. Concern is productivity for the individual.

6—The energy manifests itself as love, which is given to those close to the individual by caring for their needs and wants.

8—Energy materializing as power for achievement—if not for the world, then on a very large scale, so that it is felt in a good part of it.

AIR

5—Personal concerns make use of the energy: progress, freedom, investigation, variety. There is a striving for an understanding of life.

6—The love of earth is elevated and increases its area of concern—devotion to a wide range of people and things.

11—Energy is given to the spiritual realm where illumination that can be shared with all is sought and where beliefs are created and perfected. Concern is with ideals.

WATER

2—Harmony and rhythm are the expressions of energy. Concerns are peacefulness and individual emotions and responses.

7—Energy is used to join the mental and spiritual realms together, and the insight, ideas, wisdom, and understanding that are gained are then given to those in quest of them.

22—Represents energy of the most elemental nature, which flows through all realms and worlds. The concern is to produce in material form that which is gained through vision. What is produced must be made useful and beneficial to all.

The explanations of the characteristics of the vibrations within the elements is based on the positive aspects, and it should be remembered that it is also possible to bring forth the negative qualities instead. It is apparent that certain characteristics are common to each influence of an element.

Fire is bright, warm, useful—a tool for mankind. It can be the tended fire that provides heat, cooks food, and tempers steel, or it can be the raging fire that burns trees and homes and scars the land, leaving only ashes and charred remains behind.

Its energy is activity that can be productive or consuming. It is forceful, determined, hard to control, aggressive, fast, and a great force for good or ill.

Earth is solid, firm, productive. It can bring forth fruit, or it can be destructive if there are landslides or earthquakes. Its energy manifests itself as precise actions along logical, conventional lines that produce sure results. It can be slow because of being bound to traditional methods.

Air is light, breezy, free, formless. It is the force we cannot see that sustains life. Air can be a cool breeze on a hot day that brings a breath of freshness, or it can be a roaring wind that brings devastation to the land and fills people's eyes with dust so they cannot see their way. Its energy brings inspiration, a broad and understanding outlook, a realization of truth, and the working of unseen forces that motivate and direct. It is concerned with the spiritual side of the physical world.

Water is in all living things. It is flowing, moving, cleansing, nourishing. Directed and controlled, as with irrigation, it brings the possibility of life and growth to arid land. Unchanneled, it is a flood that lays waste the land, uproots growing things, and leaves debris in its wake. Its energy flows through both the physical and unseen worlds of man, joining the two. It manifests itself in quiet, reflective activity on the inner planes that refreshes and cleanses.

To determine the amount of influence of each element we first consider the Inclusion Table. The elemental position of the numbers is outlined in the following manner:

2–1	fire-1-1-3-3-3-9-9-9-9/9
3–2 (1–11)	earth-4-8-8/3
3–3	air-5-5-5-5-11/5
2–4 (1–22)	water-2-2-7-22/4
4–5	
0——6	
1–7	
2–8	
4–9	

We can see that fire in this case is the dominant element and within it the characteristics of the 9 are strongest, followed by those of the 3. Air is the element of secondary influence and within it the qualities of the 5 are predominant. These should be carefully noted as they provide valuable information.

Next we take a look at the major numbers of a chart. For example:

inner self	7	water
outer self	8	earth
heart self	1	fire
destiny	2	water

Considered with the elemental totals already arrived at, we now see that the element of water is gaining strength. In addition to the major numbers we should consider the secondary numbers. However, we must remember that it is the totals gained from the Inclusion Table that are the most important. The various influences tell us where we have to be on guard so that the strength of one element doesn't become overdominant, which negative aspects are apt to do. It also indicates whether or not we will receive assistance in transmuting the more physical elements of earth and water through the appearance of fire or air.

The number 6 has two positions when determining the elements because of the dual nature of the love of the 6. It can be the love that stirs the physical emotions and makes one person more important to us than another, or it can be devotional love that knows no limits.

The elements also give us insight into the compatibility of relationships and associations. Checking the table of compatibility will make clear the relationships and effects of the elements when combined. Keep in mind that there are exceptions to every rule, but in most cases the relationship of the elements will be much as described. This information can be very helpful when considering an association or choosing a vocation. It also gives us a more in-depth look at ourselves and others.

COMPATIBILITY OF ELEMENTS

fire and fire—overpowering—fire consumes fire
fire and earth—controlled—disciplined—can be restrictive
fire and air—compatible—even uplifting and inspiring
fire and water—forceful—power that can be explosive

earth and fire—controlled—disciplined—can be restrictive
earth and earth—unyielding—physical aspects—slow—materialistic
earth and air—unharmonious—not adaptable
earth and water—compatible—may be bound to physical aspects

air and fire—compatible—even uplifting and inspiring
air and earth—unharmonious—not adaptable
air and air—erratic—unrealistic—unstable—impractical
air and water—compatible—the blending of two realms—idealistic
                                          and intellectual

water and fire—forceful—power that can be explosive
water and earth—compatible—may be bound to physical aspects
water and air—compatible—idealistic and intellectual
water and water—inexpressive—introverted—insecure

Twenty-three

FURTHER INFORMATION FROM THE INCLUSION TABLE

From the Inclusion Table we have thus far determined the Karmic lessons, the subconscious, the ruling tendency, and the influence of the elements. This is the major information to be gained from the table, but there is some minor information as well. It will give us greater insight into why we are the way we are. The three areas to be discussed are weak notes; one, many, and all; and inward and outward.

WEAK NOTES

We have learned the importance of the numbers that are totally lacking as well as that of those of greatest strength. We have also discussed the influence of strong vibrations that are not ruling tendencies. The weak notes are the vibrations in the Inclusion Table that have few or no numbers present.

When there is the lack of any particular number in the table, it not only tells us that it is a Karmic lesson but it also warns of undesirable influences or characteristics that should be guarded against. It also tells of qualities that are apt to be weak or totally absent and that need to be developed. It stands to reason that if a vibration is minus and we strive to make its qualities a part of our nature, we are helping ourselves to overcome the Karmic lesson it indicates. Study of a particular vibration in this chapter and in Chapter Two, Basic Characteristics of the Numbers, will make clear what you need to develop and what to guard against. Vibrations that are present but weak are danger signals that should be noted.

If a vibration is weak or minus and appears somewhere else in the chart, it indicates that you still need to be on guard, but that you are being given help. If vibrations appear as cycles, then it indicates a particular period of your life during which you will have to pay close attention to these matters and really work to overcome them.

1—Courage is needed, also faith in yourself, your abilities, your goals, your ideas and plans. Go forth with strong, determined actions; be brave and decisive. Look for new ways to do things, new ideas that have merit, a plan for getting what you want. Don't just sit and think about it—go out and do it. You could lack aspiration and ambition or the drive necessary to go after what you want. The tendency may be to do nothing unless others lead the way. Take the initiative and go after something —let others follow you for a change.

2—No matter how trying it may be, put yourself in the position of working with others. Join in group activities. Learn to be diplomatic and tactful. Give thought to the needs and feelings of others and how your words and actions can affect them. Work at paying attention to details, regardless of the fact that you'd rather overlook them. Make a point of being on time and aware of time. Plan your activities so that you can have a well-rounded schedule. Stick to your plans. The tendency is to be careless, thoughtless, and uncooperative. Show consideration to others, and you're far more likely to get the same in return.

3—You need to cultivate the habit of putting into words the things you feel and think. At first this may be difficult, but it will become easier with time. Feelings of inferiority are apt to be a problem. Realize that each person is an individual and stop measuring yourself against others. With your own talents and qualities developed and in use, you are as good as anyone. Make time for social and creative activities. The tendency is to sit back and quietly watch others—let them watch you for a change. Break out of your shell. Learn to see the humor in situations and be optimistic about life in general. Don't take life too seriously—try enjoying it more. Don't be so conservative that you miss new ideas and things that would be good for you.

4—If your life lacks organization, then it is time to acquire it. Set up a routine and make it work. Don't be overgenerous with time spent in pleasurable activities—make sure you allow enough work time. Then, get busy and work. Don't try to push manual labor off onto others; your life could use its productivity. You tend to be disorderly and at times even lazy. You must strive to overcome these things. You are apt to be somewhat impatient and intolerant—try not to be so demanding. Make allowances for what you see as others' shortcomings and hope they do the same for you. Develop good judgment and it will work for your success.

5—A change of pace or scenery could be the answer for you. Don't be afraid to change your mind, to try something new, to believe in something different. Cultivate a fresh outlook on life by getting out and experiencing it. Stimulate your mind through contact with people, books, and travel. There could be a tendency to avoid the opposite sex—stop and face your fears. Don't avoid people, but make a point of contacting as many as possible. Be active and make change the constant thing for you. Get rid of the ideas, thoughts, beliefs, and restrictions that keep you from getting full value out of life.

6—If you've been running from responsibility, then it's time to run toward it. Seek it, accept it, and discharge it well. There are those who need your strength to help them carry their burdens, and you shouldn't withhold it. When asked for advice, don't shrug your shoulders—give it. In fact, you would do well to make a habit of counseling others when you feel there is a need. You may want too much freedom and thereby miss much happiness and satisfaction. A home could bring contentment and make you feel useful. Responsibility will make you feel wanted and that is really what you need to know. Stop neglecting the things that you know you should do.

7—Sooner or later you're going to have to stop and take a good look at things, and there's no time like the present. You could begin by taking a closer look at yourself—who and what you really are. Develop poise, dignity, and pride in yourself. Don't settle for less than the best—especially where your own efforts are concerned. The tendency is to ignore spiritual things and possibly even to ridicule the spirituality of others. This may be because you have failed to examine such things to see their worth and gain an understanding of them. You may be lacking in faith and living in fear. The study of philosophy could prove beneficial. In nature you could find the peace you want and need. Cultivate the habit of finishing all you begin. Gather all the knowledge you can—it will aid you greatly. Take time to be alone with your thoughts—and examine them well.

8—Your problems are apt to begin with a dollar sign. You need to curb impulsiveness and manage financial affairs better. You may tend to dislike the handling of business matters and are likely to give this task to others whenever you can. Attend to these things yourself. Learn from those who've mastered success and you could be successful yourself. In all matters, make sure you aren't shortchanged—or that you aren't doing it to yourself. Develop a businesslike outlook and it will profit you. Don't avoid accepting authority and leadership—seek it. Be conservative and practical when there is a need. Trying to divorce yourself from material matters is separating yourself from life—thus you are missing one of the greatest teachers. You're here because you need to learn, so don't pass up any opportunity. Otherwise you're just insuring the need to tread the same path again.

9—For you, the key is to "turn the other cheek" and to understand why you should. Tolerance and compassion are qualities that need to be developed. You need to broaden your outlook concerning both life and people. You also need to broaden your scope of concern. Don't limit yourself to caring about only those who are close to you. Give all the love you can to all the people you can—and don't mistake the type of love meant. Physical passions and affections are not true love, and what the world needs is not another "great lover." Avoid criticizing, judging and condemning others at all costs. Be generous and forgiving in nature, and love in all things. Let go of your own emotions and you'll understand the emotional reactions of others better. Until you're really in the swim, you won't feel part of the waters of life. Go on; jump in. The water's great.

THE ONE, THE MANY, AND THE ALL

This classification of the numbers gives us insight into where we are and where we ought to be. It tells us where our main concern lies and what it should be. To do this we first consider the numbers of the Inclusion Table, which tells us where our concern naturally is. Then, by considering the other numbers of the chart, we can see where our concern should be in order to fulfill our destiny, accomplish what we came to do, and develop ourselves.

This is the grouping of the numbers:

The One	The Many	The All
1 2 3	4 5 6 7	8 9 11 22 33
A B C	D E F G	H I K V
J L	M N O P	Q R
S T U	W X Y	Z

The One—The byword is *mine*. You are concerned primarily with yourself. You can be creative and pioneering, but generally in areas that pertain to yourself.

The Many—The byword is *ours*. This generally includes

your family, friends, community, and possibly country. You do not separate yourself from the masses but prefer to work with them. The numbers in the many have a sense of responsibility that goes beyond yourself. The 7 is the bridge between the many and the all but is primarily concerned with the many.

The All—The byword is *yours.* You perceive no differences between races or creeds and love humanity selflessly. You believe in service to mankind. The 33 is a part of this group and yet much above it, for its understanding of the universal and divine is so much greater.

First we note the number of vibrations in each category in the Inclusion Table. This tells us which area we are likely to be concerned with and which will be of second and third importance.

To understand where our concern is best directed we must take a look at other vibrations in the chart. We consider the inner self, the outer self, the heart self, the destiny, the foundation, the key, the ruling tendency, the subconscious, the approach, and the destiny direction. We take all of these numbers and put them in the proper categories. The category (or categories) with the most numbers shows us where we would do best to direct our thoughts, plans, and activities.

A look at the category of particular numbers will also give us information that can be helpful. For example:

1. Where the outer self number falls will tell us how we can better develop ourselves.

2. The category the destiny falls in shows where we will find many opportunities to fulfill our purpose.

3. Classifying the categories of each of the major life cycles gives further insight into the experiences during those years and the type of development needed then.

4. The category that the destiny direction falls in will give further information about the area of work of the destiny, whether or not it falls in the same category as the destiny.

The one, many, and all is a means of helping us decide what

kind of attitude will benefit us most. If you are concerned with
the one when you should be concerned with the many, you are
limiting yourself. You are also spreading yourself too thin or
are overreaching if your goal is to do something for the all. The
predominance of numbers in a category tells you whether you
have come into this life primarily to work at self-improvement,
work with the masses for their good, or work for the benefit of
all on a universal scale.

We list the numbers of the one, many, and all in the following
manner:

```
                    Inclusion
                    4. . .1
            4/7     1. . .2
                    2. . .3
                    0. . .4
            1/8     5. . .5
                    1. . .6
                    2. . .7
            5/4     2. . .8
                    2. . .9
```

The number closest to the column is the total derived from the
Inclusion Table. The numbers farthest from the column are the
totals gained from the other numbers of the chart.

INWARD AND OUTWARD

With the numbers of the individual letters of the birth name
as shown in the Inclusion Table and with the name totals, or
inner self, outer self, and heart self, we can determine these
vibrations. In this instance the numbers fall into three categories:

inward	outward	dual
1-3-5-7-9-11-33	2-4-6-8-22	1-6-22-33

We are concerned with which category has the predominance
of numbers, for this tells us more about what we are. They are
listed in the chart in the manner shown below, with the name

totals listed separately to the far right. This is because their influence is greater than that of the separate digits and therefore should not be added together.

inward—7/2
outward—6/1
dual—2/1

The Odd Numbers—indicate that you are a dreamer who seeks and works for illumination. You are inspirational, idealistic, artistic, and love beauty. You are spiritual and are a visionary who sees the broad view. You tend to test things from an emotional and subjective standpoint.

The Even Numbers—indicate that you are a doer who seeks and works for success. You are practical and constructive and are concerned with activity that shapes material things. You are conservative, want all things to be useful and efficient, and tend to test things objectively with reason and judgment.

The Dual Numbers—indicate inspirational power within that you are capable of bringing forth for material or physical use.

The totals gained from the Inclusion Table define your latent capabilities, and those gained from the name totals indicate the area in which you are most inclined to direct your efforts. If you find that both of the predominant totals fall in the same category, it is an indication of strength and harmony.

Twenty-four

PECULIARITIES

This vibration exerts a great influence toward making us the individuals we are. The number to be worked with is revealed by the total number of letters in the full birth name. Thus, with the name *John Smith,* we find a total of nine letters, which gives us 9 as the vibration of peculiarities. If the total number of letters in your name is greater than the numbers given in this chapter, reduce that number by adding its digits together. If the total number of letters in your full birth name were 39, you would have to reduce that to a smaller figure. You would add 3 + 9 to get a total of 12, and because 12 is listed, you don't have to reduce it to a single-digit figure.

4—You like to stay active and have little patience with those who don't. You are concerned with productivity, and all of your activities are likely to be aimed in this direction. You may not allow much time in your schedule for pleasure and social occasions. If others are waiting around for your praise or compliments, they could be in for a long wait. You tend to be a planner and your goal is material success.

5—You like the easy life, free from cares and ties and the practical concerns of life. Curious, possibly even to the point of being nosy, you love investigation and exploration. You can be a schemer and may go to any length to get things your own way. You are adventurous and love excitement. Inclined to live fast, you like things that are powerful and to go places quickly so your impatient nature is satisfied. A speculator or gambler, you are forever taking chances and your magnetic quality may well draw success to you.

6—Always lending a hand, you are likely to be taken advantage of because of your helpful nature. A true home lover, you domesticate any surroundings you find yourself in. You strive to promote better conditions in all things and can be a great aid to your community. Don't waste advice on those who won't listen—use your perceptive powers to determine those who will make use of your beneficial counseling.

7—To others you may seem like a dark mine shaft—cool, quiet, and unyielding. When they get to know you, they'll find great hidden wealth—but it's apt to be buried way below the surface. Why not bring it out into the light of day? Unused, a thing is worthless; shared, the value is increased. You like to be alone, but take care that you don't become a hermit or introvert. Be led by your intuition, as your hunches are good, and give away some of the treasure you're hoarding.

8—You have the ability to make the most outlandish ideas profitable. You realize the need for practicality and see how it can be achieved. You're inclined to measure success with dollar signs and material acquisitions. You enjoy finding the answers to problems and managing things and will run others' lives if they'll let you. It's not that you're bossy—it's just that you have faith in yourself and only a little in others. You are diplomatic and have a way of getting others to do what you want. If someone were to give you a pleasure-seeking bunch of loafers, you'd soon organize them into an efficient, hard-working crew.

9—You may well possess the power to soothe and heal through your voice and hands, or even just through your presence. It is the love you feel for others, working through you. But don't get carried away by it. You are impulsive and could be rash in your generosity, ending up with nothing for yourself. Quite emotional and sensitive, you are prone to spells of great happiness and sadness, almost without reason. Don't get so down that you can't see the beauty in life. Remember the healing qualities of laughter and sunshine and enjoy plenty of both.

10—You are the one who is likely to be interested today in what others won't be ready to accept for some time to come. With a little farsighted inspiration, possibly gained from a friend, you could really make others sit up and take notice. You feel that within yourself is contained all you will ever need, and you look to others for little if anything. You may not need them, but they may need you. One of a kind, you're the spark that lights new fires in the minds of men, but don't let your head swell with your own importance.

11—You run on high-octane energy that could explode at any minute, and keeping it harnessed could make you quite nervous. Find yourself some constructive outlets for it. Others may not know how to react to your ability to read their thoughts or predict events—for you may well have developed psychic powers. Because of this, you may have some uneasy moments. Your electric qualities were meant to make you a light for others, which could bring you acclaim and attention.

12—You're not always sure what you want to do, and all too often you want to be where you're not. You like to keep your life full of friends, fun, happiness, and beauty. When you're sad you're apt to cheer yourself up by going on a shopping trip or a pleasure excursion. You enjoy creating, with your hands or mind, and like to have others praise your artistic endeavors. You tend to strive for approval in all that you do. Emotional and impulsive, you may laugh one minute and cry the next. Unpleasantness upsets you and you avoid it whenever you can. Your sense of humor is a powerful tool that can aid you greatly.

13—You realize the need for work, but can't stand for it to be too routine and dull, so you strive to make it fun. Co-workers probably find you a pleasant addition and welcome the smiling way you do your job. You may not see the funny side of things immediately, but you'll laugh about them later. You like romance, but at the proper time and place. You're not likely to let it disrupt your whole life. You strive to keep your head in control of your emotions, but you don't always manage to do it. About some things you're very practical and about others you are very impractical—you may not understand why you're so inconstant.

14—Whatever you do you do in a wholehearted way and put a great deal of energy behind it. When you work, you work; when you play, you play, and you enjoy doing both. Generally practical and somewhat conservative, you have an inner desire to throw caution to the wind and do something really rash and exciting. The reason you probably don't is concern for what others would think. Inclined to have something of a temper, when you are angry others would do best to stay out of your way. Problems irritate you and if they're large you're apt to feel like walking away from it all. There's a dual nature in you that you need to work at blending.

15—Basically a homebody, you still feel the need to get away fairly often—if it's only for a day. When you feel the need to get away and can't, things are likely to bother you and others could suffer the pains. Your very curious nature is apt to be directed toward others' lives and problems—out of true concern for their happiness. Something of a talker, you are prone to giving advice and selling others on your ideas and beliefs. Your persuasive nature will make you more successful than most. You like to go your own way—although you're not always sure what it is. Others may be drawn to you because of your loving, giving nature.

16—You're apt to be known as something of a perfectionist. You feel a sense of duty about seeing that things are as well done as possible. You want to understand all things and so you search for facts and answers. When you've found the answer, it's a good bet that you'll be right, and you'll probably argue the point if challenged. You and your surroundings are usually an example of good taste, and you have a knack for creating beauty. You take things seriously, sometimes too much so, and need to develop a lighter outlook.

17—Loyal and trustworthy, you like the same qualities in others and are intolerant if they disappoint you. To you, keeping a secret is a matter of honor, as are making good your promises and being dependable. Your opinion is worth seeking, but you prefer to be asked only about things that have been given careful thought beforehand. A thinker yourself, you have the ability to turn out smooth, efficient, workable ideas and put them into action. Quality and pride are important to you, and you also value respect and strive to earn it.

18—Business matters and success are important to you, but you need to feel that you're helping others with the things you do. There's a good chance that you have the ability to make a lot of money and an equal chance that others will come to you in need. Consequently you might not end up with a large bank account. If personal gain isn't your only concern and you keep your vision and ideas unlimited, you can attract a great deal of success. Remember that success attracts leeches. Take care not to let yourself be used. Guard your health by getting away now and then. Let the beauty of nature revitalize you.

19—Fresh, new ideas are your key to success and they flow to you in an undiminishing stream. The problem may be that you share your ideas with others, and before you act they've used your plan. You also tend to become so involved with a still newer idea that you fail to bring the last one to completion and thus miss harvesting your reward. The ideas and things that tend to interest you most are progressive, new methods that will benefit others. Torn at times between personal desires and the needs and feelings of those around you, you are likely to have trouble deciding which way to go. Don't let indecision keep you from acting at all.

20—If we want to look something over thoroughly and see

feelings as well as facts, we'll call on you. You have the ability to be a self-sufficient analyst who can relay information to others so tactfully that it is well accepted. If you want to really go somewhere, get together with an "idea person"—let him or her provide the inspiration for you to make something workable. Such cooperation can take you far in this world. You're a music lover—it represents a need for harmony in yourself and your surroundings. When there is no harmony, you're petty and apt to be hurt by the slightest thing. Love is the balm that heals all wounds, so be sure to let it flow freely.

21—Progressive imagination detailed into a plan of action is your key—your gift to all. Let it begin to unlock doors for you. You have a three-sided nature: now a loner and aggressive, then needing to be with others but remaining somewhat quiet and reserved, then an extrovert who tries to steal the show. Your life should be varied because of your many facets. Youthful and active, you may amaze or shock others because you appear younger than you are and refuse to act your age. Ignore them. You're as old as you feel and those who disapprove are only jealous.

22—The world is your domain if you go after it. You may want to limit your achievements, but there really should be no limits for you. Sensitive, perceptive, practical, patient, methodical, powerful, diplomatic—the list could go on and on. Shed that ridiculous inferiority complex and get to work—you have big things to do. Politics could be your world since you have the magnetism a statesman needs. Creating something better for others is your role. Play it big. Your stage can be national or international—it's all up to you.

23—Witty and cheerful, with a delightful sense of humor, you are entertaining and great to have around. You have a bright, fresh, optimistic outlook that makes others feel better and helps them see their troubles in truer perspective. Whether socializing, selling your ideas, or looking for new interests and loves, you're always on the go. No one could call you run of the mill. You have a sharp mind that moves quickly, searches for understanding and ideas, and is very clever. Your ability to judge others well and to analyze their character is a profitable asset—use it.

24—Conservative and practical, you have your feet firmly planted on the ground and intend to keep them there. That's great, but can't your head be in the clouds at the same time? Don't limit your vision, as you have the ability to make dreams work through logic and application. Counseling others in a sympathetic, understanding manner is a way of life for you. You can't see a problem and not want to solve it or rid yourself of the desire to settle differences. Your "motherly" nature makes you care about everything and everyone, and if not careful you could smother people with concern. Adopt a freer outlook and think a little more about Number One, and you'll achieve greater balance.

25—When you decide to sell an idea to others, they ought to pay attention. Your way of investigating things thoroughly makes it fairly safe to say that if you feel something is good it probably is. Sometimes when asked for your opinion or ideas you're inclined not to volunteer information. When you do give it, you want others to heed it. To those around you, you are apt to be something of a puzzle. One time you will steal the show with your magnetic personality and wit, and the next time you will sit quietly in the corner and say nothing. One day you want to be surrounded by people, and the next day you want to be alone. For you the pendulum swings from one extreme to the other. But all of this won't bother you one bit because change is something you love.

Twenty-five

TABLE OF EXPRESSION—AREA OF ACTIVITY

Self-expression, for all of us, is managed through four areas or planes of expression: mental, physical, emotional, and intuitional. Knowing the plane in which we have gained the most proficiency, through experience and knowledge, tells us how our activity should be directed. The destiny points *where* and the planes give an indication of *how*. They tell us our area of greatest power and also which area backs that power up—to give us extra strength when needed.

The planes, which are determined from the letters of the full birth name, have their own groups of letters, as shown below:

Table of Expression

Mental	Physical	Emotional	Intuitional	
a	e	i o r z	k	inspired
h j n p	w	b s t x	f q u y	dual
g l	d m		c v	balanced

From the table we know that all *a*'s in the name go under the mental plane, all *y*'s under intuitional, all *e*'s under physical, and so on. If an *e* appears five times in the name, then five *e*'s are put in the physical plane. Each letter is listed the number of times it appears in the name.

Notice also that there are three levels within the planes. In the mental plane only *a* is on the first level, with *h, j, n,* and *p* on the second level, and *g* and *l* on the third. When you are noting the letters, be sure to put them on the right level or your information about the areas of activity will be wrong.

Each letter has its own plane of expression and its own personal characteristics. The particular letters that occur in a plane give added information about how to use the power. Each plane has three levels of activity: inspired, dual, and balanced. By studying the plane of greatest power, the characteristics of the power, and the area of activity, we can see how best to put the power and our talents to use.

For someone to say you have the ability to write is not enough. Write about what? Should you write fiction or about educational, technical, humorous, or religious matters?

The planes of expression can be invaluable in telling us where our power lies. We know from the destiny where we are supposed to be going, but there are many paths. The destiny direction points out a generalized area of paths, and now we can begin to narrow that down. Considered along with the abilities of the outer self, we will begin to see just how to use what we have been given. The number of letters on any plane determines its power in relation to the other planes.

The Mental Plane—Indicates attributes that are best expressed in writing matter that is educational, serious, technical, or scientific—something that expounds theories, beliefs, knowledge, methods, and formulas—large business operations and concerns, national and international matters, leadership and authority, investigation of new areas and ideas, invention and creativity, thinking about and accomplishing reforms in both material and religious areas. Your concern is reason, logic, facts, judgment, knowledge, and use of the intellect. You are matter of fact, decisive, determined, and forceful. Your actions are well planned and you intend to reach your goal.

The Physical Plane—Indicates attributes that are best expressed in material progress through a physical manifestation of ideas, work that makes use of both the body and the mind, construction and productivity, detailed or complex scientific projects, study and research, factual investigation, material reforms. You are interested in your fellowman and life, are completely practical and thorough, and like to see results.

The Emotional Plane—Indicates attributes that are best expressed in artistic creation and design (painter, poet, musician, architect, clothes designer, photographer), appreciation of and protection of beauty and nature and service to others. Your concern is based on feelings and has little to do with facts, logic, judgment, examination, or reason. You are moved by your heart and tend to get carried away with your ideas. You may not finish what you begin.

The Intuitional Plane—Indicates attributes that are best expressed in invention and innovation, formulation of concepts and beliefs, reception and understanding of spiritual matters, seeking enlightenment for oneself and others, instilling in others zeal and faith in ideas, teachings, and beliefs. The concern is based on revelation, intuition, and development of the inner realms and spirituality. Your actions are motivated by inspiration. Often, however, you are too detached from the material world. Living in your inner world almost constantly can make you unstable and cause you to lose sight of reality.

AREAS OF ACTIVITY

The areas of activity are determined by the three totals to the right of the Table of Expression. The planes of expression are determined by the column totals, while the areas are derived from the line totals.

Inspired—You are a starter. You begin things either by furnishing the idea or by beginning the action itself.

Dual—You take up what others have begun and see to it that what has been started is continued.

Balanced—You are a finisher. You are concerned with completion—you dislike effort that is wasted on projects that never reach their goal.

A predominance of letters in one area shows us where most of our activity is directed or where it should be directed. This will tell you your primary area (what you are best at), your secondary area of concern, and your third. If the totals are close, such as 7-6-5 , you are fairly strong in all areas and should function reasonably well in any of them. If two totals are the same, as with 5-5-3, you have two areas in which you function equally well. When there is a great difference in the area totals, as with 8-3-2, it indicates considerable strength in the area with the greatest total and definite weakness in the other two areas. In the case of totals of 8-7-1, it shows strength in two areas but definite weakness in the other area. When we know whether we're a starter, a continuer, or a finisher, we can stop wasting time trying to function in an area we're poorly fitted for.

CHARACTERISTICS OF THE LETTERS

To fully understand the importance of the planes we must realize the influence that the individual letters bring to bear. This is gained by realizing the characteristics of each letter and how they are determined.

Each letter gains its characteristics from its numerical value, plane of expression, area of activity, and the numbers behind its total. For example, let's look at the letters *a, j,* and *s.* They are all 1s but *a* is a definite, singular 1, while *j* is a 10–1 and *s* is a 19–1. *A* and *j* are mental, while *s* is emotional. The letter *a* differs from *j* in that its area of activity is inspired, while *j* is dual, as is *s.* From this we can see that no two letters are going to have the same characteristics.

The plane of greatest power is shown by the plane or planes with the most letters appearing in it. Within that plane we have the qualities indicated by the letters shown there. Within that plane the qualities indicated should be applied in the area of activity we are best at. Let us assume that in a particular chart we find the mental plane strongest with the letters *a, n,* and *p* appearing there. The area of activity indicated is "balanced." The mental plane indicates that this person could be a teacher since a teacher deals with the intellect. The *a* indicates a need for originality that may be gained through the *n*'s inspiration and imagination, that is, referred to the mind and, through the fact-seeking qualities of the *p,* is analyzed for its value. The area, balanced, indicates a finisher, and so this person would be wise to consider teaching in college or the later years of high school rather than assuming the role of a starter and teaching elementary school.

When there is more than one of a letter in the plane of power, those qualities are intensified and dominate the weaker ones. If we were working with *a, a, n,* and *p,* we would know that the attributes indicated by the *a*'s would be twice as strong as those of the *n* and *p.*

We are primarily concerned with the plane of greatest power and the letters contained therein, but it should also be noted that if there is great strength of a particular letter or letters in another plane, those characteristics are very strong within that individual. Again, using the same example, if we also found four *r*'s in the table, it would indicate a tendency to give of oneself greatly, or in this case, sharing one's knowledge fully. On the other hand, four *o*'s would make one concerned with his or her own development and power. There would be a tendency to keep information from others as much as possible. When there is a predominance of any particular letter in any plane, its influence must be considered. Remember when looking up any letter to keep in mind the characteristics of its numerical value and the digits behind that total.

THE MENTAL LETTERS

a—Inspired—1—determination that proceeds directly to its target, creative originality, leadership, and concern with self-development—all guided by inspiration.

h—Dual—8—motivation for achievement that is weakened by indecision about action; links the physical world to the mental and so is connected to both, but refers all to the intellect.

j—Dual—1 (10/1)—indecision caused by seeing the various aspects of things can weaken one's ability to lead and his or her individuality.

n—Dual—5 (14/5)—imagination and the ability to understand things intellectually, if they are seen clearly, which they aren't always. There is a tendency to instability.

p—Dual—7 (16/7)—self-sufficiency, though at times there is a tendency to be unsure, seeking facts to aid understanding, sometimes lacking drive and self-control, possibly talking authoritatively about religion and creeds but having little faith or spirituality, inability to express inner feelings.

g—Balanced—7—analytical, introspective, reserved, the true pulse of intellect—the most mental of the mental; outward expression is large, balanced, and complete, giving well of itself with strong drive and self-control.

l—Balanced—3 (12/3)—generous in giving, though it's done with some thought and in a definite manner; actions are not quick, but tend to be planned; intuition is strong, though cautiously heeded; expressive and outgoing, though not fully extroverted—there is some reserve.

THE PHYSICAL LETTERS

e—Inspired—5—turning of life's experiences into understanding, interest in scientific matters, practical application in the physical world of inspiration received, a desire to give aid.

w—Dual—5(23/5)—vision, a desire to give, high goals—all of which may be limited in expression by failure to rise out of the depths of emotion or above physical passions. The heights can be reached only if they are sought after with determination and self-control.

d—Balanced—4—efficient, practical, self-sufficient, re-served, self-contained, fairly unexpressive; reason rules emotions and gives ability to handle material matters well.

m—Balanced—4 (13/4)—practical, thorough, well-ordered handling of material matters, but with little vision; expression is stifled by repression; seeing the physical realm as being of greatest value; tending to be cold and uncaring. The most inexpressive of all the letters.

THE EMOTIONAL LETTERS

i—Inspired—9—power that can shed light on the path by spirituality and revelation, or there can be destruction through negativeness. There is no in-between—the extremes of height or depth can be reached. Mind is ruled by the feelings.

o—Inspired—6 (15/6)—conservative; inspiration is carefully guarded and nurtured; poise and charm are tools well used. Can be egotistical and concerned with self-gain, and bound to traditional concepts and beliefs.

r—Inspired—9 (18/9)—selflessness, compassion, understanding, forgiving and tolerant without limit; strength of power to be used for others or it will overtax the physical.

z—Inspired—8 (26/8)—emotional understanding that gives insight into the spiritual realms; joining of the physical and spiritual through inner knowing; inclined to excesses which create problems.

b—Dual—2—sensitive and loving, with a tendency to be withdrawn and shy. Needs to be cared about and for. Loves too easily and may be in and out of love often.

s—Dual—1 (19/1)—Great emotional extremes through relating everything to the self; feelings may limit the mind's ability; impulsiveness could lead to problems.

t—Dual—2 (20/2)—self-sacrifice, spirituality, desire for greater understanding and illumination, nervously energetic. Physical and emotional pressure comes from the weight of burdens assumed.

x—Dual—6 (24/6)—self-sacrifice beyond what is good; confusion due to adapting emotionally.

There are no balanced letters on the emotional plane, as the emotions are rarely balanced.

THE INTUITIONAL LETTERS

k—Inspired—2 (11/2)—openness to all realms; intuitive greatness that comes from revelation and can manifest itself as psychic ability; tendency to want to live in the visionary world, which is seen with such clarity that its reality may seem greater.

f—Dual—6—balance arrived at through intuition; helpful and willing to assume others' burdens and responsibilities; apt to be troubled by indecision and confusion.

q—Dual—8 (17/8)—a capacity for inspiration that can produce a genius; the ability to function in spiritual and physical worlds at the same time; ability to receive great quantities of Light, but there are problems in use of the power.

u—Dual—3 (21/3)—receptive and magnetic but able to give little and may draw the unusual in life; this can be loss and unhappiness. Positive attitude can add the strength weak areas need and reverse the flow of current.

y—Dual—7 (25/7)—strong intuitive perception; a seeking nature that needs to be followed by firm decisions, or all efficiency will be lost.

c—Balanced—3—complete, free expression that achieves

productivity; psychic power that could be unrealized; giving and generous; artistic creativity.

v—Balanced—4 (22/4)—intuition clearly received through openness to the realms above, combined with power for material accomplishment and the ability to know how to put both to their best possible use. The capability is to cut through to the heart of any matter through guidance.

Twenty-six

COLORS, GEMS, MUSICAL NOTES, AND PLANETS

Because numerology is the science of vibration, it is closely tied to colors and to musical notes. We are aware that music is vibration, but most people do not know that color is sound at a different rate of vibration. Number, sound, and color are the three types of vibration that are the easiest to identify and work with. Each number, or vibration, that we use in numerology has its own color and musical note. Each vibration is also governed by a planet and has a gem or gems that relate to it.

All of this probably brings to mind the question, "What is their relationship to numerology?" To the student of astrology, knowing the planetary influence of the numbers in a numerological chart can prove an interesting basis for a study of relating influences. A comparison of a person's astrological and numerological charts usually shows a considerable similarity of planetary influences and related qualities.

Colors, gems, and musical notes can be very beneficial in a variety of ways. To date, most of my research in this area has been confined to the use of colors and gems. This is mainly because of my limited knowledge of music. It is my belief that if music were composed that primarily made use of the major and secondary vibrations in a person's chart, it would be extremely beneficial to him or her. I am also convinced that such music must be of the quieter type and that much of our modern music, the loud and "acid" kind, causes disharmony in the body and mind.

My research into the use of colors and gems has shown that they bring certain influences to bear in a person's life. If a person is working on a particular Karmic lesson help can be gained by wearing the color or gem of that vibration. The same is true of challenges and working at developing the qualities and characteristics of any vibration in our chart, particularly the major vibrations. This works in two ways:

1. The use of a particular color or gem adds the influence of that vibration and because like attracts like, it helps us develop the corresponding qualities and abilities. In this regard it appears that gems are stronger than colors.

2. The subconscious is well aware of the characteristics of each vibration and by using one of their influences it knows to work at attracting situations that help develop these characteristics in us. It works on the principle of psychocybernetics, or setting a goal for the subconscious to reach.

For example, if one of the Karmic lessons is 7, we then know that wearing the color or gem of the 7 will aid in developing the inner resources and faith necessary to learn the lesson. When working with gems, I have found that it is not at all necessary to use a cut or polished stone and that they are most effective when worn singly next to the skin in the area of the heart. Wearing several at once, however, seems to cause some confusion and dissipation of forces, so I advise using only one or possibly two gems at a time.

For relaxation, beneficial motivation, establishing greater harmony with your soul, and developing the characteristics indicated, wear the color and/or gem of your inner self.

To increase your capabilities and aid in the development of your natural talents, wear the color and/or gem of your outer self.

To attract new opportunities and situations that will generally aid you in fulfilling your purpose, wear the color and/or gem of your destiny. For dreaming, and to help you achieve your desires, wear the color and/or gem of your heart self.

To help you add direction to your life and find the proper channel for your activities, wear the color and/or gem of your direction.

The wearing of any color or gem, regardless of whether its vibration is in your chart, aids in bringing its particular influences to bear in your life. It should be mentioned also that Sidney Omarr, the renowned astrologer, has done considerable research using numbers as symbols to the subconscious. His findings are explained in the time-machine section of his book, *The Thought Dial Way to a Healthy and Successful Life.* He has found that if a certain number is concentrated upon, it brings definite influences to bear, and so he uses numbers as we have used colors and gems. The three used together are triply effective. To anyone who finds this section of interest I highly recommend his book. To arrive at the numbers he works with, he has combined numerology and astrology. Again we see another instance in which the two fields work together in harmony and complement each other.

MUSICAL NOTES AND COLORS

When working with music, we begin by relating number 1 to middle C. When working with colors, it is best to use the purest form of each hue or color listed for greatest effectiveness.

```
1. . . . .C. . . . .red
        C#. . .red-orange
2. . . . .D. . . . .orange
        D#. . .orange-yellow
3. . . . .E. . . . .yellow
        F. . . . .yellow-green
4. . . . .F#. . .green
```

5. . . . .G. . . . .turquoise
      G#. . .blue
6. . . . .A. . . . .royal blue and blue-purple (indigo)
      A#. . .purple
7. . . . .B. . . . .violet (purple with a pinkish hue or cast)
8. . . . .high C. . . . .pink or rose
9. . . . .high D. . . . .yellow-gold (9 responds somewhat to all the notes and
               colors)
11. . . . .high E. . . . .silver and glossy white
22. . . . .high F. . . . .red-gold
33. . . . .high G. . . . .sky-blue (not pale, but deep in color)

NUMBERS OF COLORS

1—*Red* is strong, progressive, vibrant, creative, and aggressive. It is bold and full of life and is the starter.

2—*Orange* is a mixture of red and yellow—the middle ground between the two—and is balance and harmony.

3—*Yellow* is bright, cheerful, full of sunshine and light and gives forth beauty, sympathy and happiness. It is full of warmth and feeling.

4—*Green* is growth, construction, productivity, healing and soothing. It is the balance between the brightness of yellow and the cool calm of blue.

5—*Turquoise* combines the healing of green with the peace of blue. It is changeable, adaptable, seeking, refreshing, restless, and full of activity. It can calm or stimulate through its duality.

6—*Royal Blue* is deep, rich, and vital. It is solid, stable, sure, strong, and powerful in a quiet way.

7—*Violet,* the last color of the spectrum, bridges the physical and spiritual realms and therefore is reverent, mysterious, fearless, quiet yet alive, deep, reflective, and royal. It is the color of meditation and can be used to increase its depth and achievements.

8—*Pink* is red in its higher form; the physical joined with the spiritual, and so is full of love, warmth, and generosity.

9—*Yellow-Gold,* the halo that rises from the other colors, is the aura of them all and shines with the light of the sun, combining something of all the colors into a harmonious blend. It is strong, warm, and gives life to all.

11—*Silver* is pure and shining, giving light and reflecting light. It is bright, rich, eye-catching, and magnetic. Not always practical, never conservative, but always attracting; it can blind with its brilliance.

22—*Red-Gold* is sun and earth, using the energy of the former to create for the latter. It is strong, vital, powerful, active, warm, intense, and commands attention.

33—*Sky-Blue* is the color we see as we look into the heavens above. It is the color of prayer and so is full of spirit, harmony, quietness, and serenity. It is restful and calming.

GEMS

1—ruby and/or garnet
2—moonstone
3—topaz
4—green jade and/or emerald
5—turquoise and/or aquamarine
6—white pearls or blue sapphires
7—amethyst and/or alexandrite
8—rose quartz and/or diamond
9—opal
11—platinum and/or mother of pearl
22—coral and/or red-gold
33—lapis lazuli

There are other stones and gems that have the same vibratory influence, but the ones mentioned above are the best known.

PLANETS

1—Sun	4—Saturn	7—Mercury	11—Neptune
2—Moon	5—Mars	8—Sun	22—Uranus
3—Venus	6—Jupiter	9—(aura)	33—Pluto

The number 9 has no particular planet associated with it in numerology. It is called the aura of the planets because it has something of the influence of each one.

Sun—fire, life, creation. The hub around which all revolves, it is the beginning and is full of energy.

Moon—Vacillating, adaptable. It is quiet power that influences in subtle ways, as in its effect on the tides, crops, and the moods of man.

Venus—Love in its artistic expression, which creates and appreciates the many aspects of beauty.

Saturn—The planet of "The Watcher," who insures that all lessons are learned. It is discipline and systematic construction on all levels.

Mars—Power that can create or destroy. It is change, activity, and expansion, and its influence is seeking and restless.

Jupiter—Earth and air mixed, it is protective, possessive, and the devotion of the deeper aspects of love.

Mercury—Intellectual, mental, and curious. It can be insecure and fearful if the explosive aspect is attuned to. On the positive side, it is knowledge, wisdom, reflection, poise, and refinement.

Neptune—Impractical, forceful, mysterious, inspired and inspiring, and visionary. Its influence is apt to be other-worldly.

Uranus—Massive power that may tear down to recreate in better form, it is strength, energy, and activity. It is extremely electrical and forceful and destroys the useless to make a place for the useful.

Pluto—Apart and yet part of, its influence is quiet, strong, sure, penetrating, and often unrealized. If its effects are felt, they are not always understood. As the opposite pole of the sun, it is the same energy manifesting itself in another form. It pulls energy to and through the other planets and is thereby giving.

Twenty-seven

SETTING UP A COMPLETE CHART

With what you have learned so far, you can now prepare a complete chart. A full chart takes two pages: one to calculate the various vibrations and the second to compile all of the various influences, totals, and information. There are many ways to set up a chart, but the arrangement I use in this chapter is neat and easy to read.

When calculating the years of the major life cycles, be sure that you do so by figuring the closest 1 personal year to the approximate time of change.

If you should decide to use what you have learned to prepare a work-up for someone else it is a good idea to include a brief explanation of each particular influence, such as, "The subconscious deals with the unconscious actions," etc.

Remember when considering weak notes that the absent vibrations, or Karmic lessons, are weak also. It is not necessary to list them as such, as I have, but they should not be overlooked.

For the first page of the chart, I find that graph paper (four squares to the inch) is extremely useful in keeping a chart orderly and evenly spaced. It also eliminates the problem of drawing straight lines.

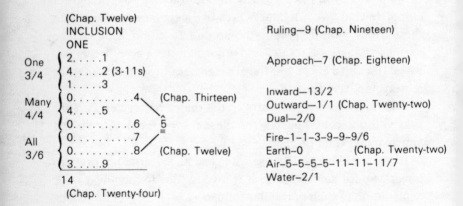

```
                18/19      +      6      +      6     =21/③   (Chap. Three)
                                                              Inner Self
                9          9      1    5      1    5
(Chap. Ten)     N I  K  K  I      K A R E N    C A B E    9–4–11 ⑥  Outer Self
Foundation—     5 9 11 11 9      11 1 9 5 5   3 1 2 5             (Chap. 4)
Key——              45/9      +     31/4     +     11   =24/6
(Chap. Eleven)
                _____      _____    _____
                5   11 11       11   9   5    3    2
                   27/9      +     25/7     +    5     =21/③  Heart Self
                                                             (Chap. 7)
```

(Chap. Twelve)
INCLUSION
ONE

Ruling—9 (Chap. Nineteen)

Approach—7 (Chap. Eighteen)

```
One     { 2.....1
3/4     { 4.....2 (3-11s)
        { 1.....3
Many    { 0.........4 ⟍ (Chap. Thirteen)
4/4     { 4.....5      5̂
        { 0.........6  ≡
All     { 0.........7 /
3/6     { 0.........8 (Chap. Twelve)
        { 3.....9
        _____
        14
(Chap. Twenty-four)
```

Inward—13/2
Outward—1/1 (Chap. Twenty-two)
Dual—2/0

Fire–1–1–3–9–9–9/6
Earth–0   (Chap. Twenty-two)
Air–5–5–5–5–11–11–11/7
Water–2/1

Table of Expression (Chap. Twenty-five)

Mental	Physical	Emotional	Intuitional	Areas of Activity
A A	E E	I I R	K K K	Inspired–10
N N		B		Dual–3
			C	Balanced–1
4	2	4	4	

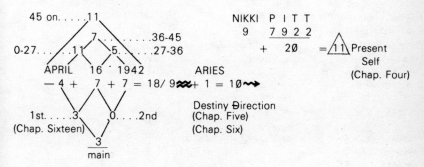

(Chap. Seventeen)
Pinnacles

45 on. 11
7. 36-45
0-27. 11   5. 27-36
APRIL   16   1942   ARIES
— 4 + 7 + 7 = 18/ 9 + 1 = 10

1st. 3   0. . . .2nd
(Chap. Sixteen)
3
main

NIKKI P I T T
9   7 9 2 2
+   20   = 11 Present
Self
(Chap. Four)

Destiny Direction
(Chap. Five)
(Chap. Six)

Challenges

Cycles
1. 0-28. . .1970
2. 28-55. . .1997
3. 55 on
(Chaps. Fourteen & Fifteen)

Date   June 1974   Name   Nikki Karen Cabe—Pitt

Inner Self— ③
Outer Self—/6\   One—4/3
                        Many—4/4   Foundation—5
Heart Self— 3   All—6/3   Key—9
                                             First Vowel—I (Chap. Twenty-one)
Destiny—9 〰   Approach—7
                                             Birth date—16 (Chap. Nine)
Direction—1 〰

Elements   *Planes of Expression*   *Areas of Activity*
Fire—6   Mental—4   Inspired—10
Earth—0   Physical—2   Dual—3
Air—7   Emotional—4   Balanced—1
Water—1   Intuitional—4

Colors (Chap. Twenty-six)   *Gems*   *Planets*
Inner—Yellow   Topaz   Venus
Outer—Royal Blue   Pearls or Sapphires   Jupiter
Heart—Yellow   Topaz   Venus
Destiny—Yellow-gold   Opal   All planets
Direction—Red   Ruby   Sun

Present Age—32   Karmic Lessons—4-6-7-8
Personal Year—5   Tests—0 (Chap. Twenty)
Present Cycle—7   Subconscious—5
Present Pinnacle—5   Ruling Tendency—9
Present Challenge—0   Peculiarities—14 (Chap. Twenty-four)
Present Self—   Weak Notes—3-4-6-7-8 (Chap. Twenty-three)
        Nikki Pitt—11
                           Inward—13/2
                           Outward—1/1
                           Dual—2/0

On the first page of the chart we calculated all the vibrations we learned in the preceding chapters. It includes the information gained from the full name at birth, the Inclusion Table, the elements—inward, outward, and dual—the Table of Expression, the present self, and all the information gained from the birth date. The second page is an orderly compilation of these vibrations and other information, which includes gems, colors, planets, and information that pertains to now, like the personal year and present challenge, cycle, and pinnacle.

Notice that the Inclusion Table clearly shows the Karmic lessons, the master numbers, and the subconscious on the right side. The one, many, and all are on the left. With the Table of Expression, the total of the letters in each plane are listed at the bottom. To the right are the totals of each of the areas of activity: inspired, dual, and balanced.

With the birth date, the pinnacles are figured above and the challenges below. Under all of this is listed the number of years of each major life cycle and the calendar year in which they will end. In this example, the first cycle will be from birth, or 0 through 28 years, ending in 1970. The second cycle will run from 28 to 55 years, ending in 1997.

On the second page of the chart, we list not only the vibrations calculated on the first page but also things like the first vowel, the birth date, which in this case is 16 for April 16; the tests as determined by the subtotals of the inner, outer, and heart selfs and the destiny; the weak notes of the Inclusion Table followed by the numbers of the Karmic lessons, with the actual weak notes underlined; the peculiarities, which is the total number of letters in the full birth name; as well as the items already discussed.

When preparing a chart, the following steps may be helpful:

1. First write out the name and letter values. The first calculation to be made is that of the inner self, or the sum of the numerical values of all of the vowels.

2. The next calculation is that of the outer self, or the total

of the values of all of the letters in the full birth name.

3. Now add up the values of all of the consonants to arrive at their sum, or the heart self.

4. The foundation and key should be noted. The foundation is the value of the first letter of the first name at birth. The key is the sum of all the numerical values of the letters of the first name.

5. Next the Inclusion Table is calculated. Begin by listing the number of times each number appears in the name. The absent vibrations are listed farther to the right, as these are the Karmic lessons. The subconscious is drawn off even farther to the right, underlined three times and with an arrow over the top so that it is clearly noted. Be sure that you make note of any 11s and 22s according to the method shown.

6. Below the Inclusion Table the number of letters in the name, or the vibration of peculiarities, is listed. To the left side we make note of the one, many, and all. From the inclusion we also get the ruling tendency, which comes from the strongest vibrations in the name and is listed on the right side of the paper.

7. Below the ruling tendency the approach is listed, which is the sum of the day of the month in which a person is born and the key. Directly below that are listed the inward, outward, and dual, which are derived from the inclusion also, and from the name totals. This is covered fully in Chapter Twenty-three.

8. Now make note of the influence of the elements as gained from the numbers in the Inclusion Table. Make sure that you list each number as many times as it appears in the name.

9. The Table of Expression is calculated by listing each letter in the name in the plane in which it belongs. The number of letters in each separate plane is then added to determine the amount of influence of each plane. Then the number of letters in each area is added up to determine their strengths.

10. The birth date is now written down and totaled up to arrive at the destiny. To the destiny is then added the numerical

influence of the astrological sun sign to determine the destiny direction.

11. At the bottom of the page the years of each of the major life cycles are listed and also the ages at which these will begin and end. This is done by first adding 28 to the year of birth. To this figure the month and day of birth are added to determine what the vibration of that personal year will be. The nearest 9 personal year is figured and the age at that time calculated. This will be the time of the ending of the first major cycle. The start of the second cycle will be the following year. To determine the end of the second cycle 28 must be added to the year in which the person turns 28. This will give the calendar year at the time the person is 56. Then determine the vibration of that personal year. Now go to the 9 personal year closest to that year in which the person will be 56 to determine the end of the second cycle. The third cycle starts the following year.

12. Next the challenges are calculated below the birth date. Begin by subtracting the month and day—the smaller of the two from the larger. This gives you the first challenge. The second challenge is determined by subtracting the day of birth from the year in the same manner. Lastly, calculate the main challenge by subtracting the two sums that you have just calculated—the smaller from the larger.

13. The pinnacles are figured above the birth date. First add the vibrations of the month and day of birth together to arrive at the influence of the first pinnacle. Next, determine the second pinnacle by adding the number of the day of birth to the year of birth. The sums of these two calculations are added together to arrive at the influence of the third pinnacle. The last pinnacle is the sum of the month and year of birth.

14. To calculate the time or years of each pinnacle, subtract the number of the destiny from the number 36. This gives you the years of the first pinnacle. To arrive at the time of the ending of the second pinnacle, add 9 years to the end of the first pinnacle. Use the same method to arrive at the end of the third

pinnacle. The fourth pinnacle begins the next year and goes on through the rest of the life.

15. Lastly, as for the first page of the chart, calculate the present self by adding up all of the numerical influences of the name being used at the time the chart is being prepared. That sum is the present self.

16. Once you have calculated all of the vibrations on the first page of the chart, then go to the summary page. On that page all of the vibrations already listed are listed, though in the case of the major cycles, the challenges, and the pinnacles, you only list the ones that are presently in effect. Also listed are the personal year, age, birth date, and the weak notes. Colors, gems, and planets are also put on this sheet.

V

OTHER INFORMATION FROM NUMEROLOGY

Twenty-eight

PERSONAL MONTHS AND DAYS

In Chapter Fifteen we discussed the influences of the personal years. Each month and day also have a personal influence that varies with individuals. Knowing what our personal vibrations are can help us plan our activities to derive the most benefit from them and enable us to see in advance what kinds of experiences are likely to confront us. It also gives us a guide as to what our general attitude should be during that time.

When considering the influence of our personal months and days, we must also keep in mind the influence of our personal year and co-relate them. If, for instance, our personal year is a 1 and the present month is a 3, then we should strive for self-expression in an individual way during the month. If the particular day is a 2, it would mean that we should not strive for self-expression in a way that would cause disharmony.

The personal month is calculated by adding the number of the particular month to the number of your personal year. If it is a 3 year for you and you want to know what kind of a month you will have in June, you add the 6 of June to the 3.

June 6
your personal year 3
9 personal month

So the formula for determining the personal month is

number of the month plus
number of the personal year
gives you: number of the personal month

When you have calculated the personal month for yourself or someone else, you can then look it up under the Chart of Personal Months to determine the influences.

The personal day is arrived at by adding the month and day in question to the number of that particular personal year for you, the year in which the day falls.

Thus:

the calendar month plus
the calendar day plus
the personal year
gives you: the personal day

If the calendar month and day are July 25 and the personal year is a 3, you would add:

7
25
3
35/8 personal day

You would then look up the 8 under the Chart of Personal Days to see what was indicated by that day.

Knowing what sort of power is working for you in any given year, month, or day can help you achieve greater successes and meet with fewer disappointments.

THE PERSONAL MONTHS

1—A time for new beginnings, for progressive, creative ideas and activities, for courage, determination, strong will, and an exploring attitude. Be independent and individual and assume the role of leader. It's a time to take the initiative. Be open to new ideas and put into action your plans. Keep busy by using energy both mentally and physically. Things begun in a 1 month are favored, and although the rewards may not be readily apparent, they usually come to fruition in time.

2—A time for making new friends, for resting up from last month's busy schedule, for doing things for others, for adding to what has been accumulated. This is a good time for study, establishing peaceful relationships, and doing things to make others happy. Be helpful and approach all situations with a desire for harmony. It's a good month for attending to all the small things you haven't had time for. Challenges could appear in the form of situations involving conflict, which you can ease if you want to. By all means, be sure that you cooperate with others.

3—A time for fun, for enjoying friends, both old and new, and social activities of all kinds, for being happy and carefree, for putting your talents to use, for all types of self-expression. This isn't a time for being too serious. The attitude should be optimistic, light, and happy. It's a good month for pursuing hobbies and artistic endeavors. Creativity is featured and enjoyment of nature and beauty is indicated. Many invitations could come your way—accept them and live it up.

4—This is the time to get your affairs in order, to set up a schedule and stick to it, to develop a plan of constructive activity, to go to work and to be productive. Attend to details, direct your efforts carefully, and put your skills into use. No matter how unpleasant the task at hand may be, see to it that it's done. It's a time to see the value of mental and physical labor and use both wisely, giving as much of both as is needed to do any job to the best of your ability. Keep social activities to a minimum; be patient, cautious, and sure. Take pride in all you do.

5—A time for travel, for promotion and advertising, for change and leaving behind the old, for growth and expansion. Be adaptable, adventurous, and investigative. Seek new things and meet new people. Try a new outlook and examine new ideas. Don't be too conventional and don't shy away from something just because it's different. Variety is likely to come your way—maybe new interests or new loves—and all could be good for you. Get out of your rut and enjoy all the freedom you can. Meet challenges head on. It can be a good time for selling yourself, your ideas, your beliefs, your business interests—just about anything. It could be a good month for vacationing. Enjoy yourself and life.

6—A time for enjoyment of home, family, and friends, for tending to responsibilities, for settling differences, for working out family problems. This is not a time to be away from home or to shirk your duties. An attitude of willingness to help others and a desire for promoting harmony are indicated. This is a good time for domestic purchases and repairs or for making home improvements. Entertain at home, or if a change of scenery is needed, try going somewhere for an evening of music or for a drive in the country. Time spent enjoying pets, animals, or children could be good. Give your love and aid freely and don't withhold advice if it is sought.

7—A time for quiet, for reflective and introspective thought, for study and learning, for books and intellectual discussions, for being alone. Look over plans and ideas and examine all things thoroughly. Self-examination can bring new understanding, which can be very beneficial. An attitude of patience and tolerance while quietly waiting is indicated. Examine your fears and doubts closely and try to replace them with faith. The influence is spiritual, and study involving spiritual matters could prove enlightening.

8—A time for business and financial matters of all kinds, for taking control and heading in a definite direction, for well-planned expansion, for going forth positively. Organization is the key to all activities this month. Develop an attitude of efficiency and an outlook that could be called authoritative and executive. Take the managment of affairs strongly in hand and proceed in an assured manner. Be dignified, cautious, and diplomatic. Use good judgment and be honest in all you do. Give only your best in all situations. Advertise and promote your business. Expect success and achievement and they can be yours.

9—A time for completing all things possible, for thinking of the welfare and happiness of others, for loving in unselfish ways, for activity that is not directed at self-gain. Personal achievements, desires, and goals are not well aspected this month. Keep your outlook broad and have compassion for your fellowman. Seek contact with others and opportunities for artistic endeavors. All public appearances are favored, as are all things you do to aid others. Give of yourself and your love— and it will be a good month.

11—A time for the study and examination of philosophy and religion, for any activities that can be furthered by enthusiasm, for working inventively, for use of the imagination. Actions based on intuition could easily bring success this month. Your attitude should be one of human understanding, unlimited faith in inspirations, and a desire to better conditions in any area. Make practicality a habit and don't get too caught up in your personal interests. Give of yourself through sharing your beliefs and ideals. Fame and fortune should not be sought this month —though anything could conceivably come your way.

22—A time for the practical application of ideas, plans, and dreams, for initiating large projects, for material concern on any level. Energy should be directed toward providing service to others in any way possible. Visions of accomplishments should be examined for ways to make them a reality. Then proceed with strong will, determination, and unyielding faith that you can reach your goal. An attitude that allows no thoughts of limitation is needed, as well as one that desires to do things for others. Inactivity should be avoided. Think on a large scale in all circumstances and believe that you are capable of accomplishing whatever you go after. Pettiness can halt all progress if you let yourself fall into its trap.

33—A time for kindness, for really striving to live what you believe, for caring about and for others, for attending to whatever comes your way and showing no displeasure or begrudging anyone anything. This influence is very spiritual and all things of such nature can be of considerable benefit during this time. Enlightenment and increased understanding will come if the mind is kept open. The attitude should be one of humility, compassion, and love. This is truly the month to turn the other cheek and to do unto others. Look upon everyone as your friend. Spend time with people and seek to increase your understanding of everything.

PERSONAL DAYS

1—Anything new or progressive is good today. Creativity and ideas should receive attention. Anything that concerns you is highlighted today. It's a good time for thinking of yourself, your desires, your goals, your needs, your success. Put your plans into action today. Be independent and assume the lead. Be willing to work on your own—you'll probably go farther if you do. Take matters into your own hands. Be determined and don't let others' opinions change yours if yours are well founded. Be different. It's your day for individuality. Changes you've been considering could be well made today. Avoid laziness. Don't share your ideas with others, on the chance that they could dampen your ideas and shake your faith.

2—Take it easy and go forth quietly today. Work at cooperating with others. Don't make waves if you can help it. Peacefulness is to your benefit today. Be patient in the knowledge that your time is coming. Acquire anything useful that comes your way: friends, knowledge, material possessions, facts. Let others do the talking and leading. Keep your temper under control and help others to do the same. Be nice to others, do the work that comes your way without protest, and try to be helpful—

even if it means doing someone else's job. Apologize if there's a need and make amends for any unpleasant situation. Keep your mind off yourself and on others. Be amiable and the day will ultimately benefit you.

3—If you can't sing, whistle or hum today—even if it's only inwardly. Put a smile on first thing and look for reasons to keep it there. Don't let gloom or depressing thoughts gain a moment's foothold—keep optimistic and cheerful. Put your sense of humor to work and laugh at whatever comes your way. It's a time for fun and play—if you have to work, then find a way to make play of it so that it's enjoyable. It's a good time for social engagements, shopping, tending to your personal appearance, and doing anything that involves art and self-expression. Time spent on a hobby could be very enjoyable. Spread some joy around—happiness can be contagious. Displaying some of this attitude every day goes a long way toward making life better.

4—If you didn't plan a schedule of activities the night before, then do it bright and early. Stick to it as closely as possible. Make all your efforts productive. Do things in a slow, sure way that allows you to attend to all the details. Put forth all the mental and physical labor you need to do the best job. Pride in work will help today. Be practical, serious, thorough, and patient. Avoid haste, waste, and shortcuts. It's a day of work and shirking it won't benefit you. Obedience in all situations is called for. Be conservative, conscientious, dependable, loyal, and exacting. Give attention to correspondence and finances.

5—Today is a good time to break away from yesterday's routine and seek something different. Change, variety, and freedom are the order of the day. Travel if you can; it's bound to be beneficial and educational. Seek to understand another's point of view or beliefs. It's a good day for selling just about anything you can think of, for advertising and promotions. Enlarge your circle of friends. Whatever you usually do—don't do it today. Be versatile and enthusiastic. You can make your own luck today by using your intellect and personality and seeking advantageous changes. Stay active and stimulate others in the hope that they'll do the same for you. Go somewhere. Do something—be adventurous.

6—This is a day for making adjustments wherever they are needed—in yourself, your family, your home, your relationships, your job, your goals, your friends. First, situations must be clearly looked at, realistically understood, and objectively approached. Seek the best solution for all involved. Be responsible and care well for all your "charges," whatever they may be. Give advice when you see the need—be sure it's sound and well meant. Solve problems to the best of your ability. Tend to your home and family—and to others and their concerns if they're unable to do so. Keep things balanced and in harmony. Strive to see justice done. Be an advocate of fair play. It's a good time for domestic purchases and for spending time with family and friends at home.

7—Keep calm and quiet today and try to arrange your schedule so that it includes plenty of time for being alone. Read a book, listen to some peaceful music, or go see a play. Keep poised and avoid haste, confusion, noise, and conflict. Study something that interests you. Spend time taking stock of yourself. Decide what characteristic of yourself you are going to eliminate or alter. Remember that like attracts like and that what we fear will come to us. Don't settle for less than the best. Heed your intuition and devote some time to things of a spiritual nature. Rest and wait and perfect your ideas and plans. Don't be concerned with material possessions and values—see them for their real worth. Analyze carefully all that comes along. Replace talk with thought. Replace fear with faith. Say a prayer—and put all your feeling into it. Get out and enjoy nature. Replenish your energy and establish stronger contact with the stillness within.

8—Take stock of your finances. Make sure your books balance. Look at your business dealings. Is everything in order?

Could you be doing things more efficiently? Today is the day to organize, arrange, streamline, and perfect your operations. See that things are well managed. Put commercial plans into action in a big way. Think success and you'll draw it to you. Advertise your business—promote your goals. Put your energy into determined actions. Seek advancement. Be dignified. Make your appearance businesslike and your personality and presentation dynamic. Develop a better system or routine than the one you have. Eliminate wasted efforts and be productive.

9—Say a good word and do a good deed. Enrich others' lives through your words and actions. Give generously in any way you can. Go out of your way to be thoughtful. Share whatever you have if others need it. Sacrifice your personal desires and give no thought to your own achievements. Help others to reach their goals. Be a humanitarian. Be cheerful, sympathetic, tolerant, and understanding. Buy someone a gift or send flowers. Tie up all the loose ends and complete the things you've been putting off. Try your own prejudices on for size—the fit is apt to pinch a bit. Get rid of useless clutter to make room for things of value—possessions, ideas, actions, relationships, occupations. Be of goodwill and don't let the sun go down on unresolved conflicts and misunderstandings.

11—Shelve concerns about money and business. Be only as practical and as material-minded as necessary. Zero in on ideas and inspirations. Allow yourself some quiet moments so that your intuition can function without hindrance. See through excuses to your own strengths and weaknesses. Ask for enlightenment and be ready to receive it. Share your knowledge with those you come in contact with. Don't strive for self-gain today, or you're apt to suffer losses. Look for beauty in everything—especially people and life. Let your enthusiasm light a spark in others. If you can help someone else, don't fail to do so.

22—Ideals and ideas are useless unless followed through with practical planned action. Build something today—or at least make a start. Take the initiative and look for ways to improve conditions for others. Get out and participate in community activities. Outline an orderly plan for a worthwhile achievement so that others can understand how it can be done. Then help them bring it into being if necessary. Consider all aspects of situations carefully. Be tactful in dealings with others and help enlarge their vision. Accept no hint of limitations from any source. Stay busy and create something worthwhile.

33—Relax and take things as they come. Release all worry and tenseness. Be optimistic and *know* that there is a solution to every problem. Let your own inner strength and peace radiate so that others can see and feel it. Put all thoughts of self aside—crucify the ego and receive the greater glory. Let go false pride. Keep yourself free of resentment, anger, and bitterness —no one can harm the real you, no matter what they do. Strive to see through illusion to reality. Give time to spiritual matters and to your fellowman. Make this day count for something through service. Be as the little child who is full of love and forgiveness. Don't be corrupted by the ugliness around you— know that negativeness comes from lack of understanding. Be tolerant and compassionate—and above all, judge not. Accept any job that comes along and do it willingly and well.

GENERAL DAILY TRENDS

Regardless of what the influences are for any given day, we should not put off doing anything that is necessary—anything that absolutely must be done on that day. We cannot live our daily lives according to numerology, we can only arrange those things which are possible and practical for the daily influence that is best. If we do have to do something that is not well aspected, we can aid the situation by adjusting our attitude to the influence of the day in mind.

Always *start* on a 1—don't try to finish.

Always be agreeable on a 2.

Always be cheerful on a 3.

Always put forth constructive effort on a 4.

Always get up and out on a 5.

Always plan as much time at home as possible on a 6.

Always stay quiet and thoughtful on a 7.

Always stay in control on an 8.

Always *finish* on a 9, don't try to start.

> 1—Best for asserting and promoting yourself.
>
> 1-2-3—Best for purchases of clothing, jewelry, art, and decorative items.
>
> 3—Best time for planning activities for your own enjoyment and that of friends.
>
> 4—Best time for repair and detail work and practical projects.
>
> 5—Best time to sell, advertise, promote, speculate, and make most changes.
>
> 6—Best time for practical purchases and domestic purchases, for seeking a new residence or moving into one.
>
> 7—Best time for savings deposits, buying or enjoying books, serious discussions.
>
> 8—Best time for handling large financial matters, for business decisions.
>
> 9—Best time for buying or giving gifts, for public appearances, for making large donations, for charity work.
>
> 11—Best time for selling ideas and beliefs to others.
>
> 22—Best time for instituting large projects.
>
> 1-2-4-8-22—Best time for checking-account deposits.

Twenty-nine

UNIVERSAL YEARS,
MONTHS, AND DAYS

We are all affected by our own personal vibrations, and these influence us strongest. Underneath there are very subtle currents—universal vibrations—which in their quiet way touch the world. These influences do not tell us of specific happenings but indicate general trends that men and nations unknowingly follow.

From the universal year we can get an idea of what kinds of things the world as a whole will be interested in and what kinds of things we can expect to happen. The universal year is determined by adding the digits of the calendar year.

$$
\begin{array}{r}
1 \\
9 \\
7 \\
4 \\
\hline
21
\end{array}
\qquad 2 + 1 = 3
$$

In this manner we determine that the year 1974 is a 3 universal year, while 1975 (1975-22) is a 22 universal year. With the yearly influence we find that it comes into its greatest power or strength on or about January 1. In September its influence begins to fade and the influence of the coming year begins gradually to seep in. By the end of the year the influence of the old year has faded almost completely. The new has come into power by degrees, eliminating an abrupt change. (This change begins to take place in September because it is the ninth month, and 9 is the number of completion.)

UNIVERSAL YEARS

1—Inventions, new ventures, progressive plans and activities, exploration, creativity. Great strides are made in 1 years, feats of daring are attempted, and often independence is sought. Beginnings are made but often results are unrealized until later years. Often the start of changes, upheavals, and dissension takes place in a 1 year. Exploration flourishes in a 1 year and people and nations tend to be more courageous and strong willed. Many pioneering activities have taken place in such years, as in 1927 when Lindbergh, Chamberlain, and Byrd all made flights that were firsts. Other 1 years have been 1945, 1954, 1963, and 1972.

2—Efforts to establish peace, work in cooperation with others, signing of agreements, preservation of institutions, and conferences between nations generally have agreeable results. The influence is conducive to peaceful relationships on all levels, to working with data, and to the spreading of goodwill. The Kellogg peace treaty was signed in 1928, a 2 year. Other 2 years have been 1937, 1946, 1955, 1964, and 1973. (In 1973 President Richard Nixon visited China to establish a relationship with that country from which we were so long estranged.)

3—The spending of money, enjoying of the lighter things of life, restlessness, increased use of recreational and entertainment facilities, and public interest focused on pleasure and a desire for luxury are all part of a 3 year. The trend is to be reckless and unconcerned with serious matters. Considerable energy is put into use in a 3 year, but more for pleasure than for anything constructive.

1929 was a 3 year—a year of fun. People bought cars, clothes, and pleasure items and took chances in the stock market—and then came the crash. Other 3 years have been 1938, 1947, 1956, 1965, and 1974.

4—Building, taking matters into firm hands, slow but determined progress, concern with the more solid things, increased productivity; often there are hard times when considerable work is needed. The influence is good for manufacturing and for education. It is a time of organization and reorganization, when systems are made more workable; spending is cut and the world settles down some. Our last 4 year was 1930, when people in the U.S. were trying to pick up the pieces after the crash and adjust to the hard conditions of the Depression. Since then, all possible 4 years have been 22s.

5—Working conditions are improved; there is an interest in new things, a surge in creative thinking and writing, increased international trade, and a considerable rise in amount of travel. Activities of a speculative nature usually increase, as does interest in metaphysics, the psychic, and the occult. Youthfulness commands attention and often we see young leaders come to the fore. People and nations are concerned with freedom, with discarding outworn restrictions, and with the forming of more realistic controls and livable situations. Some 5 years have been 1931, 1940, 1949, 1958 (when we began to really hear about John F. Kennedy), and 1967; 1976 will be a 5 year.

6—Improvement of conditions and situations—especially those dealing with health and medicine; there is a concern with education; responsibilities receive consideration—particularly those of an international nature—adjustments are made and the solutions to problems are sought. Great international dealings go on in a 6 year—very often in an effort to resolve problems. As history proves, however, when solutions are not arrived at peacefully, conflicts arise. Both 1914 and 1941 were 6 years—the beginning of World War I and the entry of America into World War II. Other 6 years have been 1932, 1950, 1959, and 1968. The year 1977 will be a 6 year.

7—Patriotism takes an upswing, agriculture receives attention; there is greater quality in work and products; financial aspects are good except during war; very few new projects are launched as interest is directed toward examining and perfecting those already begun. It is a thoughtful, quiet time. Conservation and ecological activities gain power, as there is greater interest in nature and in preserving its beauty. It can be a time full of controversy. Travel and construction concerning water (tunnels, etc.) are more prominent in a 7 year. Columbus discovered America in a 7 year. Recent 7 years have been 1942, 1951, 1960, and 1969.

8—Business mergers, great increase in commercial activity both at home and abroad, expansion, interest in business matters, prosperity; there is an upswing in the economy, establishment of controls, and advances in engineering. This influence could well be represented by a dollar sign because financial affairs come to the fore. Large-scale plans are set in motion; amalgamations occur; new businesses are formed and the business machinery increases its pace. At the outset there can be instability as reorganization takes place in an effort to make things run more smoothly. An 8 year is known for its material progress. The years 1934, 1943, 1952, 1961, and 1970 were all 8 years.

9—Completion takes its toll; a kind of spring cleaning takes place, and much gets swept out from under the rug. During this time, things that have outlived their usefulness are discarded. This is the completion of a cycle in universal vibrations. Old business is finished with, loose ends are tied up, unsatisfactory relationships are severed, things are lost. It is a year for humanitarian deeds, for friendliness, tolerance, and understanding. Greed, jealousy and selfishness bring stronger reactions than usual. Many past efforts, deeds, and words reap their like reward in a 9 year. From September on, new ways of life begin to present themselves. Some 9 years have been 1935, 1944, 1953, 1962, and 1971.

11—Psychological thought receives great attention, and many new leaders in the teaching and expounding of it appear. People begin to think more about religion and spirituality. It's a year of dreams, inspired inventions, and concern with improving conditions. There are usually religious revivals everywhere. Beliefs and ideas are shared and enthusiasm runs high. It is not a time of practical concerns, though plans may be formed for later use. Reforms often take place in an 11 year. Our last 11 year was 1910 and 2009 will be our next one.

22—Expansion on a grand scale—great accomplishments; world conditions are improved, advances are made, projects for improving the conditions of mankind are initiated. People in general think in large terms and often idealistically—their sights are fixed on higher things. Dreams and plans become a reality and there is much concern with progress and improvement. Industry takes great steps forward, huge plans are conceived that have far-reaching effects, and constructive activity is primarily the goal striven for. Visions of greater things and a better world give rise to efforts to bring them into material manifestation. Often before creation can take place, room must be made, and so in many cases there must be destruction of the old to prepare for the new. Some 22 years have been 1939, 1948, 1957, and 1966; 1975 is one.

THE UNIVERSAL MONTH

To determine the universal month we add the number of the universal year to the number of the calendar month. For example, July 1974 was a 1 universal month.

$$
\begin{array}{rr}
\text{July} & 7 \\
1974 & \underline{3} \\
& 1\emptyset
\end{array}
$$

In the same way, we would calculate that November 1975 is a 33 universal month.

November   11
1975   <u>22</u>
            33

After we have calculated a universal month, we have only to check the chart to determine the influences of that month and what they will mean in terms of situations and attitudes.

UNIVERSAL MONTHS

1—Growth is seen, promotions are made, new leaders take charge, ideas are formulated into plans of action. It is a good month for opening new businesses, starting projects, and forming committees. Inventiveness has a good aspect and working alone is good.

2—Diplomatic discussions, political adjustments, gathering of data, collection and accumulation of all kinds. Favorable for coming to agreements, working out differences, amiable relationships and situations. The trend is to get down to the meat of matters.

3—Stock market activity increases, pleasurable pastimes are sought, spending on nonessentials is greater, optimism tends to prevail. Favorable for creativity, amusement, enjoyment of people. The trend is toward impracticality and extravagance. People are more inclined to be candid in speaking what they believe or feel.

4—Need for skilled labor is more acutely recognized, adherence to routine and order is strengthened, errors are rectified, details receive attention, efforts to increase productivity are made. Favorable for constructive activity, institution of discipline, conservative ideas and projects.

5—Taking chances, increased advertising, the unusual or extraordinary receives notice; products of a different nature make their way into the market, sales rise. Favorable for theater activity, selling of anything, travel, change of pace. The general trend is to be more receptive to anything new.

6—Educational activity, domestic and community matters, concern with health, general improvements, receive greater attention. Favorable for solving problems, establishing more balanced relationships, and for purchases for the home or family. People tend to stay at home and get involved in redecorating activities.

7—Increased interest in things of a scientific nature, analysis, improved monetary conditions, surge in intellectual activity; educational facilities receive greater support and use. Favorable for close examination of anything, perfecting of plans, conservation activities. The trend is toward being more peaceful and in general things are quieter.

8—Business organizations established, commercial growth and expansion; plans are put into action. Favorable for purposeful, directed activity, dealing with finances, making business decisions of a large nature. The trend is for business conditions to improve and financial matters to be more favorable.

9—Well-known personalities are in the news and receive attention. Businesses eliminate unnecessary personnel; inventories are taken, personally and commercially, of stock, efficiency, and productivity. A cycle has come to an end, and so the trend is change and adjustment. A favorable time to finish anything, for enjoyment of friends, for giving gifts, and doing kindnesses for others.

11—Increased activity by churches and religious organizations, and increased patronage of such institutions—evangelism —things of a psychic nature receive more attention. Zealous groups strike out for improvements; inspired ideas can come forth to benefit all. A favorable time for religious or philosophical study, enjoyment of the impractical, making reforms, and sharing of thoughts and ideas.

22—Greater activity in international politics, large betterment projects conceived or begun, corporations formed in larger numbers. A favorable time for all constructive activity, for putting plans into progress, for expansion. The trend is toward forming and implementing large plans and projects.

33—Understanding atmosphere, greater patience, attempts to establish or maintain peace, concern with bettering conditions in all areas, spiritual study and seeking of truths. A favorable time to search for answers, solve problems, deal with others, make new friends, do charitable work.

THE UNIVERSAL DAY

Each day has its own vibratory influence, and the circumstances of any day are colored greatly by the characteristics of its vibration. By knowing what to expect we can plan our day accordingly. The universal day is calculated by adding the calendar month, day, and year together.

$$
\begin{array}{ll}
\text{July} & 7 \\
4 & 4 \\
1776 & 3 \\
& 14 \quad 1 + 4 = 5
\end{array}
$$

Thus the universal day for the day the Declaration of Independence was signed was a 5. After we have calculated a day, we have only to look it up in the chart of days to see what its influence will be.

UNIVERSAL DAYS

1—Strong stock market; acts of independence, such as strikes and picketing. New ideas are brought forth; people feel explorative and more individualistic than usual. At the same time they may be somewhat uncooperative and desirous of being alone.

2—Rest, inactivity, efforts toward collection, increased death notices, pettiness. People are more interested in small things; more apt to pay attention to details. Although they may be easy to get along with, they tend to put off making decisions and doing things. Vision tends to be limited and so it's not a good time for sharing ideas.

3—Nervousness; flourish of activity, though often poorly directed and therefore wasted; stock market unstable and fluctuating; places of entertainment and amusement busier than usual. People are more interested in pleasure than business; restlessness prevails.

4—The stock market is more stable, business runs more smoothly, efficiency is greater, restrictions and controls are imposed, schedule is important. Often pressure is applied that causes rebellion; therefore demonstrations, strikes, and unrest may occur. People are more business-minded but cautious. Possibly an increase in deaths and illness.

5—Shedding of restrictions; changes, speculations, stock market activity usually great; restaurants and entertainment establishments crowded; travel, intellectual interests. People want to be free of the routine and therefore seek pleasure. Sporting events receive more interest. Strict discipline causes problems and freedom is strived for.

6—Musical events are popular, solutions to problems are sought, people feel inclined to stay at home, spending is conservative, stock market usually stable and better adjusted, domestic matters are the greatest concern. Community activities are usually well attended.

7—Rural areas are quiet, whereas there is tension in the cities—the day depends a lot on where you are. Intellectual and educational pursuits, the stock market tends to go up, scientific projects are favored. People tend to look at things more analytically, decisions are carefully considered, and efforts are made to put the finishing touches on things—perfection is desired.

8—Business activity increases, large decisions and plans are made, expansion and promotion take place, organization is strengthened, financial matters are reviewed. People on the whole are more active and industrious, and there is usually greater efficiency in business dealings.

9—Friendliness is more prevalent, as is tolerance; public matters receive attention; romance is in the air, as is emotionalism; concern for others is at a high. People tend to be more charitable and generous and are swayed a lot by their feelings. The stock market is apt to be erratic.

11—Idealistic activity, impracticality, spreading of ideas, expounding of beliefs, possible rise in crime, interest in spirituality. A day of extremes, for this vibration can lend great energy in either direction. People are nervous and flighty and can make poor decisions unless they heed their inner guidance.

22—Efforts directed more constructively, expansion, plans put into action. The stock market is good. People tend to view things from a realistic standpoint, with material results in mind. Inspiration put into practical use is the pattern of the day.

33—Compassion, forgiveness, solving of problems, making adjustments, giving service, friendliness, stabilized activity. People seek advice; they are more likely to forget their own desires and enjoy artistic activity and beauty. On the whole, conditions are harmonious, though often there is disruption until adjustments are completed.

Thirty

CHOOSING A VOCATION

Much can be learned about vocation from the destiny, the destiny direction, the outer self, and the key. It's true that our vocation does not have to have anything in common with our destiny and destiny direction because we can fulfill our purpose without using our job to help us. But since so many hours of our life are devoted to working, we may well wish to put them to use toward what we came to do.

Our outer self tells us much about our natural talents and abilities, and any job that doesn't make use of at least some of them is wasting our attributes. Our key tells us how we can best accomplish things, and since this is generally what employment is all about, the key should be considered.

If we still wish further guidance, we can gain it from the formula that calculates the vibration discussed in this chapter, which we will call "vocation." This formula determines its vibration by adding together the subtotals of the inner self, the outer self, the heart self, and the destiny. For example, if we were to determine the vocation of Nikki Karen Cabe, it would be done in the following manner:

```
  9   +   6   +   6   = 21/ ③
NIKKI  KAREN   CABE                    April   16   1942
  9   +   4   +  11   = 24/ 6            4  +  7  +   7   = 18/9
  9   +   7   +   5   = 21/ ③
```

Having determined that the subtotals are 21, 24, 21, and 18, we would then add them together:

```
21
24
21
18
84      8 + 4 = 12      1 + 2 = 3
```

So, the vocational vibration for Nikki Karen Cabe is a 3. In the example, I have underlined the subtotals only to make it easier for you to see what numbers I am talking about.

If we were to calculate the vocation of Catherine Marie Thompson:

```
  2   +   6   +   3      = 11
CATHERINE MARIE THOMPSON
 11   +   1   +   3      = 15/ 6    July 23  1922
  9   +   4   +   9      = 22        7 + 5 + 5 = 17/8
```

we would add:

```
11
15
22
17
65      6 + 5 = 11 the vocation
```

In this case there are no subtotals for the inner self and the heart self, so we must use the totals, or 11 and 22.

When calculating the vocation, we can use the subtotals of the full birth name or those of the present self. When we take on a different name we tend to change more than we realize, and so a vocational change may be indicated.

THE NUMBERS OF THE VOCATION

1—Vocation that provides opportunities to put into use: leadership, creativity, ideas, strong will, determination, inventiveness, forcefulness, initiative, ability to work alone, and energy.

2—Vocation that provides opportunities to put into use: co-operativeness, diplomacy, ability to work with others, attention to detail, obedience, taking orders well, keeping the peace, and service.

3—Vocation that provides opportunities to put into use: sociability, a way with words, artistic talents, sense of humor, cheerfulness, friendliness, love of beauty, seeing the importance of the less practical things of life.

4—Vocation that provides opportunities to put into use: system and routine, efficiency, thoroughness, caution, practicality, taking directions well, self-discipline, loyalty, dependability, and conservatism.

5—Vocation that provides opportunities to put into use: adaptability, intellect, curiosity, salesmanship, contact with people, travel, varied situations, inventiveness, character judgment, magnetism, and lack of restriction.

6—Vocation that provides opportunities to put into use: reliability, patience, conventionality, understanding, service, responsibility, morals, making adjustments, solving problems, giving advice and counsel, educational matters, domestic affairs, and a desire to better conditions.

7—Vocation that provides opportunities to put into use: pride, mental ability, desire for quality and perfection, poise, calmness, analysis, knowledge, educational interest, working alone well, studiousness, intuitive powers, spirituality.

8—Vocation that provides opportunities to put into use: good judgment, efficiency, dignity, management potential, executive attitude, control, organization, large plans, handling of money, dealings with large concerns.

9—Vocation that provides opportunities to put into use: charitable activities, service to others, generosity, feelings such as compassion, sympathy, and tolerance, artistic abilities, love of beauty, human understanding, contact with people.

11—Vocation that provides opportunities to put into use: inspiration, enthusiasm, ideals, ideas, inventiveness, zeal, spirituality, knowledge, intuition, perception, service, excitement, moral values.

22—Vocation that provides opportunities to put into use: practicality, construction, service, improvement of conditions, large plans and operations, civic and national projects, analysis, diplomacy, outlines for activity.

33—Vocation that provides opportunities to put into use: service, harmony, peacefulness, inspiration, knowledge, humility, reliability, compassion, willingness to work, giving of advice, contact with people, calmness, love of nature, music, and art and all things of beauty.

Thirty-one

AFFAIRS OF THE HEART

Through numerology much can be told about how a person will act in a close relationship especially when love is involved. This is determined by the vibration of the outer self. The outer self is the total of the numerical values of all the letters of the full birth name. (See Chapter Four.) The characteristics described are, of course, generalities, and not all of them may be evident in an individual. It must be remembered, however, that they are inherent and could appear at any time.

To varying degrees, some of the other vibrations in the chart modify the characteristics. The heart self can have a definite influence because we generally feel freer to be what we want to be when we are with the people we know well. The Karmic lessons can have an effect since they may indicate an area where we are weak because we have not yet learned that lesson. The major life cycle we are in can also have its influence upon our thoughts, actions, moods, and attitudes. Lastly, there is the ruling tendency, and it definitely has its effect upon what we do and the kind of person we are. All the vibrations in our chart are colored to some degree by each other. Still, from the outer self alone we can get a fair idea of how someone will respond in affairs of the heart.

Check the number of the outer self for yourself or someone

else, and then look it up in the following chart to determine how a person will most likely respond in a close relationship. (The following numbers refer to your lover and not to you, the reader.)

THE NUMBERS OF AFFAIRS OF THE HEART

1—You relate almost everything to yourself. You can be very generous and giving, but you generally weigh what you will get in return for your actions. Not usually very emotional or impulsive, you could seem even cold and uncaring at times. You use judgment in all things, and your brand of judgment says that everything should profit you in some way. Since you find it hard to show your emotions, you could care more than you let on. You are apt to say things more matter-of-factly than romantically. When romantic, you act with strength rather than with a lot of "mush." You are usually quite direct and once your mind is made up, you're awfully hard to deter. You can be determined to the point of stubbornness!

You like attention, praise, and to know that you are appreciated. With your ego well fed, you can then turn to thoughts of someone else. You are usually active but time alone is necessary for you. Don't expect to conform to a pattern or to conventions, for you make the molds that others fill.

You are progressive in your thinking. You like new ideas—ideas that go forward. You are full of the pioneering spirit. You may not get involved in every new thing that comes along, but you will usually have to check it out to see if you are interested. With some, this may even extend to members of the opposite sex. At the same time, you are usually quite possessive and not inclined to share. To you, what is good for the goose is not necessarily good for the gander. This may seem unfair, but as I said, you are inclined to think about yourself.

You may not like to argue, but your opinions are so strong

that you feel forced to. You are rarely able to back down. Your opinions are matched in strength by your will and forceful nature. Keep in mind that you also appreciate strength in others and abhor weakness of any kind. You expect to win and enjoy the battle—it makes the victory sweeter and feeds your ego. So even when a friend agrees with you, he or she should resist a little anyway. Afterwards, you will shine with pride and the good mood that comes from winning.

Another thing to remember—you can see the value of any good idea, but sometimes it takes you a little while if the idea isn't yours. You are sometimes upset if someone thought of something before you did. You really need a companion who has gotten his or her own ego under control and can help you with yours.

As a lover you are usually creative. You like to be the one in control at all times, and times like these are no exception. A creative lover can be quite a pleasure if the other person doesn't mind. You can also be aggressive—even to the point of acting like your cave man or cave woman ancestors.

You may be dominant, self-centered, and forceful, but remember, if you ever decide to make someone a part of your world, he or she will be just like a part of yourself.

2—If a person has been lucky enough to land one of these thoughtful, sensitive people, congratulations. If not, then he or she should bait a hook well. Part of the reason you are considered desirable is because you usually think of others first. You also can have an uncanny way of sensing others' feelings, needs, and desires. You really care about people, especially those close to you, and will go out of your way to make them happy. You like to give and can be generous to a fault, but you usually provide for yourself and those you are responsible for by accumulating in advance. What you like to give most is service. You find it awfully hard to resist a distress call. You have to feel needed and useful, and that is something others should keep in mind. If they want to keep you around, they shouldn't let you think that they could get along without you—even if it happens to be true.

You have a lot of friends. This is because you are friendly and dislike being alone. Loyalty is one of your major characteristics, and people can generally rely on your faithfulness. You are the kind of person who is apt to send cards for every occasion, bring your sweetheart one rose because you've been dating a month, or remember your sweetheart's favorite foods and prepare them for him or her. To you the small things are very important and you rarely overlook them. At the same time, you don't like others to overlook them either. If people want to make you happy, they should show you that they care in the little ways as well as the big ones.

Usually you are very emotional and arguments and disagreements upset you terribly. You like harmony and will do almost anything to keep peace. Consequently, you are considerate, diplomatic, and kind. It is this need for peace and doing almost anything to get it that can make you seem spineless. Often others don't understand your tendency to give in so easily to people. You are really just agreeable, adaptable, and easy to get along with. You see many things as too unimportant to fight over. Sometimes an impression of weakness arises from your dislike for making decisions and being the leader. Others should offer decisions or choices. People shouldn't put you on a spot and make you miserable by expecting you to do something that can be so hard.

As a lover you're thoughtful and always striving to please. You are very aware of people's unspoken needs and desires. Because your desire to please is so great, be sure that others don't take unfair advantage of you. No matter how agreeable you are, you can be pushed too far. If people abuse your thoughtfulness you are likely to find someone else who will appreciate you better. Your sensitive, emotional nature makes you easily hurt. Tears may come frequently, as well as emotional highs and lows.

Don't be surprised if you are petty at times. It is just the negative aspect of your concern for small things. You can truly be picky about the littlest things, which may be of no importance at all to others. You want things to be right, and at times others may find this nerve-wracking. You love music and have an inborn rhythm that makes you a good dancer. A gift of good music is usually a hit with you. You are a collector and generally have at least one collection of some sort, even if it is only old love letters. You find it hard to get rid of almost anything —even worthless items.

If others are thoughtful and loving and keep things as peaceful as possible, you ought to be happy. Others will come to you with their problems and they'll get not only sympathy but help in solving them. You are a true lover of beauty, and the beauty you admire most is that which is found within others.

3—You are often called a charmer and the description fits you well. Usually you are very outgoing and friendly, and when you're happy you seem to sparkle and bubble all over. You are subject to spells of the blues even if you are a born optimist. You may be something of a social butterfly because you love people and all kinds of social events. It gives you a chance to show off your sense of humor and ability to talk. Sometimes you talk even when you really have nothing to say. But you can make it sound so interesting that others may sit there and listen anyway.

You are a romantic and a lover of beauty. It's all due to your very emotional nature. You laugh easily and the tears may flow just as freely. In fact, you can be the most emotional person around. You may be thrilled at finding a wildflower or seeing a beautiful sunset. Your tears usually last. Your feelings are genuine and deep but you also can see the better side of most situations. You can be serious but your nature is directed toward the lighter side of things.

Part of the reason you enjoy social occasions so much is because they offer opportunities for flirting. This shouldn't upset your sweetheart unduly because despite the flirting, you will probably be faithful. It's just your way of building your ego. You feel a great need to reassure yourself that you are attractive and desirable. If others want to see you really glow, then they should just feed your ego by letting you know how great they think you are.

Usually you dislike fights—but arguments and discussions are apt to be another story. Defending anything gives you more chances to talk, and you'll usually jump at the opportunity. Besides, you just seem to have to tell people how you feel about anything that comes along. If others don't like to argue, they should keep you talking about all your good points and accomplishments. Your gift of gab usually makes you very expressive. Others probably won't have to wonder how you feel about them —they're apt to hear it often and in many different ways. You can be very good at making flowery speeches and using all sorts of pretty phrases. The word *Blarney* probably best describes this kind of thing.

You like to be important and noticed and thrive on praise. As a lover you are usually creative and strive to make things as beautiful as possible. You are very affectionate and tender and like others to be the same way in return. Governed almost completely by feelings, you generally aren't too practical and you can be very impulsive. You are often a dreamer also—not infrequently a romantic one.

Others should be sweet and loving with you and keep their party clothes ready. They shouldn't let their jealousy show too clearly, and they shouldn't try to outshine you. You want to be the center ring attraction of the circus.

4—If you lived in a beehive, you'd be one of the workers. You are usually practical and productive, thorough and exacting. You'll usually only play when and if the work is done. You're a builder who does things slowly but surely. This may not sound like much fun, but in the hive the workers provide for the queen bee—and being taken care of isn't a bad deal. If

276 Other Information from Numerology

others are looking for a few fun evenings or for a light-hearted romance, they have to go hunting for other game. If they have a permanent mate in mind, they could probably do a lot worse. You are usually serious and not overly social, but then you aren't frivolous or flighty either. Extravagance isn't generally part of your make-up.

You are inclined to be dependable and loyal. Others will find that you're very faithful—and won't be tolerant or understanding if they aren't. You believe in fairness, justice, and honesty in all things. Usually set in your ways, you prefer to have others see things your way and will argue the matter, trying to prove a point. You aren't a patient person and foolishness is one of your pet peeves.

Judgment generally rules and you are apt to think things over slowly and carefully. You don't like to make hasty decisions and rarely act on impulse. You like to check into every detail and proceed with caution. Often you give the outward appearance of being cold and unfeeling. People shouldn't let your icy bluff fool them—you feel things too. In fact, you feel things so deeply that you need a lot of love. The trouble is you can't seem to show this need and have difficulty responding when love is given. People shouldn't expect you to spill forth with mushy love talk or even show much affection. They'll have to learn to understand that this is the way you are.

Take care, however. You could become a "green-eyed monster." Jealousy can be one of your major shortcomings. You are possessive because you care a lot about the people close to you. People should keep things neat and orderly and not let your habit of systematizing everything get to them. Generally, if you feel secure, people will get their way unless what they want is very unconventional or extravagant. You feel secure when you know that you are loved and needed. One thing others can fairly well count on: you usually take good care of your own. Your hive buzzes with constructive activity.

5—You are always on the go, and others could use track

shoes just to keep up with you. You could find your thinking cap useful also, as you're just as active mentally as you are physically. Winning an argument with you can be quite a feat, unless others happen to encounter you on a day when you aren't up to par intellectually. You respect knowledge and will back down if others can show you that they're right.

Others may find themselves agreeing with you because you are born salesmen. You not only have a way with words but have a way with people as well. You are an excellent judge of human nature and are usually very intuitive—a hard combination to beat. Getting your own way is a challenge, and there is rarely anything you enjoy more than proving you are equal to any challenge. You jump right in and it's no holds barred! You are apt to go to almost any lengths to get things the way you want them. If others don't intend to lose every fall of this wrestling match, they'll really have to be on guard. The whole thing spells excitement to you and without it you would just wither away.

Another big problem for you is your fascination with physical pleasure—be it food, drink, or sex. For example, you are greatly attracted to members of the opposite sex. You don't generally mean to overindulge in anything—it just seems to happen to you and then you aren't sure why. When you are unfaithful, it's not because you intended to be. You just find things so attractive or enjoyable that you get carried away. Others should try not to become suspicious and start checking on you and doubting your word—it won't help matters. Nor is it wise to try and tie you down or keep a watch on your every move. The best bet is for them to strive to be exciting, and then you will be far more inclined to just look around rather than play around.

What can others be sure of with you? They can be sure that you may be different from one moment to the next. You can be something of a modern-day gypsy, so they should keep their bag packed and ready to go. You can be very emotional and loving and then be cool and unfeeling. As a lover you are original, try hard to please, and can be a real "sweet talker." People will probably never figure you out completely—just when they think they have, you'll pop up with some surprise. If they're smart, they'll try to do the same thing to you. You may not take well to responsibility, so people shouldn't try to burden you.

If others can hold your interest, they can pat themselves on the back because it means they have accomplished something. If they can hold on to you, they have learned the art of holding with an open hand. If they have mastered all these things, they won't have a tame animal to lead on a leash but they will have an exciting lover who can make every day a new adventure.

6—If people are looking for someone with whom to spend many a fun evening, doing everything from dancing and partying to sitting quietly by a fire, they will have found the right person in you. If they happen to be looking for someone to settle down with, they may also have found the right person. You are usually a home-lover to whom the family is all important. You work hard and care for your family well. You are inclined to go overboard in caring for the people and things that "belong" to you and are capable of giving a lot of devotion to them.

Generally you are conservative. There are exceptions, of course, but on the whole, you just are not naturally inclined to be a swinger. If you decide to try to be one, you'll probably feel very guilty.

You like to do things for others and therefore take on responsibilities and burdens. There may be times when your home seems like an orphanage because of all the strays that find their way into it. You just believe that everyone ought to have a home. The fact is that everyone who comes to your house will probably feel at home and will be eager to come back.

If others have been feeling somewhat neglected and would like you to pay a little more attention, they should develop a problem and go running to you with it. They will make the most of their troubles and will even muster up a tear or two. You will be genuinely concerned and will be far more apt to look after them more closely for some time thereafter. A word of warning —you can be very possessive. "What's mine is *mine* for good" is generally your philosophy. You usually have very set and clear-cut beliefs, are convinced that you are right and want others to abide by what you believe. You don't like arguments, but you will argue long and hard for a principle. You don't really mean to be one-sided, you just feel so strongly that you're right that you don't understand why your way isn't right for everyone. Knowing this, others can see that the way to get around you may well be to pretend they agree with you. Then gradually, they can begin changing you.

Having told you all the pros and cons about 6s, I have saved the best information for last. Your lover has probably found in you a loving, giving, and caring person. If 6s come to really care, their love is likely to manifest itself as devotion, and they are even capable of idolizing someone out of all proportion. In such cases they are inclined to look with rose-colored glasses and see only the good. Keep in mind that you love praise more than the average person and need to know for sure that you are cared about and appreciated. Given this you will generally remain faithful to the very end. Withhold this, and you are likely to go out in search of someone who will give it to you.

7—You can be a great puzzle when it comes to love relationships. You act uncaring at times and even appear cold and unfeeling. This is because the feeling and thinking natures of 7s are fairly well balanced and they are not sure which to listen to. When listening to their feelings they are very warm and affectionate, capable of speaking words of love and demonstrating that they really care. When the head holds sway, they are usually reserved, somewhat aloof, and say or do very little to let you know that they feel at all. Some of these people are all one way or the other, while some of them add to the confusion by being a mixture of both. If someone is involved with one of the cold, reserved types, he or she should remember that under that brittle exterior is a sensitive and emotional nature. Often it is a fear of being hurt that makes a 7 put up a front. If someone makes you feel safe and secure, you are apt to relax. If you are a 7, the chances are you will show your feelings far more with actions than with words, as you are not very verbal.

Usually quiet, you are far more likely to enjoy a day in the country than a social event, and if you go to a party you would rather watch than get into the swing of things. When you are standing on the sidelines, people should just leave you alone. They might as well get used to not being included in all of your activities. You require time by yourself, and your desire to be alone is not an indication that you don't care for others. You are basically a great thinker who needs quiet time. You like to talk with knowledgeable people, and education, however gained, holds a great attraction for you. You will be far more talkative when you feel there is something worth talking about. People should keep one thing in mind—you often tend to be something of an authority on the things that interest you, and they should avoid arguments with you unless they know their ground.

Quite often you have an annoying habit of being a perfection-ist—you do things to the best of your ability and expect the same of others. This can make you very demanding. You are refined and like "class," or your idea if it. You are likely to be concerned with things like etiquette and good behavior. You usually have excellent taste and tend to like good paintings, books, antiques, heirlooms, and anything that is full of tradi-tion. You like occasions like Christmas or Valentine's Day and want to make big things of them.

As a lover you are generally thoughtful unless you get too involved with your own thoughts, in which case you can be forgetful and preoccupied. If you seem to be off in your own little world, you probably are. Your thoughts are also apt to be concerned with things of a spiritual nature, the psychic or occult. Kindness is one of your strong points—you can't stand cruelty or brutality of any sort. You respect physical strength but only if it hurts no one. Another thing that you aren't fond of is conflict, because it disrupts the quiet atmosphere that is so necessary to your happiness and emotional balance. When you do give in to an argument, it's because you feel that you are right and others should know it also. You can become very withdrawn when confronted with petty bickering and upheaval.

If others want to get their way, they should present a good case and go armed with the facts—all of them. You will want to examine the whole thing before you make a decision. Music has a very soothing effect on you. People should give you a lot of love—even if you throw cold water on it. They should be sincere and honest and faithful to you. Others should share your interests but not give up their own.

8—No ruffles or frills here—just a very matter-of-fact approach to almost everything—even love. Eights show they care, but it won't be with a lot of mushy phrases. When you do display affection, it is in a firm, direct manner that leaves no doubt about how you feel. Eights have a natural tendency for organization and efficiency and the urge is so strong it's hard to resist following it in any and all areas. You also have a great desire to manage and control—and you can usually do so quite well. You're a born leader and may be prone to bossiness and giving orders, but your judgment is usually such that it's hard not to agree with your decisions.

You respect dignity and take great pride in yourself and anything you're involved with. One thing you don't understand is lack of personal pride in others, and consequently you have little to do with such people. You like to make a good impression and so are careful about your words, actions, and appearance. You tend to do well in anything you set your hand or mind to. Solid, dependable, loyal, and conscientious are good adjectives for describing you. If you are unfaithful, at least you will be very discreet. Basically, though, you are the faithful type

—your conscience doesn't give you any peace when you do something you feel is wrong.

You can be both extravagant and penny-pinching, but you usually believe in getting full value for your money. You can be quite generous and may even be inclined to give large gifts. Usually very diplomatic and tactful, you try to avoid arguments whenever you can. You prefer quiet discussion to loud fighting. But others shouldn't push too far—you can be as loud and as forceful as anyone else. When you speak you like to have others pay attention and don't appreciate it if they don't. If others want to put you in a good mood, they should make sure that everything is neat and in order. Give you something to manage, let you make plans, and you're happy. When asked for advice in business and financial matters, you glow with pride.

As a lover you're thoughtful, kind, generous, and put forth considerable effort to please. You thoroughly believe in looking after the people and things you care about. Being largely concerned with material matters, you usually believe in living as well as possible and will spend a lot on clothes, home, and car —all carefully chosen and in good, somewhat conservative taste. You think in large terms and don't care about petty matters. You love without reserve—fully, deeply, and usually lastingly. You do all things in a complete way or not at all. That's your strength.

9—Prone to great emotional highs and lows, you may be ecstatically happy one moment and in the depths of depression the next. Don't be surprised if you go to a movie and cry at the sad parts. Nines feel things so deeply that they have to respond. Some of you have established strong outward control, but nothing can stop you from feeling deeply inside. You are usually ruled by your heart and feelings, unless this has brought you much pain and trouble. The beauty of 9s is that their feelings are not all for themselves—in fact, all too often their thoughts are so much of others that they shortchange themselves. Others can be fairly sure that you will be considerate, thoughtful, generous, compassionate, and understanding. Because you are so emotional, you can be easily upset by things that a stronger person wouldn't even notice.

If someone has made a 9 a permanent mate, or plans to, he or she had better be prepared to share him or her with the world if the occasion arises. What occasion? Simply feeling that they can help others. If someone calls at 3 A.M. and wants to talk over a problem, they are just as apt to rush quickly to their side as not. The 9 really does belong to the world, but sometimes he or she tries giving in the wrong way. Some 9s consider themselves "Great Lovers" as well. If people love them, they may be in for some sharing that is hard to put up with. It may not seem like much compensation, but they can at least look forward to a warm and tender lover, no matter where a 9 roamed before coming home. Nines truly can be great lovers and can even be so sweet and charming that others may be inclined to forget the times they have been left in bed alone. Part of the problem is that 9s have so very much love to give.

Don't let my talk of unfaithfulness make you run from a 9, or make you so suspicious that you become distrustful. When they are loyal, 9s are completely so, and even those who feel inclined to play around can be made to change their ways by someone who is clever enough to provide them with what they need. Nines need a lot of love, reassurance, and a feeling of security. They tend to be possessive and if a 9 tries to hang on with a stranglehold then you must make him or her realize that you have no plans to leave. Nines are the true romantics who love things like dinner by candlelight, and they like to make something of even the smallest occasion. If others want to get their way, they have only to play on a 9's emotions and they'll usually win. They shouldn't bother with reason and facts. If someone says things to really hurt them, they are apt to forgive easily but rarely forget, for the scars are deep and lasting. If the world has hardened a 9, he or she can be the hardest person around. Say "I love you" often and give him or her a valentine on the eighth of June; celebrate a rainy day or do any silly thing. It's a fairly safe bet that a 9 will tell you what love is all about.

11—You are a dreamer—one who sees visions as real as the world we live in. It seems necessary for you to spend part of your time in this make-believe world that no one else can ever really share. If you'd just learn to be practical, many of your dreams might be very useful. You generally have strong morals, though not necessarily conventional ones. In fact you may be somewhat idealistic and find it hard to live up to your own standards. You are inclined to impose your beliefs on others and do so with such zeal that often they find it hard to resist you.

You're an odd mixture of nervous energy and bubbling enthusiasm, which are both contagious. You rarely do anything in halfway measures. When you love, you go all out and may even promise the moon. An 11 probably won't be the most thoughtful and considerate lover around. Elevens don't mean to be forgetful either—when a person lives in two worlds, it's hard to keep track of both and do a good job in each. Others won't have to compete for your attention with anything or anyone but that other world, so loving you has its compensations. Your tremendous energy is apt to make you tense and irritable at times—especially if you don't keep busy. When this happens, think up some project, quickly, or engage in an intellectual discussion. A battle of wits is something you generally enjoy and are good at.

You tend to know things before they happen, to anticipate others' thoughts, and to have strong hunches. This unnerves some people and they had better just steel themselves against such things. You are generally very intuitive—even to the point of being psychic—and for you it's an unconscious, effortless thing that just happens. You're so perceptive that people will have a hard time deceiving you. Honesty is the best policy for them. If others want to get on the good side of you, they should just ask questions about your beliefs and ideas and then agree with you. They should plan outings in the country, send flowers, or give you a book of poetry—appeal to your love of beauty, for it's closely tied to your heart. They shouldn't get into debates about principles or religion with you because you usually feel especially strong about such things and will argue long and hard. If others play their cards right, they'll gain your love and attention—and if they're really lucky they'll even get included in your dreams.

22—You could be the picture of self-confidence or could have the worst inferiority complex ever. You tend to be super-positive or super-negative. At least your ego doesn't usually get out of hand because you tend to feel that you are less capable than others. If you ever realize, even in part, what you are capable of doing, everyone better stand back. You should be given all the encouragement you can get; people should never throw cold water on your ideas and visions. You abound in human understanding and if listened to can enlighten any situation. You may not always see things the way the majority does, but there is a good chance that much could be learned from you if your opinion was sought. If others want to have something analyzed, they should take the time to ask you about it, and chances are they will be amazed at how talented you are in this area.

Generally you like things to be well organized—order and system are important to you—and when chaos reigns, you are apt to become somewhat disgruntled. In this state you will be inclined to set about, in a very determined manner, to put things to right. You have a real talent for saying and doing the right thing at the right time. You are a master of tact and diplomacy. You are charismatic—and it can be catching. When things don't turn out right for you it is because you fouled up your highly developed intuition with intellectual reasoning. You need to pay attention to your visions and ideas and not underestimate your ability to bring things to pass.

Doing things for others truly makes you feel good and useful.

While you can be very loving and generous, you can also be indifferent. If the latter is the case, it happens when you sense that people are getting too close. You do have the ability to sweep people right off their feet if you want to turn on the full power of your charm. You like and need people. Even though others may have to put up with sharing you, by and large your activities are harmless because you tend to be basically faithful and honest. If you aren't, then chances are you will go all the way and be really nasty. You tend to be unsure of yourself in your role as a lover and will seek frequent reassurance. If you are confident, you have the ability to make love a beautiful experience. However you may seem on the surface, people can be fairly sure that love is important to you and you have a tremendous amount of energy to devote to it if you so choose.

33—The 33 is so high-powered and spiritual a number that generally where love is concerned the holder of this number reduces it to its lower aspect of 6. Six is the number that should be read. The reason for this is that where close relationships are involved we become almost if not totally concerned with the material and the emotional, and the pure spiritual aspects of love are generally unrealized in such personal situations.

Thirty-two

NAME INFORMATION

INHERITED TRAITS

It may seem odd to consider that we can inherit traits numerologically just as we can inherit characteristics genetically, but we definitely can. Our inherited tendencies are determined by the total vibration of our last name at birth. For instance, if someone's last name at birth was

$$\begin{array}{ccc}
\text{M A I N} & & \text{H A L L} \\
\underline{4\ 1\ 9\ 5} & \text{or} & \underline{8\ 1\ 3\ 3} \\
19/1\emptyset = 1 & & 15/6 = 6
\end{array}$$

the vibration of the inherited traits of *Main* would then be a 1, while for *Hall*, it would be a 6, or the sum of the numerical values of all the letters in the last name. Inherited traits are calculated in the same manner as the outer self and the present self, using only the last name at birth.

1—You have inherited an independent spirit that is concerned with progress and creation. You also have a forceful nature, a strong will, and the ability to produce original ideas.

2—You have inherited a peaceful nature that believes in cooperation, makes use of diplomacy, adjusts to differences, and inclines you toward being sensitive and loving.

3—You have inherited an outgoing personality and a sense

of humor. Your enjoyment of people makes you welcome almost anywhere and gives you lots of friends. You have the ability to talk well, be artistic, and brighten the day with your optimism.

4—You have inherited an attitude that sees work as the path to productivity, believes in system and routine, sees a need for handling details well, and inclines you toward self-discipline, thoroughness, and caution.

5—You have inherited a freedom-loving spirit that chafes at restriction, limitation, and routine and thrives on change, travel, and investigation. You have a curious nature that seeks new experiences and enjoys challenges.

6—You have inherited a conservative attitude that sees acceptance of responsibilities as necessary, that believes in helping others and in improving what you can. Your nature causes you to seek harmony through solving problems.

7—You have inherited a desire for knowledge and a respect for quality, tradition, facts, and theories, as well as a spirituality that seeks truths and increased understanding. You tend to seek help through prayer.

8—You have inherited an attitude of material concern that causes you to see the importance of business and financial matters and that makes you feel a need for efficient organization. You have also inherited qualities of leadership and believe in well-made plans.

9—You have inherited concern for others, generosity, a very emotional nature, and a great love for your fellowman. All of this is combined with an attitude of compassion, sympathy, tolerance, and service.

11—You have inherited an enthusiastic, zealous spirit that causes you to go into things with energy and an intuitive nature and a desire to do something great, preferably to benefit mankind. Idealism and spirituality have also come to you through this vibration.

22—You have inherited the power for great material accomplishments, as long as they provide service for others, and the ability to make your visions and ideas realities and to conceive workable plans for progress and achievement.

33—You have inherited a desire to be of service. You have an understanding, compassionate, and loving nature that can make you a fine counselor, a helpful friend, and a good example for others to follow.

NICKNAMES

Most of us acquire a nickname sometime during our life. A nickname has far more influence upon us than we realize. We have not only been the recipient of nicknames but we may have given some as well. There are names that are derivatives of our given name or names: *Kathy* for Kathleen, *Joe* for Joseph; or initials derived from names: *B.J.* for Brenton Jack. We also use names like Buddy, Butch, Doc, Sonny, Shorty, Sissy, Lassie, Princess, and Missy.

What influence do these names have on us and do they conflict with or complement our original vibrations? To determine the vibration we must add the value of all the letters of the name, or its outer self:

K A T H Y	B U T C H	S I S S Y	D O C
11- 1 - 2 - 8 - 7	2 - 3 - 2 - 3 - 8	1 - 9 - 1 - 1 - 7	4 - 6 - 3
29/11	18/9	19/1Ø	13/4

We will use these four names to show how to balance the nicknames against the original numerology.

We will consider my own numerology for *Kathy.* The 11 is in harmony with the 11 foundation of the *k* and is the higher vibration of the 2 totals found elsewhere. It is a powerful vibration for a child and indicates a need for strong guidance from parents as well as a spiritual atmosphere that aids in the development of this aspect of the vibration. Now, when I am in an 11 major cycle, it is a helpful vibration because it aids me in attuning myself to the influence that I need at this time.

In the case of *Butch,* let's assume that this person has a 4 outer self, a 2 inner and heart selfs, and a 1 Destiny. The 9 vibration would then be in conflict with the major vibrations, and unless a strong need for this was indicated, the name would only cause confusion. The confusion would come through the materialistic attitude of the 4 and the self-centeredness of the 1, which conflict with the impersonal, nonmaterial influence of the 9.

In the case of the 1 of *Sissy,* we will assume it is a child with a 1 outer self. Giving a nickname of this same strong-willed, independent influence would tend to make a child extremely desirous of doing what she pleased, causing great difficulties for parents, teachers, and all those associated with her in positions of leadership, guidance, and control.

The name *Doc,* a 4, could be in conflict with the majority of the major and secondary influences in the original chart, and still be a good nickname if the particular person had, for instance, a 4 Karmic lesson. It would then give assistance in developing the qualities needed to learn the lesson. The same could be true if the present cycle, challenge, or pinnacle was a 4.

Many times the nicknames we use create problems we are unaware of. For instance, 5s are hard vibrations for children to carry because they make them feel rebellious toward regulations, restrictions, and responsibilities. Unknowingly, we had given my older sons names that carried the 5 influence, and this was aggravated by the fact that it was not in harmony with their original charts. *Pat,* for Patrick, was having problems with boredom and accepting authority, while *Tommy,* for Thomas, resented all restrictions put upon his activities. After becoming aware of this, we shortened *Tommy* to *Tom,* giving him a 3 influence, which is much easier for him to carry. With my oldest son we didn't change his nickname but changed the way we spelled it: *Pat* became *Patt.* By adding the extra *t,* we gave him the influence of 7, which complements his original influences. Since doing this, we have seen the elimination of the conflict that was within him.

NAME CHANGES

When I speak of name changes in this instance, I don't mean the change of name that occurs when a woman marries or a child is adopted. I am talking about changing your name if the original numerology produces conflicts, and you feel it could be causing your present problems.

Before we go into name changes fully, let me explain more about original numerology. The parents of a child are guided subconsciously to choose a name that the soul of the child knows it needs. Generally the parents believe they've picked a name they liked or wanted. There are situations where this guidance is ignored or completely blocked out, or where a child is bound to a particular name by family tradition. For example, with "Juniors" or those who carry a name through several generations, the soul knows this in advance. But the name is chosen to harmonize with the destiny of life's purpose, not vice versa. Therefore, the soul has to settle for conflicting vibratory influences in the chart.

In reality, no vibrations will conflict if their higher aspects are attuned to, but we must deal with vibrations lowered to one degree or another by our own negativeness. At the human level, there is conflict between some influences. We can either work to harmonize them through developing more fully their positive aspects, or we can consider changing our name.

Before a total name change is contemplated, the original chart must be carefully studied and compared with all of the changes the new name would bring into being. There are no hard and fast rules in name changes—each change is an individual matter. In all cases the big "do" is *do* study the matter thoroughly and *don't* overlook any aspect. Consider every changed effect for its full influence. Sometimes the conflict occurs because we need to learn to overcome the lack of harmony. We must therefore ask ourselves if we think this is the case before we change our name. There is considerable disharmony in my original numerology, but I have learned a great deal by working at bringing myself into greater balance while under this influence.

NAMING CHILDREN

This is a matter I feel very strongly about and cannot emphasize the importance of enough. Sometimes people who study numerology find that they or someone they know is going to have a child. Immediately they sit down and begin to calculate the influence of various names—ruling out those they feel wouldn't be good and picking those they like the influence of. *Don't do it!*

Again, the soul of the expected child knows what influences it needs—*we do not.* In our efforts to be helpful, we may hinder the child. We also tend, through this method, to block the guidance that will help us pick the right name. One of the biggest mistakes is trying to pick a name with no, or even few, Karmic lessons. The lack of a vibration doesn't create a lesson. The lesson exists already and its existence creates the need for the minus influence. The subconscious is then aware of the vibration it must work on, and the lack of that vibration brings situations and experiences into the life that will aid in the learning of the lesson. In purposely choosing a name with no minus vibrations we rob the child of this very helpful influence —assistance it needed.

If you are concerned with naming a child correctly, I give you the advice that I followed during my recent pregnancy. Ask for guidance in picking the name the child needs, and then have faith that you will be guided to the right choice. When a name comes to you that feels right, don't begin to doubt but continue in faith. If it's a name both parents agree on with no feelings of prior dislike or family tradition involved, then chances are you've received the guidance. *Never* check the numerology of any name until you have decided definitely upon a name. Then, whatever the name works out to numerologically, don't change your choice. After the child is born—taking the destiny and the information gained from the birth date—work up the child's chart. See what help the child is going to need from you to do what it has come to do, to learn its lessons, to meet its challenges, and to develop its natural talents and abilities. In this way you can help your child greatly, and you won't hinder it before it can get on with doing what it actually needs to do.

APPENDIX

ADDITIONAL INFORMATION FROM NUMEROLOGY

BUSINESS INFORMATION

By using some of the formulas that we use to calculate the numerological influences for individuals, we can determine a great deal about businesses. This can be a considerable help if we are considering starting a business of our own, investing in one, or going to work for a company. Numerology can tell us what the primary function of a business should be, where the concern of its personnel should be aimed, and how it should go about reaching its goals.

By determining the outer self of the business from the total of all of the numerical values of the letters of its full, registered name, we can see what kind of activity it needs to develop and the image it needs to project. The business outer self can also tell us a lot about the people we should employ, or whether it would be a good place for us to go to work. If the name of the business were Hale's Place, for instance, then its outer self would be a 1. With a 1 outer self, the business should be progressive and creative and should employ people who possess those qualities, along with ambition, foresight, and individuality. This is a very brief example, but it should give you some idea of how this works.

The date of the conception of a business, such as the day the business was actually begun, gives us its destiny, which tells us what its goals should be. If the business opened its doors on August 7, 1974, for instance, then its destiny would be a 9 (8 + 7 + 3 = 18; 1 + 8 = 9). The destiny for a business is calculated in the same way as a person's destiny. (See Chapter Five.) A 9 destiny would indicate service to others, placing them first and striving for their welfare and satisfaction. A 6, on the other hand, would point to domestic matters, community affairs, and acceptance of responsibilities.

By studying the influences of the various numbers of a business chart, you can soon learn to determine the effect of the various influences in relation to a business. Of prime importance are the outer self, the destiny, the foundation, the key, and the plane of expression. When considering going to work for a company, it is not necessary to do a complete chart. Doing a very brief work-up can tell you whether there is harmony between its influences and your own major numbers. At times, if you feel the need to strengthen the qualities of your secondary numbers, they can be considered also.

When considering opening your own business or investing in one, a more complete chart should be done. This will help you understand how to run your business for greatest success and achievement. When choosing a name for your business, remember that it should be in harmony with your own numerology and the destiny of the business. Another rule to keep in mind, things usually function best when the outer self is in harmony with and of a higher vibration than that of the destiny. So, if the destiny of your business is a 5, it would be best to pick a name that vibrated to a 6, 7, 8, 9, 11, 22, or 33. At the same time, while all of these numbers are higher, the 6 and 8 do not tend to be very compatible with the 5, and so should be avoided if possible. Later on in this appendix we will discuss the compatibility of numerical influences more fully.

PARENTAL COUNSELING

Numerology can be a great help to parents, teachers, and anyone else who deals with youngsters. By knowing the influences governing and affecting a child, you can better understand, deal with, direct, and aid the child's development.

The foundation has a considerable effect upon children, especially during their early years. It can tell us much about a child's actions, attitudes, and interests.

The first major cycle has a great deal to do with a child's behavior, outlook, thought processes, and interests. It can help us understand what kinds of activities children should be encouraged in, how they will do in learning situations, how best to try to teach them things, and how they will respond to authority.

The outer self indicates the talents a child should be aided in developing and the qualities and capabilities that come to him naturally.

The key gives further information about abilities that children should be aided in developing.

The plane of expression tells us which area a child has the most knowledge and experience in, and this should be considered when directing a child's activities and interests.

The ruling tendency tells us what kinds of hobbies and activities are likely to interest a child.

The inner self tells us what qualities the soul wants the individual to acquire and make use of and the attitude that should best be assumed. Helping a child to bring forth these can be of benefit during its adult life.

The destiny tells us what children are supposed to do with their lives, and they can be helped in their early years to strive toward that goal and be made to see the importance of such activity. The destiny direction gives us added information about the specific area that a child should be headed toward.

The Karmic lessons should be carefully considered by parents, because aiding their children in developing the habits and outlooks that will promote learning of the lessons is of prime importance. Possibly this is the greatest help parents can give to their children.

The first challenge is something a child needs to be helped at meeting and overcoming. In many ways this is the hardest challenge because there are so few adult years in which to work on it.

The heart self can give us an idea of the personality traits that are most likely to begin appearing, particularly as the child gets older.

The method of approach can aid us in understanding why children approach situations as they do and can help us to anticipate their response to experiences.

The spirituality aspect of the first vowel aids us in understanding how best to present things of a spiritual nature to children so that they can better accept and understand them. It can also give us an idea of their outlook on such matters.

The effect of nicknames as well as the present self should be taken into consideration.

NUMBERS IN YOUR LIFE

We are surrounded by numbers and are affected by them to some degree, whether we are aware of it or not. There are numbers for bank accounts, charge accounts, telephones, licenses, and addresses. In almost every case, if we determined the best influence for a particular number and requested it, we would find things far more likely to go better for us.

It seems a coincidence that once we begin attuning ourselves to our numerology, the numbers that come into our life seem to be more attuned to us also. For example, when I recently went for my license plates, I was given a plate that adds up to 7. Seven is the number of my outer self and one of my Karmic lessons. The primary use of my car, other than for mundane uses, is to take me places that help me in the development of my inner resources. Also my phone is used largely for helping others and for counseling. I took the number that the telephone company gave me but was not surprised when I later found it vibrated to a 33. To others this may seem pure coincidence, but I am too aware of the power and workings of the subconscious to accept such an answer. I know that the influences we need in our lives are drawn to us by our subconscious, especially when we open the door to help this very strong part of us.

CITIES AND STATES

You may find it very interesting to calculate the influence of your place of residence, place of birth, or other places you have lived. The influence of a place is derived from the total of all of the numerical influences of the name. Anyone who's been to San Francisco is well aware that its 5 influence manifests itself in its being a great place for fun, a city of variety and considerable differences. Las Vegas is a good example of the 5 also, for who could deny that the speculative, chance-taking, gambling nature of the 5 has been capitalized on and manifested to a great degree there. Chicago and Los Angeles are both cities of progress, creation, and leadership, as their 1 totals indicate. New York City is an area of great expression in a multitude of forms, where people go to be what they are, as its 3 total indicates. Amarillo, Texas, is my present home, and it is fairly well attuned to its 9 influence by being a very friendly city. Having been to Alamogordo, New Mexico, I feel it truly lives up to its 7 by being a center for some of the greatest minds of the U.S. and because of the research and study that go on there.

Often, by checking the influence of the city and/or state we live in, or plan to move to, we can determine much about its expression and whether or not it is a good place for us. It is also interesting to calculate the influences of places we have been or lived in just to see if they are in tune with their vibration.

CRAVINGS AND DIETING

At some future time I intend to research dieting and numerology to a greater degree, but I have done some checking that you may find interesting and useful. So far, most of my study concerns cravings.

Through cravings, our subconscious is trying to give us messages. I don't mean short-term cravings—when we want a particular thing to eat just before dinner and forget about it as soon as we are full. I am speaking of the cravings that plague us for many days or for several years.

To determine the message our subconscious is trying to give us we must calculate the influence of the craving. This is done by adding up the total numerical value of the item as we think of it. For example, for years I craved a particular type of soft drink that has a two-word name, but I used the common one-word nickname when referring to it. To calculate its influence for me, I added up only the numerical influences of that one-word nickname.

How can this benefit us? Because our subconscious is pointing out what we need more of in our life. For instance, the total of the one-word nickname for the soft drink I craved was an 11. This told me that I needed to concentrate on greater spirituality, to be of service to others, to develop my intuition, and to open myself to inspiration and revelation. Having discovered this method of receiving messages from my subconscious, I immediately tried to bring these things into my life in greater force.

This information can be helpful when we are dieting because more often than not the items we crave are high in calories and also generally provide little of value to the body. When we have determined the numerical value of the item craved, and if its caloric count is high, we can then search for a substitute with the same numerical influence but with fewer calories and more nutritional value. As in the case of the soft drink, I found that iced tea vibrates to an 11 also, and I successfully managed to substitute it for the soft drink, so my caloric intake was decreased considerably.

Remember, calculate the influence of whatever you crave *as you think of it*. If you are craving Mexican food in general, calculate *Mexican food*. If it is enchiladas that you want, then calculate *enchiladas*. If you crave steak, then calculate that, not beef. If you have a thing for apples, the general rule would be to use the word *apple*, as we don't usually eat more than one at a time. On the other hand, if it's peanuts, calculate *peanuts* because we rarely eat just one. I have found that the people I have talked to can relate to the influence their cravings indicate and have felt a desire or need for such in their thinking and feeling natures.

I have been speaking primarily of food cravings, but the same is true of other cravings. I found myself strongly drawn to a particular brand of cigarette that vibrates to a 5, at a time in my life when I was striving hard to discard old feelings and habits and to adjust to a new way of life. By calculating your own cravings, you too may be able to learn much about yourself and what you have need of in your life.

BEHAVIOR PATTERNS, HABITS, FEELINGS

I present this, not so much as a matter of absolute fact but as something to think about. The thought I'd like to place before you is that, from the vibration of our behavior patterns, habits, and feelings, much can be learned about the reasons for our actions and needs, as well as those of others. We can also get some idea about the underlying cause of these actions, which may have a foundation in our childhood, and for students of reincarnation, even in past lifetimes, as we are truly creatures of pattern.

I have experimented with this somewhat and have found a strong relationship between the action and the influence that its numerical total indicates. Below is a list of some items, so that you can see the relationship between them and their influence and then draw your own conclusions.

1—BED-WETTING, HOLLERING, TREMBLING

Influence indicates a need for originality, independence, positiveness, activity, and strength. There are tendencies toward laziness, imitation, overdependence, selfishness, egotism, fear, and weakness. The chance is good that it is a response to instability, bullying, force and suppression of individuality, creativity, will, ideas, and opinions.

2—REBELLION, GAMBLING, HATRED, FOOT-STAMPING

(All of these are 11/2 totals, for in the case of negativeness, the 11 is generally reduced to the 2 unless the negativeness goes to great extremes and then it is vice: dishonesty and the like.) Influence indicates a need for love, gentleness, consideration, and peace. There are tendencies toward oversensitivity, discontent, dishonesty, aimlessness, and indifference. It may be a response to cruelty, anger, deceptions of the past, the strong will of others, and degradation.

3—SCRATCHING, FEAR, DRUG ADDICTION, YELLING, SNIFFING

Influence indicates a need for freedom from worry and to use talents or self-expression and kindness. There are tendencies toward jealousy, worry, superficiality, and extravagance. It may be a response to intolerance, criticism, hypocrisy, and possibly jealousy. There may also be a strong tendency toward cowardice and impracticality.

4—THUMB-SUCKING, FOOT-TAPPING, CRYING

Influence indicates a need for dignity, trust, loyalty, practicality, security, and calmness. It indicates repression, hatred, resistance, and a tendency toward crudeness and vulgarity. It may be a response to restriction, rigidity, narrowness, vulgarity, hatred, inhumanity, and destruction.

5—EXTRAVAGANCE, DRINKING, TEMPER TANTRUMS, PESSIMISM, DESTRUCTIVENESS

Indicates a need for freedom, variety, progress, companionship, and understanding. There are tendencies toward irresponsibility, self-indulgence, sensuality, possible perversion, procrastination, and carelessness. It may be a response to inconsistency, abuse, thoughtlessness, restriction, dullness, regimentation, and repression.

6—PANTS-WETTING, SELF-INSISTENCE, BLINKING

Influence indicates a need for harmony, love, security, balance, justice, sympathy, and responsibility properly chosen and bestowed. There are tendencies toward worry, smugness, anxiety, despondency, and the possibility of mistaken ideals. It may be a response to drudgery, insecurity, suspicion, unfairness, and lack of protection and stability.

7—SMOKING, NAIL-BITING, FINGER-TAPPING, SPEEDING, POSSESSIVENESS, RESENTMENT

Influence indicates a need for peace, faith, refinement, spirituality, poise, and introspection and analysis. There are tendencies toward nervousness, melancholy, fear, deceitfulness, skepticism, coldness, and negative attitudes. It may be a response to humiliation, suppression, deceit, confusion, and turbulence and any actions by others that cause great fear.

8—KNUCKLE-CRACKING

Influence indicates a need for discrimination, judgment, organization, control, self-reliance, recognition, and directed energy. Cracking of the knuckles helps to release energy blockages in the fingers, and so the subconscious is indicating a need for greater and directed flow of energy. There are tendencies toward materialism, intolerance, worry, carelessness, and impatience, and a desire for revenge. It may be a response to bullying, abuse, injustice, cruelty, strain, leadership and power, and lack of direction.

9—JEALOUSY, ANGER

Influence indicates a need for love, understanding, sympathy, and generosity, along with security and stability. There are tendencies toward emotionalism, bitterness, fickleness, and stinginess. It may be a response to immorality, vulgarity, indiscretion, lack of love and tolerance, fickleness, and the inability to accept the loss of things that we weren't ready to let go of.

At this time, I have calculated no behavior patterns, habits, or feelings that total 22 or 33.

NUMERICAL HARMONY

Study of the characteristics of the numbers will show that there is greater harmony or compatibility between some numbers than others. For instance, it is easy to see that the 1 and 5 are more compatible than the 1 and 2 or 2 and 5. Considering the harmony, or lack of it, in a chart is helpful, especially with the major numbers. If there is disharmony between the inner and outer selves then it indicates a problem area that you will need to work to smooth out, modifying each influence to create a compatibility that does not naturally exist. Generally speaking, the odd numbers are more harmonious with each other, and the even numbers with themselves. There are also groups of numbers, called triads, that are harmonious due to their relationships even though they might not immediately appear to be agreeable with each other.

1, 4, 7—THE MENTAL NUMBERS

Always concerned with the mind and intellect—the inspiration and creativity of the ideas of the 1—the form and practicality of the 4—the introspection and mental and spiritual analysis of the 7. These are the angular numbers.

2, 5, 8—THE CURVED TRIAD

Concerned with outward expression in various forms—the peacefulness, cooperation, and diplomacy of the 2—the adaptability, versatility, and curiosity of the 5—the dependability, constructiveness, and organization of the 8.

3, 6, 9—THE TRIANGULAR NUMBERS

Multiples of the basic trinity, their expression is emotional—in the artistic creation and friendliness of the 3—the devotion, service and concern of the 6—the love, compassion, and sympathy of the 9.

INDEX